Objectives and Perspectives in Education

Objectives and Perspectives in Education

Studies in Educational Theory (1955–1970)

Ben Morris

Professor of Education, Bristol University
Visiting Professor of Education, Harvard University 1969–70

Routledge & Kegan Paul London and Boston

First published 1972
by Routledge & Kegan Paul Ltd
Broadway House, 68–74 Carter Lane,
London EC4V 5EL and
9 Park Street,
Boston, Mass. 02108, U.S.A.
Printed in Great Britain by
Northumberland Press Ltd, Gateshead

ISBN 0 7100 72473

For Margaret
and our family

In general, our approach to education suffers from a one-sided emphasis upon the child who is to be brought up, and from an equally one-sided lack of emphasis upon the deficient character of the adult educator ... In fact, I suspect our contemporary pedagogical and psychological enthusiasm for the child of a dishonourable intent: people speak of the child, but should mean the child in the grown-up. For in the adult there is hidden a child—an eternal child, something that is always becoming, is never completed, and that calls for unceasing care, attention, and fostering. This is the part of the human personality that wishes to develop and to complete itself...

Perhaps we misconstrue the pedagogical need, because it would remind us uncomfortably that we are ourselves still children in some ways and are in urgent want of bringing up.

C. G. Jung, *The Integration of the Personality,* chapter 6, 'The Development of Personality', Kegan Paul, 1940, pp. 283–5.

Contents

Acknowledgments

I should like to thank a number of publishers, institutions and periodicals for permission to publish the essays in this collection which first appeared under their auspices. A list is given below.

It would be pleasant to be able to acknowledge individually what I owe to the many people who have influenced my thinking, amongst them my colleagues in Bristol and elsewhere. This is clearly impossible. My major intellectual debts will be fairly evident from the text and from references listed. In the introduction, I mention my debt to my students.

For practical help in the production of the manuscript my sincere thanks goes to my personal secretaries who over the years have dealt skilfully and faithfully with complex and often barely legible drafts; the librarians and other library staff of the Bristol University Institute (and School) of Education library for unfailing helpfulness over references; and to my wife for her limitless patience and support, not least in typing (and criticizing) successive drafts of chapters 11 and 12.

Finally, I should like to thank the President and Fellows of Harvard College for their invitation to spend a year within that remarkable university as a visiting professor, to the Dean and members of faculty in the Graduate School of Education there for their warm welcome and stimulating company, to the authorities of the University of Bristol for granting permission to accept Harvard's invitation and to my immediate colleagues in the University School of Education in Bristol for making acceptance possible. Without the promise, and the actual stimulation of my Harvard visit, this book would not have been completed.

Thanks are due to the following for permission to use all or part of the articles indicated:

Bretton Hall College of Education: *Arts and Sciences in Education*, Eleventh Annual Foundation Lecture, May 1961.

Evans Brothers Ltd: 'Guidance as a Concept in Educational Philosophy', in *Year Book of Education 1955*.

Evans Brothers Ltd and London University Institute of Education: 'Mental Health in the Classroom', in Studies in Education no. 7 (1955), *The Bearings of Recent Advances in Psychology on Educational Problems.*

Excerpta Medica Foundation: 'Personal Growth through Professional Education', in *Excerpta Medica*, no. 45 (Proceedings of the 6th International Congress on Mental Health, Paris 1961).

The Institute of Physics and Physical Society: 'Examinations as Instruments of Educational Reform', in *Bulletin* of the Society, August 1964.

Journal of Education: 'Research for Education', I and II, October 1955 and January 1956.

Monographs of the *Sociological Review*: 'Personality Study: its Aims and Implications for Students of Education', in *Sociological Review Monograph* no. 1, July 1958.

The New Era: 'Sigmund Freud—Promethean Man', vol. 39, no. 3, March 1958; 'Dr William Boyd', vol. 43, no. 8, October 1962; 'Towards a Creative Education', vol. 49, no. 3, March 1968.

New Horizons in Education, no. 23, autumn 1960.

Tavistock Publications Ltd: 'An Educational Perspective on Mental Health', in *Towards Community Mental Health* (ed. Sutherland), 1971.

University of Bristol Institute of Education: Inaugural Lecture, *The Study and Practice of Education*, printed as a Lyndale House Paper, May 1957.

Whitelands College, Putney: *Objectives and Perspectives in Education*, Winifred Mercier Memorial Lecture, October 1966.

Introduction

The various studies usually grouped together under the title of 'education' occupy an exposed position in the academic world. They are uncomfortably poised between the rigorous demands of 'pure' academic disciplines, and the often harsh realities of practical life. Students and teachers of 'education' often pray for deliverance from this situation. But the prayer, though understandable, is mistaken—for what is undeniably a cross to be borne is also the only possible source of life for these studies. Without a creative tension between practical and theoretical demands, educational studies tend to lapse either into irrelevant academicisms, or into a rationalized defence of unreflecting practice.

The task of maintaining the necessary tension is complex. Adequate and varied experience of children and young people, in and out of school, and of educational institutions themselves as on-going social systems, stands at one pole. But unless this experience is well guided and thoroughly discussed and reflected upon, it is only too likely to generate unthinking conformity. At the other pole stand theoretical studies, not only 'education', the so-called general foundation disciplines of philosophy, sociology etc., but the arts and sciences as well. All these studies, to be 'educational' for the professional student of education, have to be relevant to his calling. But relevance in this case is a very complex matter indeed. It is not merely, and in some cases not at all, a matter of having 'educational' or classroom examples or illustrations in the syllabus, of trying to give these studies direct, obvious, instrumental relevance, but rather of ensuring that they *inform* the student's vision of life, including his professional activities, attitudes, beliefs and values (Morris, 1966b). They degenerate into academicisms when they fail to generate and maintain such vision, and causes of such failure can be found both in a 'descent' into practical trivialities, as well as in an 'ascent' into theoretical ones.

But a fruitful tension between the practical and theoretical polarities requires that they enter into meaningful relationships with one another, so that each can illumine the other, and this is what educational thought and discussion are about. This is the domain of 'educational theory', 'the irreducible core of educational study' (Morris, 1966a), a domain the existence of which is sometimes denied. This is perhaps not surprising, for educational theory is from one point of view a theory of practical judgment (Morris, *ibid.*; see also Hirst, 1966), and so resists definition as a clearly delimited domain of knowledge. Nevertheless it 'has a life of its own, and is best exhibited in the process of dialogue or dialectic, i.e. in confrontations. What the dialogues are about are educational issues and problems, which always beckon ultimately towards action' (Morris, *ibid.*). But in preparing the ground for action, theory has to take account of a range of issues and presuppositions, in the formulation and analysis of which facts and values are subtly interwoven. Of course in carrying out its work theory depends very greatly on the foundation disciplines—philosophy, psychology etc. —but it is not constituted by these. As an activity of thought it is not disciplinary in the ordinary academic sense, nor yet simply inter-disciplinary, but *interpretive* in the sense that it is concerned with the generation and elucidation of *objectives* and *perspectives* in education, for it is in relation to these that practical judgments are formed, and it is these which sustain action.

The field of educational theory is infinitely large, not just because of the enormous range and complexities of the issues involved—these would make it vast but finite—but because it is a living open system of thought, continually having to deal with fresh issues as these arise out of man's changing actions and experiences. Of course one may discern within educational theorizing a finite, and indeed limited, number of major themes such as the rival claims of innovation and tradition, the individual and his social groups, reason and emotion, but these continually present themselves in new forms and have to be tackled afresh in every generation. Workers in this field continually feel the need to erect systematic systems of thought which will in their time, at least, help to provide uniform frameworks or inclusive perspectives within which practical judgments can be made. The history of educational ideas is a memorial (both an inspiration and a warning) to man's capacity for this kind of thinking and his need to undertake it. The use of techniques of linguistic analysis in philosophy has tended in recent times to bring systematic and constructive thinking in education into disrepute. It has provided a cleansing but rather bitter wind and, to change the metaphor, has tended to destroy the wheat as well as the tares. It is simply nonsense to suppose that man can or will do without attempts to systematize his knowledge *and* his beliefs and thus help to give explicit coherence to his actions. And it is much better when these systems of thought and feeling, these perspectives, are avowed, made explicit, for they may then be criticized and modified, and action tempered by greater rationality and sympathy. It is the ultimate in philosophical aggression, and despairing and self-destructive aggression at that, to insist that critical thought must always in the end be nihilistic.

This book is a collection of writings spread over some fifteen years on a variety of topics which can claim to fall within educational theory thus broadly conceived. Any unity among them is more implicit than explicit, but something in the nature of a general inclusive perspective is indicated in terms of certain major, interrelated themes.* The separate chapters, while for the most part arising from requests to speak or write in a particular setting, do reflect my own permanent professional preoccupations. Their publication now indicates a belief that the issues dealt with are of continuing major relevance for educational thought, despite many changes in educational practice and in the presuppositions of large areas of theorizing. The division of the book into sections was suggested by the material itself which seemed, in the broadest terms, to be dealing with general ideas in educational theory (in particular the relation between theory and practice), with the form of the personal as a mode of thought for education, and with the concept of renewal.

The relation of theory to practice in education has been one of the themes in this introduction itself, and it is always the foremost issue in teacher education, a perennial bone of contention. The need to have such a bone of contention is probably why the misconceptions surrounding the issue can never, it seems, be finally dispelled. Yet we must work on the presenting centre of resistance, even as we realize the trouble goes much deeper, and that we are only dealing with a symptom. The basic misconception takes the form of the belief that it is possible to practise an art, like the art of helping others to learn (i.e. teaching), without having at least a rudimentary and implicit theory about it. Any meaningful action carries with it presuppositions both of value and fact, i.e. theoretical presuppositions. The denial of having a theory —'I'm just a practitioner'—is a huge defensive self-deception. Criticism and modification of action is a first step in theory, hence the resistance to it. The study of education—reflection upon the educational enterprise—is a search for a more adequate under-

* I am at present engaged in an attempt to formulate a more explicitly systematic viewpoint which I hope to publish later under the title 'The Educational Enterprise'.

standing of what we are doing, and no one likes to be told that 'they know not what they do', no matter how (relatively) true this may be for all of us.

Theory is therefore to be seen as largely an activity of critical reflection and, in pursuing such reflection, empirical knowledge, conceptual structures and value judgments are all required. This serves to place 'research', particularly empirical research, in its proper setting. If theory forms the major target for critics of 'educationists', research comes perhaps a good second. Empirical research in education has lately enjoyed a much higher prestige than it did when chapter three of this book was first written. Yet, since attitudes towards research are always apt to be ambivalent, and the claims of some of its practitioners omnipotent, one fears that its current popularity may breed fresh opposition. It is always apt to arouse expectations it cannot fulfil, and thus is quite likely to be written off in the end by many who have championed it. Attitudes swing between the poles of omnipotence—the ascription of magical power—and impotence—the assertion of total lack of power. So long as men—even apparently very rational men—are swayed in major ways by these ambivalent attitudes derived from infantile experience, so long will they search for some magic substitute for personal responsibility and decision. And this search for magical components in education runs right through our innovations and developments, whether in curriculum, in learning and teaching strategies, or in the structure of institutions.

The indispensability of personal responsibility, and the huge odds with which it has to contend in both the non-rational and irrational elements in human life (let alone in the huge complexity of the 'natural' and man-made universes), would seem to emphasize the importance of understanding human development from a fully personal standpoint. My own thinking in this respect has been profoundly influenced by psycho-analysis on the one hand, and by personalist and existentialist philosophies on the other. Working from the clinical foundations, rather than from the obviously nineteenth-century biological presuppositions of the theoretical superstructure of Freud's work, modern developments in psycho-dynamics have increasingly remoulded the image of man in a direction which makes it easily compatible with some versions of the personalist and existentialist perspectives. Moving from the work of Erik Erikson, or of Fairbairn or Winnicott or Guntrip, in the psycho-analytic field, into that of John Macmurray or Martin Buber in the philosophical, one is not conscious of any massive radical and unreconcilable differences. (The famous dialogue between Carl Rogers and Martin Buber is a case in point; Buber,

1965.) Rather one's vision becomes more clearly bi-focal and results in a profounder grasp of both man's greatness and his tragic littleness, as he struggles to come to terms with, that is to discover, what he is.

The second part of the book is concerned with developing certain themes within this 'perspective of the personal'. One major theme is the attempt to show how the personal is the most inclusive form under which to consider man's nature, and how the biological, the social and the individual frames of reference are necessary and complement one another in illuminating both behaviour and experience. Likewise there is considerable emphasis on the cardinal importance of inwardness, of the meaning of experience, as distinct from causal influences on behaviour, which is all that the behavioural sciences, if strictly defined, can deal with. In particular this perspective stresses three key conceptions, relevant to education. First, that a state of 'well-being', necessarily compatible with the levels and kinds of achievement which furnish an individual with the raw material for a personal identity in any particular kind of society, is an aim that can be held in common by workers in education and in mental health. Secondly, education, instead of being viewed as either child-centred or adult-centred, should be seen as basically transaction-centred (Murphy, 1961), in that it always involves an interaction between the generations which results eventually in modifications of culture. And finally, that extending human well-being implies extending the domains of love and reason, and that this in turn means coming to terms with our own capacity for hate and unreason. Essentially this involves deepening our self-knowledge, and increasing our capacity for self-acceptance and hence acceptance of others. This is regarded as *a fortiori* an essential task for the educator.

It is clear that a major thrust in my own thinking is towards the possibility of a better world, in the making of which a better education has an indispensable part to play. But this is not for me a search for Utopia. I do not believe in the perfectibility of man or of human society in this sense.* I do not think the kingdom of heaven will come upon the earth, except in the sense that it is already here, when, in moments of illumination we are capable of

* Passmore's *The Perfectibility of Man* (1970) is the latest in scholarly treatises aimed against Utopianism. While agreeing with much of his analysis it seems to me he has lost sight altogether of the human need for 'the vision without which the people perish'. That they may and do perish because of some visions is no argument against all visions. To suppose that men are incurably unable to discriminate between destructive and constructive visions is to come close to giving up all hope for man.

seeing it, whether it be in the natural world, the works of man, in children and young people, or in the lineaments of those we love. Rather I believe in the necessity of a continuous renewal, which is not mere innovation, but is a rediscovery by individual men and women of their own fundamental natures in which love and hate may be reconciled in creative action. This renewal may be thought of in conceptual terms as 'individuation' in a Jungian sense, personal integration in a Freudian sense, the explicit understanding of knowledge as personal in Polanyi's sense, the discovery of self and other in Macmurray's sense, the encounter of I with Thou in Buber's sense, or in much simpler terms as feeling in tune with the cosmos, or of being fully alive. To me these are modern ways of speaking the truth inherent in the myths of resurrection and redemption which have informed human thought throughout recorded history. Thus may the gods be brought to earth, but without being mocked. Renewal is always, *au fond*, a personal event, a 'happening' or inner change, resulting in a reaffirmation of faith, but it is often inspired by example. I have been fortunate in having been asked at various times to write about people who have greatly influenced me and/or others. These tributes drawn together in the third section of the book look a rather chance collection, and so in a sense they are. But, while Sigmund Freud, William Boyd, Winifred Mercier and Herbert Read might at first have felt themselves in strange company had they ever met ensemble, it would surely not have been long before vigorous and constructive discussion would have begun! Such people play a unique role in educational renewal and in pointing towards new horizons for man.

But, for myself, renewal has always come first and foremost through personal relationships, and particularly through educational relationships with my students. It is in this sense that I have tried to interpret teaching, making of it, as far as possible and with its own appropriate safeguards, a personal encounter. Thus in Bristol over the years my students have played an indispensable part in the development of my thinking. Recently I have also received powerful intimations of educational renewal in some aspects of the revolt of youth and in what is loosely referred to as the sexual revolution. These movements, like all great movements, seem to me inherently ambiguous and ambivalent. They carry both threats and promises, and I have tried to lay bare something of their double nature in the last two chapters of section II. These chapters were begun in England and virtually worked through during a visit to the USA. They owe a great deal to the capacity for friendship, the vigorous sense of life and the fervent desire for human betterment I found in my Harvard students. I am particularly indebted to those who worked with me in seminars concerned with the transformations the human individual lives in, and lives through, in his development through relationships with others. These young people and others like them in other parts of the world sustain my hopes that, despite his genocidal tendencies, man as a species may continue to redeem himself. If this is to happen, education must become, more than it is at present, a major means of nourishing man's powers of love and reason, and this objective must become throughout the world part of a more adequate and more commonly accepted perspective.

Bristol—Harvard

References

Buber, Martin (1965), Appendix: Dialogue with Carl Rogers in *The Knowledge of Man* (M. Friedman, ed.). Allen & Unwin.

Hirst, Paul (1966), 'Educational theory' in J. W. Tibble (ed.), *The Study of Education*. Routledge & Kegan Paul.

Morris, Ben (1966a), Discussion. 'The graduate study of Education', *Harvard Educational Review*, vol. 36, spring 1966.

Morris, Ben (1966b), 'The contribution of psychology to education' in J. W. Tibble (ed.), *The Study of Education*.

Murphy, Gardner (1961), *Freeing Intelligence Through Teaching*. Harper.

Notes

The following appear to me to be recent contributions of major conceptual importance to the development of 'a perspective of the personal'.

Buber, Martin (1965), *Between Man and Man*. Macmillan.

Erikson, Eric H. (1959a), *Young Man Luther*. Faber.

Erikson, Eric H. (1959b), *Identity, Youth and Crisis*. Faber.

Fairbairn, W. R. D. (1952), *Psychoanalytic Studies of the Personality*. Tavistock.

Fingarette, Herbert (1963), *The Self in Transformation* (Psychoanalysis, Philosophy and the Life of the Spirit). Basic Books.

Guntrip, Harry (1971), *Psychoanalytic Theory, Therapy, and the Self*. Hogarth.

Macmurray, John (1957, 1961), *The Form of the Personal*: vol. I, *The Self as Agent*; vol. II, *Persons in Relation*. Faber.

Polanyi, Michael (1958), *Personal Knowledge*. Routledge & Kegan Paul.

Schachtel, Ernest (1963), *Metamorphosis*. Routledge & Kegan Paul.

Winnicott, D. W. (1965), *The Maturational Processes and the Facilitating Environment* (Studies in the Theory of Emotional Development). Hogarth.

Part I

Contributions to general theory

One

The study and practice of education

Being a professor is customarily thought to involve professing something, some subject or body of knowledge. What is it that professors of education and their colleagues in departments of education, training colleges and institutes of education profess? This question is often asked, sometimes maliciously, the questioner being aware of the difficulty of giving it a direct answer, sometimes from a genuine wish to know. It is a question that we teachers of this so-called subject, in our more candid moments, are prone to ask ourselves, and to find quite often some dissatisfaction with the answers we give.

You might think the answer straightforward. Departments of education exist to train teachers, that is their obvious though perhaps not their only justification. Our business, therefore, you may say, is to turn students of the various subjects into teachers of them. That is certainly the expectation with which most graduates enter on their training year. They come more or less full of a subject, expecting to be told 'how to put it across'. They are prepared to be reasonably tolerant of any 'frills' of history and theory etc., which they may be expected to acquire as well, so long as they receive this essential practical instruction. A similar, if somewhat less marked, expectation is to be found among students in colleges of education. This expectation of students puts us, those of us who work in departments and colleges of education, into the role of instructors in a particular art or skill. We should perhaps be masters of this art; certainly we should be sufficiently competent and experienced practitioners of it to be able to communicate it to others. And in this act of communication itself it might be expected of us that we would reveal by example the skill we are attempting to communicate. By this token the best teachers should be found in departments and colleges of education! These implications are, of course, eagerly seized upon by our detractors, and they are not few—though perhaps growing fewer. If, they say, in effect, there is an art or skill in teaching, tell us how it can be communicated directly, how it can be acquired otherwise than through experience. Further, they will ask whether the quality of teaching in a department of education itself is so outstanding that it should convince the sceptics, that if there is a key to be passed on, it is really in the possession of those who are carrying out the education of teachers. In any case, they will ask whether this sort of thing is proper work for a university.

As it happens, I think few of us would be willing to attempt to justify our work solely in terms of our own teaching skill, not so much through modesty perhaps, but because we reject the conception of our role as that of instructors in an art, i.e. as technicians. Yet the expectations of our students that they should be taught how to do the job is reasonable and must be met—in so far as it can be met. There are limitations in meeting it, and the nature of these limitations, and the grounds upon which they rest, form part of the theme of this lecture.

Some of the difficulties concerning the nature of teacher training and the esteem, or lack of it, in which it is held are illumined by historical perspective. The idea of professional training for teachers is very new compared with teaching itself. Even newer is the professional study of education, as the essential core of that training. The training college, or normal school as it was called, grew out of the pupil teacher system, and that system left marks upon professional training, some of which are still discernible. The first training college in England was that founded by Kay-Shuttleworth at Battersea in 1840. It had been preceded by normal schools on the continent and in Scotland. Battersea was founded deliberately on the Swiss model. Mr Kay, as he then was, encountered the fiercest opposition, albeit the purposes of his new institution seems limited enough now. 'Its purpose,' says Frank Smith (1923), Kay-Shuttleworth's biographer, 'was to prepare teachers for workhouse and district schools, for schools of industry, for schools which would reconcile the children of the poor to a life of honest toil, while tasting the delights of mental activity and religious communion.'

The history of university education departments goes back only to 1890 and the first training college provided by a local education authority was established in 1904. True, Joseph Payne was Professor of Education at the College of Preceptors in 1873, and chairs of education were established in St Andrews and Edinburgh in 1876. For all that, newness has been and is still an important factor in the lack of regard with which the training of teachers is held in some quarters. In Bristol the Chair of Education, carrying with it the headship of the Education Department, was established in 1919, and to date has had only three occupants. Apart from newness, another important factor is origins. We saw how Battersea began, and the aura of poverty, which hung about English elementary education until recently, left a deep mark on the training colleges. In 1944 the McNair Committee, of which our own Vice-Chancellor* was a member, stated: 'What is chiefly wrong with the majority of the training colleges is their poverty, and all that flows from it.' Commenting on the fact that university departments of education do not suffer from the same poverty, the report said: 'They have other difficulties to overcome. These arise partly from the poor regard in which education has in the past been held by some universities, and partly from the related fact that training departments tend to be conducted as self-contained units.' The creation of university institutes of education as 'organic federations of approved training organizations', so strongly argued for in the McNair report, and of which Bristol came first in 1947,† is generally taken to have been a crucial step forward. The McNair report recommended that

> the universities should accept new responsibilities for the education and training of teachers and, to that end, should establish University Schools of Education. Some universities may find it desirable to establish more than one such School. We wish to state with the utmost frankness that we are not proposing something which is comparatively unimportant and which will make no substantial difference to the work of the universities. On the contrary our scheme asks much of them. It demands of the universities a richer conception of their responsibility towards education.

The acceptance of this recommendation and the further decision of the majority of the universities that the directorship of such an institute should carry with it a university chair of education, or that the directorship should be linked with an existing chair, may be taken as further evidence of the seriousness with which universities are now regarding their responsibilities in this field.

Poverty and isolation have gone, but some fundamental problems remain. Although we believe we have now a grasp of some of the essentials of a teacher's preparation, criticism is still rife and that there is room for criticism is not to be denied. The

* At the date of this lecture, Sir Philip Morris, K.C.M.G., C.B.E.

† This priority is disputed by Birmingham. It is a question of which of a number of closely related events is to be taken as signalling the actual birth of institute organization.

introduction in 1960 of a three-year course for all teachers in training colleges is eagerly looked forward to by many, as an opportunity to re-design the content of teacher training and to imbue it with a new spirit. What are the essential problems of that training? Let me take one only—the one which implicitly contains all others. How are we to conceive of education as a subject of study, and how can such a study be effectively related to the practice of education? For a considerable time, and even now in some places, the major emphasis was put on reading and reflecting upon the doctrines of the great educators of the past, and upon the history of educational institutions. Conducted in a particular way by a skilled tutor, this approach has still a vital contribution to make—for the older, abler, and more philosophically minded students. It came as a great step forward from imparting the tricks of the trade. But for the most part students imbibed uncritically, rather than reflected upon, what the great educators had said. Theory and practice were but distantly related. Another important step came with the recognition that the teacher's business was not only to teach subjects, but to teach children. That is now accepted as a fundamental idea, and is the justification for the child study and educational psychology which now figure prominently in most training courses.

These developments, however, have not solved the problem of education as a subject. Nor has the further introduction of courses in sociology and comparative education. In fact, all such introductions have served only to highlight the fact that in studying these disciplines, as they are often presented, the student is not studying education at all, but something else; something which is no doubt bound up with it, but which cannot be said to constitute it. Moreover, the more that is added, the more impossible does the task of preparing the teacher in this way seem to become. And the more impossible becomes the task of the teacher of education. The sheer range of the material he is expected to know about leaves him in constant danger of becoming a charlatan. Lastly, all these approaches to the study of education stress either what someone else has thought or done in the name of education, or stress those aspects of education which make the study of it one of the social sciences. The latter approach, already valuable, and increasingly important as its contribution is likely to become, where it is an over-riding one, inevitably tends to dehumanize the study, because the business of science is with natural objects and their manipulation. Personal and moral aspects are always in danger of being overlooked, subordinated to manipulative considerations, and even of being banished altogether, as evidence the ease with which *persons* become *personnel* and the study of *morals* turns into questions of *morale*. Moreover, the vital problem of linking all these different studies with practice in the classroom remains.

The educational enterprise

There is need, it seems to me, for us to reconsider the nature of education and the study of it. Perhaps we require some such reminder as that given by Robert Redfield (1955) when he said: 'Education is a desirable experience of a particular kind, in this respect like falling in love, joy and the state of grace. It is a good thing that happens to people.' And again: 'In my own self I feel now and then the educational experience, and in the lives of others I see its signs.'

Leaving aside the embarrassing consequences that might ensue were I simply and boldly to declare myself a professor of an experience, which was rather like that of falling in love, let us recognize that Redfield is looking at education from the inside, as an experience which someone undergoes, enjoys and perhaps suffers too. He sees himself as partaking in this experience, and that is a vital step forward. But his participation appears to be entirely passive, and here I think he just fails to take another crucial step. Have we not also to recognize that we can partake fully of the educational experience only by participating actively in it, not merely as creatures of stimulus and response, nor even just as beings in whom some hidden leaven is at work, though that this should be happening is vital, as Redfield suggests, but in some measure as agents, and as consciously free agents at that? Here it seems to me is the vital key. Education is after all not primarily a 'subject' at all, but rather a practical enterprise in which many adults are joined together and joined together with children and young people. It is the personal experience of this enterprise and the part that we actively play in it, which constitutes our own education. The enterprise of course has its objective, social, impersonal aspects—to be studied in their extension in space and time—but it has its subjective, inner personal aspects also, and it is these which ultimately give it meaning for us.

How do we study an enterprise on which we are engaged, and study it in a way which will affect our actions? Surely by reflecting upon what it is we are doing in this enterprise, and upon how what we are trying to do is related to what others are doing, have done, or have tried to do. Such a change of viewpoint does not at one stroke solve all our problems, but it puts them into a different framework of thought within which it may be possible to find solutions. One immediate consequence is to help to rid ourselves of the notion that in preparing teachers for service we are under an obligation to turn out the finished article. On the contrary, what we have to do is to provide the intending teacher with some preliminary equipment for a life-long engagement, and suggest to him some of the best ways of discovering what his enterprise is really about, ways which will enable him to tackle problems for himself as they arise and enable him to some extent to assess the results of what he has done. In short, our task is to give the intending teacher the essential life-saving equipment he will need at the start, and to awaken in him an impulse to try to understand what he is doing, that will last him for the rest of his life. The study of education is therefore largely a matter of finding out what it is that one is doing in the educational enterprise, and of discovering the conditions under which some degree of success can be secured.

This is a normal requirement. Professional people expect to be able to say what the nature of their enterprise is. They want to have some conception of what it is about, to be able to give some intelligible form to it, and to their own part in it. It is a normal demand that a competent professional person should not simply be a skilled practitioner, but that he should have a clear idea of the scope of his undertaking, the means employed in it and the ends it attempts to serve. Moreover, we believe that in the last resort a man's skill in the practice of his profession is intimately bound up with his understanding of what it is. He may be judged competent, we say, if he knows what it is he is doing. The discovery of what it is that he is doing, of the nature of the enterprise in which he is engaged, is a task that will surely occupy the student of education all his life. If it does not, this will not be evidence that he has discovered all that there is to be found out, but rather that he has given up the attempt at discovery altogether, and by doing so, has ceased to be a student. And this will also mean, we believe, that he has given up the attempt to educate, although he may continue to instruct.

Some features of the enterprise

There is one striking feature of the educational enterprise which perhaps tells us as much about it as anything else. That is, that we all tend to believe that we know what it is, and what its objectives are, while at the same time whenever we attempt to say what it is, and what its objectives are, we fall into disagreement. Hence the proliferation of definitions of education which now grossly encumber the literature and to which it is certainly not my intention to add anything new. We may think it is not too difficult to get assent to some simple, fundamental, and very comprehensive statement, such as that education is the fundamental means whereby man as a species is able to maintain and develop the achievements which differentiate him from the rest of the animal kingdom. But immediately this authoritative sounding socio-biological statement is uttered, it will be countered, perhaps by a theological one, sounding no less authoritative, to the effect that in the last resort education has a religious purpose and is essentially concerned with man's redemption from a state of nature, to a condition in which he is able to perceive, and realize in action, his kinship with the creator and sustainer of the universe. Or the retort may be only a still small voice, saying that education is a special kind of inner experience, a series of creative happenings inside a person which progressively make him a more mature being, and a more responsible agent. It is not too difficult to see some important connections between these various statements and perhaps to attempt to reconcile them through a conception of the attainment and maintenance of civilization as the central concern of education—the state of being civilized being essentially concerned with the quality of the values which men uphold, rather than with the state of their technology, although the two are always to some extent inter-dependent. But the disputes will, of course, immediately break out again over the interpretation of the values which it is considered constitute civilization.

This feature of the educational enterprise draws attention to another familiar and closely related one. It is not only difficult to say what it is we are doing in education, but apparently impossible ever to know in any complete sense whether we have done it. It is commonplace but nevertheless instructive to reflect that, as H. G. Wells put it in *Joan and Peter*, we teachers are necessarily 'sowers of unseen harvests, reapers of thistles and the wind'. We all know this in our everyday work, we accept it and may even take comfort from it. We recall that the failure of Charles Darwin's schoolmasters seriously to engage him in the orthodox studies of his time seems to have contributed to the advance of human knowledge in a way which they could hardly have foreseen. We may wonder what those teachers in Vienna who helped Sigmund Freud to become a master of languages, ancient and modern, thought they were doing. Freud, in addition to being a distinguished stylist in his native German, was completely at home in Latin and

Greek, had a thorough acquaintance with French and English, and could read Italian, Spanish and Hebrew. An unorthodox, even inappropriate, preparation you might think for the future physician, for work in the laboratories and consulting room. Being wise after the event, we can now glimpse how these studies contributed to the growth of a mind which was destined to illumine for the first time, in a systematic way, a fundamental but hitherto dark dimension of the human personality.

But the major point here is not the apparent impossibility of knowing the ultimate results of our educational actions, in the sense that these results will only be manifest after we are dead, but the fact, at once commonplace and profound, that what we think we are doing, so often in the event turns out to have been something quite different. We are here touching on the great question of the notion of predictability in human affairs—a matter which could detain us as long as we pleased—but our present purpose is simply to draw attention to what appears to be a radical uncertainty about the results of our enterprise. This can also be illustrated on the large scale of social action. For example, as Professor Roger Wilson reminded us in his own inaugural address (1954), one important conception running through the movement for reform in nineteenth-century England was that of 'education as a stabilizing force, a process which would make the poor more amenable to the discipline of their society'. That has an ironic ring today. So also has the fact that many revolutionary spirits have firmly believed that the expansion of education, without qualification as to what kind of education it should be, would necessarily and of itself enlarge the sphere of human freedom. There is a somewhat staggering contrast, is there not, between this difficulty of saying what we are doing, this uncertainty of knowing whether we have done what we believe we intended to do, and the vast scope of the enterprise itself and the boldness and lack of apparent doubt with which we carry it out every day. To say this, of course, is only to say that education is a process which has important unconscious origins, and which in many, if not most, of its forms remains to a large extent unconscious. From one point of view, to educate our children seems almost as natural a process as having them in the first place, but this obscures the fact that education in the sense of what happens in schools is a relatively new feature of human life. In fact, at this day, only about half the children of the human race ever go to school at all. Schooling is a conscious creation and has had to be fought for, and has to continue to be fought for, as we well know. It represents the major indication of our growing concern of being involved in the educational enterprise. But as yet the consciousness of what we are doing in school, and of what schools are in fact *for*, is only sporadic, and only at intervals attains any depth. A vast amount of our educational practice is carried out with only a minimum of awareness of what we are doing. There is not meant to be any element of superiority in this criticism, for those of us whose recognized business it is to be as conscious as possible about what we are doing in education, succeed in being so only to a very limited extent. Rather, it is intended to suggest what the study of education as an enterprise should fundamentally be, namely the attempt through reflection and experiment to attain a more explicit understanding of our aims, and of the implications of our actions in relation to them.

Approaches to the study of the enterprise

We may safely distinguish three approaches to the study of education viewed in this way, provided that we remember that in the explicit study of any one of them, the other two are present implicitly. All of these approaches emphasize that the evidence provided by what we *do* in the name of education is at least as important for our understanding of our intentions in the doing of it, as that provided by what we *say* we have done or meant to do. The contrast between act and statement, between result and conscious aim, reveals something of the nature of those influences which are in conflict with our declared aims, whether they be hidden intentions of our own, often indeed successfully hidden from ourselves, or the opposed intentions of others. We cannot, of course, neglect the study of stated aims, since attempting to make clearer statements about our intentions is an indispensable aid to achieving a clearer comprehension of what we are doing.

The three approaches are: first, in terms of social process, of the institutions concerned in education; second, in terms of the vehicles or instruments through which education is conducted in these institutions; and third, in terms of the human relationships involved in education, the encounters between the persons engaged in the enterprise.

The study of the educational enterprise as a social process is best begun by participating in the enterprise and by reflecting on the experience of doing so. Practical involvement in the life of a variety of contemporary educational institutions very quickly gives an idea of the scope of the enterprise, and the apparent variety of purposes which exist. If such practical experience can then be illumined by some genuine historical understanding, and if the concepts thus arrived at can be further generalized through a study of contemporary societies at different stages of development, then the universal commitment of education to a moral purpose, variously conceived at different times and places, becomes apparent. The role of education in the maintenance of the culture of any society can thus come to be accepted as a basic fact. By an examination of our own society we can see that it is in important ways being continually re-shaped, and the question of the influence of education on social change, its direction, and what values should guide it, become matters for discussion. In a world in which education is becoming, in more and more places, a consciously accepted means for the production of a certain type of citizen, it becomes our plain duty to ask what kind of citizen we consider we are producing in a society which refers to its basic aim as the maintenance of freedom. And as we wrestle with this question, as Sir Fred Clarke did in his last book, *Freedom in the Educative Society*, we have to ask what we mean by freedom in this sense and in what ways we can enable our children to grow up so that they are capable of exercising it. If we consider that men act freely when their actions are neither entirely the result of duress, nor of inner compulsion, then we have to discover how children may be helped gradually to achieve both independence of mind and control of impulse. We have to discover how to help them to develop powers of discrimination and choice and to become eventually possessed of what Sir Fred called 'an instructed conscience'. And we have to ask ourselves whether such development is likely, or even possible, unless parents and teachers conceive it as their task to create situations in which children and young people can be helped to discover for themselves the claims of freedom and authority through life in a genuine community.

The approach through a study of instruments and vehicles of learning may lead us in the same direction. Much of what we do in home and school, particularly in the early years, is concerned with helping the young to form stable and resilient personalities in terms of what we regard as desirable conduct. Much of it is concerned with providing them with skills needed in later learning and life, and much appears to be concerned with the acquisition of knowledge, not all of it useful. What is the function of such knowledge? Arguments about usefulness, and about knowledge for its own sake, never take us very far. We are left uneasy, unless we can show that the subjects we study have a general educational value in themselves. Apart altogether from their obvious utility, the sciences may be defended in terms of the power they have to teach us how to observe, describe, experiment, reason and draw conclusions from data in an orderly manner. For classical, literary and historical studies it may be claimed that in addition to possessing some of the virtues of scientific study, they awaken our sympathies with our fellow men, widen our understanding of social affairs, sharpen our powers of moral discernment, and hence strengthen our capacity for moral decision. Through the expressive arts we may experience freedom directly in the creation of the various means whereby we deepen our grasp of beauty and of the meaning of our common human experience. Ultimately we may point out how all these studies contribute to making men free, through developing their creative powers, and their capacity to ask fruitful questions about their experience, and to rely on their own judgment in answering them.

At this point, however, psychologists will remind us that none of this development of generalized powers of the mind will take place at all unless certain important conditions are first fulfilled—conditions which are all too often absent. It is important to consider what these conditions are. The first condition is that the virtues and powers we wish children to develop, they can develop only through learning to practise them. Learning *about* them is useless by itself. In the expressive arts this might appear so blatantly obvious as not to require mention, were it not that we are still far from providing all children with adequate opportunities to develop their creative powers. The point may be illustrated also in relation to the moral virtues like unselfishness, tolerance and co-operation. To what extent at present do we provide children with opportunities to practise these virtues—and to make the necessary mistakes in doing so—in the way we provide them with opportunities for practising arithmetic or writing skills? The second condition is that they should gradually be made conscious of what they are doing. If for example they are ever to be able to recognize moral behaviour in themselves and others, and to deliberate upon it, they have to be given opportunity to practise these virtues and powers in a variety of situations, and have to be helped to see that they are in fact learning to be unselfish, tolerant and co-operative, and to see to what further questions regarding conduct these ideas give rise. Here the teachers' guidance is indispensable.

Turning to the intellectual virtues, W. D. Wall (1955) summarizes the results of experimental investigations, as follows:

> The teacher who wishes his pupils to generalize their skills and knowledge, must plan for it. He must so shape his methods and materials as to lead children to draw the parallels and

applications in related fields. Only a few and those the most intelligent will spontaneously transfer thinking skills and methods acquired, let us say in geometry, or in the learning of a language, to other tasks. The teacher must in fact teach for transfer, not only between disciplines but within any given discipline like mathematics. Once again the role of the teacher is fundamental.

Third, the development of all these general virtues requires that children should experience their presence in others and by sympathy and identification take them into themselves. This is in fact one of the most basic of all the learning processes, and is, for example, as psycho-analysts have shown, the way in which in early childhood we lay the foundations of our characters. It follows, of course, that vicarious experience gained through story, history and imaginative literature may act in the same way, provided that the teaching is of the kind that will assist children to refine their powers of identification and discrimination. Thus all the conditions under which learning is truly educative, in the sense of assisting in the development of these powers most easily recognizable as human, make special demands upon the teacher. We may thus remind ourselves that by approaching our enterprise through the study of social processes and by way of vehicles of learning like subjects, we may be in danger of leaving out the salient feature of it, namely that it takes place through a relationship between persons—between pupil and teacher.

How then can we reconcile a conception of our educational enterprise as essentially a commerce between persons, as an adventure in mutuality, with a study of it as the acquisition of knowledge and ideas, of skills and of powers of creation and appreciation, or the study of it as a social process. Some degree of tension will no doubt always exist between these approaches, but we can point the way to reconciliation if we will recognize two very simple facts. The first is that, as Professor John Pilley has pointed out (1953), anything we learn or invite others to learn represents a human achievement, and that we constitute our own minds through studying the achievements of others. Chemistry, for example, represents a human achievement and its educative value, as distinct from its utility, lies in understanding how it was created through the activities of observation, experiment, imagination and reason. Secondly, studies of social process, whether historical, sociological or psychological, derive their ultimate significance from the fact that, again as Pilley (1957) puts it, 'Men's lives, though in part the result of environmental influence, are also an expression of their capacity for conceiving of values, for discriminating between values, and for bringing into being the things that are valued.' Prominent among the ways of bringing into being the things that are valued is the educational enterprise. But the power of the enterprise to do this rests largely on the extent to which those engaged in it can become aware of what it is they are doing.

Our study is so far, therefore, conceived as being a reflection upon what we are doing in terms of values and of the relation of means to ends. Where is its discipline? Apart from the disciplines of its ancillary studies, scientific, historical etc., which must be invoked, but which I think we may sometimes be inclined to overstress at present in our teaching, has it any more characteristic discipline? My answer is that it has, and it is one which is common to all studies which have for their aim the understanding of an enterprise in which one is engaged. The discipline of this kind of reflection may be said to have two components and can be seen to have two different aspects in practice. The first component is unmistakably philosophical; it is concerned with the creation and clarification of the concepts required in order to think about what one is doing. Its instruments are constructive and critical thought, and its aim is logical clarity. The second component is as unmistakably psychological; it is concerned with the discovery and clarification of intentions as these are disclosed in the details of behaviour, and more directly, through self-awareness. Its instruments are intuition (insightful interpretation) and emotional honesty, and its aim is psychological illumination. Taken as a unity this reflective discipline has two practical aspects, which bring in other disciplines—an aspect of statement, involving the discipline of language—and an aspect of action involving the discipline of will. As a member of the educational enterprise, the student has to be able to formulate and discuss his own conception of what he is doing, and he has to try to modify his actions in accordance with the understanding he has achieved. Thus, in being called upon to come to grips honestly with what he is doing, to arrive at adequate ideas about it, to embody this understanding in clear statements and, most important of all, to render reflection effective in his own behaviour, the student of education is faced with the most exacting of tasks.

If there were time, it would be important to consider some of the constraints within which we work, and some of the limitations to which the enterprise is subjected. Such consideration would take us into the socio-economic and political fields on the one hand, and into the psycho-biological and medical fields on the other. Some of the personal limitations of which account must be taken, appcar to have their origin in differences of natural endowment among individuals, but the extent of such natural differences has not been determined with any accuracy. Far too little attention has so far been paid to the subtler environmental influences at work in early childhood. What is certain is that many of the individual limitations encountered arise from the way in which societies, in both conscious and unconscious ways, utilize distinctions like social class, sex, religion and race as criteria for regulating or maintaining differential development among their members. Within our own society, the extent to which all children are now officially within the school system, contrasted with the limited degree of success we have so far had in really engaging the energies of a considerable proportion of them, is an important study in itself. Of great significance, too, is the study of the hazards of the enterprise, and of its failures and casualties, partial and complete. Some of our deepest insights into the meaning of education have been gained through the study of casualties, and we must never forget the burden of maladjustment and mental illness our community carries, and that in some measure our enterprise is responsible for these casualties. In fact, the whole of what may be called the pathology of the enterprise is now among the most important branches of its study, For example, it is difficult to refrain from labelling as pathological many of the features of our examination systems which lay such heavy stress on children and young people. It is now being recognized that the careful study of examinations or of assessment systems in general, and the effect they have on what is done in the schools, can do much to help us understand some of the ways in which we are failing. In approaching the enterprise through the study of its limitations, casualties and failures, there is thus a vast field for research. But we must now turn to a discussion of some of the conditions under which our enterprise may be successful.

Some conditions for the success of the enterprise

To speak of the success or failure of our enterprise is at once to invoke some criterion by which it may be judged. The consideration of questions of assessment is in itself a vast topic, into which I do not propose to enter. I am not indeed thinking here of public criteria like examinations, but of the teacher's own criteria however arrived at. These are not something extraneous or new to the enterprise, but are simply re-statements of whatever it is we consider ourselves to be doing. If we are trying to help our pupils to develop powers of discrimination and taste in literature, the criteria we use will be precisely those conceptions of discrimination and taste we ourselves have arrived at, as setting our aims. While success, even in these terms, is partly dependent on our conception of our aims, we know full well that we may and do fail, while in some sense being clear what we are trying to do, and that we can succeed, without being at all clear what in fact we were after. On what other sorts of conditions then does success depend? I suggest that the understanding of these conditions depends on our realizing that the encounters that comprise education are always double encounters. There is the encounter with our common culture—the world of experience to which we are trying to introduce our pupils—and our encounter with them.

A great deal of our enterprise and its success depends upon the principles in terms of which we select and arrange the educational experiences we propose for our pupils. There in a nutshell lies the whole problem of the construction of curricula. There appear to be three main criteria on which to base selection and arrangement. We must first have regard to the capabilities and the powers and interests of our pupils, their experience and stage of development. This regard must inform all that we do, and of this, more later. Second, we must have regard to what is likely to be relevent to them in an instrumental sense—the equipment they will need for later studies and to face the world. We can never be certain of what it is best to include here, for we are unable to predict the demands of future life in any detail. At best our selection will be a reasonable or even an inspired guess; at worst it may include, and I fear it often does, much, the relevance of which, in an instrumental sense, has passed forever. Third, we must have regard to what is pre-eminently required for their *education, that is for them to develop those powers, virtues, and sympathies which seem to us to constitute the essence of what we mean by being human.* I would perhaps add one further criterion governing the relations of the last two. We should arrange that as far as possible everything our pupils learn and experience should have both instrumental and educational value, and that they should be expected to acquire as little as is absolutely necessary of what can only be of instrumental value to them. This is much more a matter of method than of content for there are few, if any, wholly illiberal, that is uneducative, studies. The fruitful way to set about this is not to minimize whatever seems directly useful—and therefore perhaps likely to engage our pupils' interests—but to ensure that whatever they learn of instrumental value is so taught that any real educational value it contains is maximized.

This principle is clearly deeply involved in our current controversies about the liberal education of scientists and technicians. Part of the answer to this problem should be plain. In so far as the sciences are taught as human achievements, their real educational value will be maximized. This is, of course, a partial answer only. While it is more correct to speak of liberal and illiberal ways of teaching any subject than of liberal and illiberal subjects, is it not also correct to say that some studies have more inherent educational value than others? It is difficult to refute the argument that what are generally recognized as humane studies—literature in our own and other languages, and history, for example—*can* have special educative value denied to the sciences because their subject matter, as well as representing human achievement, is about humanity. I say *can* have special value, for often I fear they do not have it. These subjects when educationally conceived, and what that means we shall see in a moment, nourish directly our sympathies, our imagination, and our powers of moral discernment, because they are mirrors for ourselves and our times. Hence there would appear to be a strong case for including at least one of these subjects in the general education of the scientist. But there is an equally strong case for including at least one of the sciences in the education of the non-scientist. Without some understanding of scientific achievements and of the scientific attitude no one can enter fully into the heritage of our culture. Hence I do not think the debate about subjects goes to the heart of the matter. It seems to me that just as much emphasis must lie on the *way* subjects are taught and on *who* teaches them as on what they are apparently about. A man may become civilized by learning a subject, perhaps apparently more instrumental than liberal, from someone who is himself a civilized person, and who understands the kind of achievement his subject represents. The essence of education appears to me to reside at least as much in this personal relationship as in terms of the subjects or activities in which the relationship may be conducted. I am tempted in fact to go further and to assign to subjects only subordinate roles in education, but such a judgment raises issues much too complex to be discussed here. Certainly I regard most of the special claims for particular subjects, taken apart from the teaching of them and apart from the teachers, as suspect. This does not, of course, detract in the least from the wisdom of ensuring that everyone's education embraces both humane and scientific studies.

This is part only of the story of the teacher's encounter with his culture. Having selected from it, how does he come to possess what he has selected in a way which makes it readily communicable to his pupils? What conditions govern its communicability?

Here my own views run counter to many which are widely proclaimed at the present time. It is claimed that the teacher needs to make a special study of at least one subject, for its own sake, for the sake of his personal education, and this is the important point, that he should study it without reference to the fact that he may and probably will teach it. Surely this is a contradiction. For a subject to minister to his personal education he must study it as a human achievement in such a way that his learning of it is a species of communion with those who created it. When studied in this way, it becomes his own possession through his having shared it with others—its creators—and the capacity he has developed for such sharing is one of the conditions for the development of the correlative capacity of his being able to share it in turn with others again—his pupils. Another condition is that he learns how to reflect on what this sharing has involved in the way of augmenting the powers of his own mind. Not that it necessarily follows that he will then be able to share it. There are still other conditions, but the relationships indicated are sufficiently strong to justify the common sayings that the greatest teachers of a subject are to be found among the greatest masters of it, and that there is no better way to become master of a subject than to learn to teach it. A further and crucial condition is, of course, that he should *want* to share it, that his motives in acquiring it are that he wants to pass it on, that he is as much concerned with *giving* as with *getting*.

Now there is nothing obscure or very novel about this way of looking at how a teacher should best encounter his own subject, nor does it in the least imply that in all his dealings with it he must all the time be constrained by consciously considering how he could set about teaching it. To put the point quite bluntly, until a man is able to help others to understand what he has learned, can he be said to have fully understood it himself? Doubtless there are exceptions to this principle—the occasional scholar, creative artist or scientist, for example, who is apparently a poor teacher. Such an exception, however, is of a kind that does surely prove the rule. Moreover, it is legitimate to wonder whether, whatever his subject may do for such a man, the odds are not heavily against it having a truly educative effect on him. And finally it is surely reasonable to suppose that the man who needs to learn a subject so that it becomes his own private possession—not to be shared—is likely to be a poor teacher.

The communicability of our knowledge to our pupils is also conditioned by the extent to which we are able to interpret it in a way suited to their needs and powers. To do this presupposes that we not only understand what these are, but that we can re-interpret our subject to ourselves in *their* terms. The development of the ability to do this is one of the most important ways in which we ourselves may become masters of it, and this reinforces the argument that all that a teacher learns in the course of his own education should be conceived in a way which makes it readily communicable to others. Communicability is thus a function of the teacher's powers of interpretation. The crux of the kind of interpretation of his subject a teacher has to make for his pupils is that it should reveal the 'subject' as having some definite form, and yet as being flexible. The definite form of the subject springs, for example, in mathematics from its own inherent nature expressed in its own logic and conventions. It is through this revelation of its form that pupils can encounter the discipline or authority of the subject. But it is just as important to have regard to the freedom of the subject. This springs from its inherent flexibility, and again with regard to mathematics this is a function of our capacity to discover from the infinite variety of relationships which comprise it, the particular selection and arrangement of these through which our pupils can best explore it and master its meaning.

What about the teacher's other encounter—his encounter with children? What is vital about this, is what it means, and how we seek to bring it about. It is by no means the same thing as making a study of child psychology, as this is portrayed for us in lectures and text-books, nor is it simply making the acquaintance of children in the classroom. I have deliberately used the term encounter, because I think it the best term, and because I want to make clear that 'getting to know children' means much more than is commonly supposed. We may recall that Freud (1913) once said about this: 'Only someone who can feel his way into the minds of children can be capable of educating them; and we grown up people cannot understand children because we no longer understand our own childhood.' This was meant, in part at least, to be a challenge. Thus, in order that we may truly encounter children, we have to understand what it means to be a child, and there is no possible basis for this understanding except a living contact with the experiences of our own childhood—albeit this contact need not take the form of conscious memory—that is quite secondary. This idea is not something trivial, but absolutely fundamental. It means a number of things. On the theoretical side it amounts to a denial of behaviourism as a doctrine, not of course of behaviourism as a research programme, in the sense of the necessity for what is called behavioural data in the study of human conduct, but behaviourism as a possible model for conceiving of how we come to know other people. We are only able to interpret our observations of the behaviour of others because they are pointers to experiences which we know at first hand in ourselves, or are so closely related to our own phantasies, conscious or unconscious, that we can infer their meaning by analogy. Of course we may be mistaken in our interpretations and these have always to be checked against further behavioural observations and further reflection, but that does not falsify the principle. On the practical side it is only through the re-activation within ourselves of the feelings, thoughts, and phantasies of our childhood that we are able to enter into the minds of children and share their experience, and so help them to come to share ours. Moreover, the more we become aware of the childhood impulses that still lie within us and which we not infrequently still obey, the greater our capacity to deal individually with children's emotional difficulties. As anger boils up within us, as we make the cutting or catty remark, or play tit for tat, or take elaborate steps to bolster our self-confidence—for instance, by always being on our dignity—do we not catch a glimpse of the child that was?

All this serves to remind us that our childhood is not dead and gone, but lives actively within us. Unfortunately, many of us lose touch with it and in practice attempt to deny its existence—and none of us is aware of it enough. It is for this reason that perhaps the most fundamental problem of all in training teachers is how to help students to regain access to it. There is no certain way of doing this, although all experiences that kindle the fires of imagination and feeling may contribute. One way of course is continuous first hand contact with children. This is essential in any case, for while access to our own childhood is a necessary condition for encountering children, it is never a sufficient one for the teacher. It is generally a condition for the success of our enterprise that whatever spontaneous understanding of children we possess is built upon, and strengthened in various ways. In addition to providing them with opportunities for first hand contact with and observation of children in a variety of situations, we may encourage our students to reflect upon what it means to be a child, through the agency of literature for children, or through a study of children's productions, whether literary or in some other expressive medium, or through reading books in which children recognizably figure as their true selves. For example, we may suggest that before reading books on child psychology, students would be well advised to have read such works as Edward Blishen's *Roaring Boys* or Joyce Cary's novel, *Charley is my Darling*. This is not infrequently a shock, particularly to the graduate student, and he may regard it as a rather frivolous exercise, not worthy of consideration in a university. It may take him some time to realize that there are more profundities readily to be glimpsed in *Charley* than in many textbooks. None of this means of course that we can afford to neglect the scientific study of learning and development, including physical development and well being. It is one of the great discoveries of this century that the child's mind (or the adult's for that matter) cannot be understood apart from his body, his feelings towards it and his use of it. Not only has modern linguistic philosophy made us very conscious of the deceptive nature of concepts such as 'mind' and 'body', and of the care necessary in their use, but we have also the powerful biological conceptions of organism and of psycho-somatic unity to help us. The potential broadening and deepening of our understanding brought by child study is of course enormous. We may mention the importance of well-established conceptions such as those of maturation, individual differences in abilities and temperaments, and the role of discovery and meaningfulness in learning. We may then go on to stress the way in which meaning is rooted in concrete experience and how such experience is related to the formation of the child's concepts of time, space and causality. Above all we may point to the basic role of motivation in learning, and its dependence on personal relationships. All of this, if we really assimilated it and discovered how to put it into practice, could revolutionize our educational system overnight and drastically reduce our failures and casualities. That is why I spoke of the potential power of these things. But, alas, as yet much of this is unassimilated knowledge, just as unassimilated as history or chemistry or other subject matter may be in some of our students. It has not yet fully entered into teachers' encounters with children—maybe because we teachers of teachers have not yet fully assimilated it ourselves and are therefore not as yet very skilful in discovering ways in which it may truly inform our students' understanding of their pupils and themselves. It has not yet fully become active wisdom in Whitehead's sense.

The circumstances of our encounter with children—its setting in school and educational system are of course important conditions of success—and an understanding of their true educational significance can be achieved only if we have first hand knowledge of a variety of circumstances. But on this I will not dwell, for I want to say something about the teacher's conduct of his encounter with his pupils. This is of course the core of the whole business. If it is inept, or a continually unresolved struggle for mastery, then all else is brought to nought and it matters nothing that he may have exhaustively thought about what it is that he is doing, or that he may be a walking encyclopaedia of child study. Our students are well aware of this and their greatest demand for help is always here. Of course the problem tends at first to be thought about only as how to put subjects across, how for example to arrange material so that children are interested. These matters are certainly important, but success with them depends eventually on the teacher's relation to his subject, his relation to children and his relation to himself. It is because of the part his own personality plays—and that includes his attitude to his subject, to children and to himself—that it is so often claimed that teachers are born not made. Undoubtedly some teachers have a good start in the matter—they are nevertheless often improved through a well-conceived study of their enterprise. For a very few intending teachers there is not a great deal that can be done to help them—but for the majority considerable development while in training seems possible, and most of us are persuaded that it quite often takes place, even though definite proof may be lacking. Some reasonable time is needed for the transition from learning to teaching, and it is not to be expected that the time which can be spent in training will ever be sufficient for the purpose. We offer no more than initiation into a role and into relationships whose possibilities can only be realized through experience. One of the major difficulties is that this transition or role reversal involves the teacher's relationship with authority both within and outside himself. From *being under* authority he has to get used to being *in* authority and to learn how to use his authority wisely, with some understanding of children's needs and of his own needs for both freedom and control. But at the heart of this change in his role from learning to teaching is the change from *getting* to *giving*. The ease with which the change is made depends partly on the quality of the teacher's encounter with his own subject, as I have already suggested, but ultimately it depends on the quality of the teacher's regard for children, that is on the quality of his love for them. The essential thing is that his love should be unconditional, that is, that it should imply unconditional acceptance of children for what they are. This means that it must be independent of their ability, interest, and attractiveness, independent of their dislike or even hatred of him and his subject, independent of whatever unlovable characteristics they may actually have. It is only within such a context of unconditional acceptance (which has nothing to do of course with being sentimental about children or letting them do as they please), that children feel free to express the best and most creative aspects of their own natures. This is a hard saying and it is all the harder because it implies that the teacher must first be able to accept whatever is unlovable about himself. It is to this inner integrity, based on an acceptance of self, and to which children immediately respond, that we have to look for the secret of the good teacher. This integrity and quality of regard for children is something the teacher or student cannot command by himself, if he does not have it already, nor can we give it to him. What we can do, however, is to give him opportunities for discovering and developing his own capacity for it.

This is but a brief review of some of the conditions for the success of our enterprise, and at the heart of these conditions we find one which has much more to do with what we are as persons than with what we know or are able to do. Depending so obviously on human quality, how can our enterprise be sustained?

How the enterprise may be sustained and renewed

The sustaining of an enterprise such as ours is a vast and complex matter, and yet also a humble and simple one. To attempt fully to understand its origins and the way in which it has grown and has in the past often declined, would involve us in profound questions such as the growth and decay of civilized communities. But a more personal approach is possible. There is an aspect of the maintenance of our enterprise which involves guarding it against its enemies without and its enemies within—and ultimately the latter are always to be found within ourselves as individuals. Like liberty, its maintenance depends on our eternal vigilance. For each of us it is a personal matter of continually renewing our contact with the sources of power from which the enterprise draws its energy. These are the impulses of the human spirit which most clearly characterize it as human. We can gain access to these sources in many ways, but one fundamental way is through fellowship with one another. That is why we who are occupied in the initial preparation of teachers are so concerned to bring about a sense of community among all those involved in that preparation. It is why we are so concerned to provide opportunities for serving teachers periodically or continuously to renew themselves. These tasks are the essential justification for the existence of university institutes and schools of education in their aspect as organized communities of educators.

In essentials the requirements for both initial preparation and renewal are the same. They are opportunities for coming to understand more deeply the nature of the enterprise itself, opportunities to make or renew our commitment to it, opportunities to discover or review the nature and conduct of our encounters with our own learning and with our pupils, and opportunities to augment our sense of partnership with each other—to discover more fully our mutuality of purpose. This sense of partnership is of supreme importance, and at all levels. For example, what I have said about the study of education should be sufficient to indicate how necessary to the teacher of education are his other academic colleagues—and I would dare to add, how necessary he is to them. We truly require one another and what that means we have as yet scarcely begun to find out. The teacher whose study is labelled 'Education' has not and cannot have any monopoly of understanding of the nature of the common enterprise, but he has an important part to play in revealing the unity of the principles which underlie all our separate endeavours, and in helping to make our common purpose explicit.

Finally, what are the ultimate springs of the spirit upon which we all draw? They are various, but one alone is central, because it is the universal feature of the enterprise, to be seen in every true educational experience. As we have seen, this is love; not of course simply erotic love, nor even Christian charity, but that union of both which transcends both, the coming together of Eros and Agape, the creative and the cherishing, which is the hallmark of parental love, and which it seems to me inspired Christ when he said: 'I am come that ye might have life, and that ye might have it more abundantly.' This statement would appear to express precisely our purpose as educators. But it is a purpose which as individuals we can embrace only in a spirit of true humility, because the best that we can expect is to be allowed to play a small part in the great enterprise which seeks its fulfilment.

Originally an inaugural lecture in the University of Bristol (May 1957) and published by the Bristol University Institute of Education.

References

Clarke, Sir Fred (1948) *Freedom in the Educative Society*. University of London Press.

Freud, Sigmund (1913) *The Claims of Psychoanalysis to Scientific Interest—The Educational Interest*. (Vol. 13 of Standard Edition.)

McNair Committee (1944) *Report: Teachers and Youth Leaders*. HMSO.

Pilley, John (1953) 'Educational theory and the making of teachers', *Educational Theory*, vol. 3, no. 1.

Pilley, John (1957) 'The humanities and the technologist', *Universities Quarterly*, vol. 2, no. 2, p. 129.
Redfield, Robert (1955) *The Redfield Lectures.* Fund for Adult Education, Pasadena, California.
Smith, Frank (1923) *The Life and Work of Sir James Kay-Shuttleworth.* John Murray.
Wall. W. D. (1955) 'Teaching methods' in *The Bearings of Recent Advances in Psychology on Educational Problems* (Studies in Education. no. 7). Evans.
Wilson, Roger (1954) *The Teacher: Instructor or Educator.* Lyndale House Papers, Bristol University Institute of Education.

Two

Arts and sciences in education

To speak at the present time about arts and sciences in education is to ask for trouble. Many people appear to be committed either to what they regard as the unique values of the arts or of the sciences, or to the view that the alleged (and equal) failure of artists and scientists to understand one another is a serious and perhaps even fatal threat to our civilization. This threat can be removed, so runs this view, only if somehow in education the future artist can have his mind tempered by the admixture of some science, and the future scientist be rounded out into a fuller man by engaging in one of the arts. This crude formulation of a currently popular view may satisfy no one, but its very crudity reflects what I hope to show is the superficiality and misleading nature of some of the ideas involved.

In some ways the present scheme resembles old-fashioned trench warfare. Positions have been consolidated, there are longish periods of apparent disagreement—while the next offensive is being prepared—punctuated by periodic salvos fired across, not indeed no man's land, but rather everyman's land, the territory of our educational system. In other ways the conflict is more like all-in wrestling, with a number of educators and other well-meaning dilettantes trying to act as arbiters, and pointing out—in vain—that the quarrel is a mistake. In vain, because they too are caught up in the struggle and get kicked by both sides for their pains. I dare not hope to escape this fate, and in any case my qualifications as an arbiter are not propitious. I am only an ex-scientist, and cannot claim to be any kind of artist, unless some share in the art of trying to teach be allowed as a qualification.

The disquiet, not to say alarm, with which many view the present scene has two major sources. The most obvious source of anxiety is the threat of disaster facing mankind from the misuse of physical science. At the centenary celebrations of the Massachusetts Institute of Technology, President Julius Stratton said:[1]

> The prospects of potential evil or disaster are so many and so frightening, that thoughtful people everywhere question how

> far dare we proceed. They ask whether science has not begun to trespass on forbidden territory ... To this I reply that there is no retreat. We have no alternative but to follow truth wherever it may lead us. One cannot escape evil by ignorance ... Only our will for right or wrong stands between us and disaster. We must seek salvation not by withdrawal from the quest, but in man's conscience. Science gives us knowledge and power of action. It tells us what we can do; we must turn elsewhere to learn what we should do.

Some four hundred years ago François Rabelais put this matter rather more neatly. 'Science sans conscience est ruine de l'âme.' (Of course for him science meant all knowledge, not just what we call the sciences.) This view is probably shared by many present day scientists. It is noteworthy because it apparently denies to science any moral values—although one would expect scientists to claim the search for truth as a virtue—and it shifts the responsibility elsewhere. Upon whom, then, does this responsibility—the responsibility for the nurture of conscience—rest? The champions of the arts—if not all artists themselves—are not slow to claim a major share of it and to base their demand for a considerable share of educational time upon this claim. In particular the claim is pressed most strongly on behalf of those artists who use words as their medium of communication, poets, novelists, dramatists, biographers and literary historians. Part of the strength of this particular claim derives from the history of our European culture, and so strongly has it been pressed that this group of the arts has tended to become identified with 'the Humanities'. This claim by the verbal arts to represent the humanities, either exclusively or even *par excellence*, is a piece of arrogance which as an arbiter I must sharply disallow. The denial of the title 'humane' to the visual and plastic arts, to the crafts, to music, to dance and the physical arts of the body, to studies of human affairs other than historical ones, and to the sciences, seems to me to be one expression of the basic misconceptions which lie at the heart of our current conflicts. It is for this reason that I have chosen to speak, not of the 'sciences and the humanities', but of the arts and the sciences. In saying this I am denying neither the fundamental importance nor the unique role of both language and the literary arts in the development and maintenance of civilization. They are indeed essential and make their own unique *contribution*, but they are not by themselves sufficient and have no *unique claim* to the title of humane studies. This is no mere opinion of mine, rather it is the fairly unanimous view of those who have given most thought to this question. For example, in *The*

Meaning of the Humanities, Professor R. B. Perry says: 'I define the humanities to embrace whatever influences conduce to freedom',[2] and by freedom itself he means the power of enlightened choice.

All this may appear as a digression, but it is a necessary one, and its full significance will only appear later. The claims of the arts, and here I include their full range, to be custodians of human conscience, in a way in which the sciences are not, has both a negative and a positive aspect. Negatively it is urged that the sciences are by nature impersonal and abstract and that their aims of understanding the natural world and of controlling it are achieved at the expense of reducing the human person to an automatic observing and calculating machine—a kind of undesigned television set and self-programming electronic computer all in one. In 'pure' science the human person is apt to disappear in an apparently impersonal and objective system of facts, experimental events and logical arguments. If the scientist himself remains visible, it is as a distant and inhuman image. In technology and the social sciences the human being reappears, but only as a producer or consumer, or just simply as an 'object' to be controlled and manipulated like any other part of nature. The major threat of science may thus be considered to be not so much the annihilation of mankind through its misuse of scientific discoveries, but the perhaps more probable disaster of the loss of our essential humanity through the impersonal nature of scientific work. An education involving extreme scientific specialization is therefore regarded as a dehumanizing experience.

On the positive side, the argument is that for the nourishment of a civilized conscience, i.e. one sensitive to human values, the growing human being requires those experiences provided by the arts which make plain to him his dependence on other human beings, which enable him to enter imaginatively into their joys and sorrows and share with them the perception of beauty, and which convey to him and remind him in concrete images and symbols of the glory and tragedy of his personal humanity and of the human condition. The case for the arts as the foundation of general education is thus to be established on the grounds that only through them can all men enter fully into their humanity and can scientists in particular retain an adequate hold on that humanity and a proper respect for it.

The case for the literary arts as the unique, or at least the supreme, custodians of humane values was argued in a very similar way by Matthew Arnold. In his Rede Lecture of 1882 Arnold said: 'I am going to ask whether the present movement for ousting letters from their old predominance in education and for transferring the predominance in education to the natural sciences ought to prevail.' He concluded that it ought not. Literary culture has indeed, if not entirely held its own, continued to exercise a very powerful influence, an influence which has had its effect on the very way in which science has now developed to the point at which it threatens to become predominant. The effect seems to have been that many scientists themselves have come to accept the conception of their subject displayed in their opponents' view of it—as an essentially objective, morally neutral and impersonal activity. Such scientists have, as we have seen, sought their moral values elsewhere, in the arts or perhaps in a social system or in a revealed religion. As scientists they pursue science for its own sake, but as men living in society, they are prepared to allow that man cannot live by science alone.

There are however others who find in the potentialities of science for human welfare the major moral purpose of their lives. Some of them like Sir Charles Snow nevertheless believe that in order to harness science to human welfare pure science by itself, unaffected by the arts and in particular by the art of understanding one's fellow men, will not do. In his Rede Lecture in 1959 Snow drew attention to the phenomenon of what he called 'the two cultures'—the artistic (again mainly literary) and the scientific.[3] Alarmed alike by the intellectual loss which this split expresses and by the existing moral vacuum in practical human affairs which he largely attributes to it, he sees the remedy in educational reforms which would secure a broad education in which science would play a dominant part at an advanced level for a much larger proportion of our people than have ever before enjoyed higher education. The major purpose of this reform would be to produce large numbers of men and women 'trained not only in scientific terms but in human terms' to combat what he sees as the three major menaces facing humanity—H-bomb war, overpopulation of the world and the gap between rich and poor nations. What the world needs, in Snow's view, is primarily scientists and engineers, with linguists to help them, but scientists and engineers who are democratic, humane and wise. To ensure that they possess these virtues Snow prescribes a humanistic element, presumably mainly literary, in their education. The arts in their own right scarcely appear, and pure science, although essential, exciting and wonderful, acquires and exhibits humane values principally through its applications.

This is roughly the state of the popular argument at present. Literary humanists defend their studies as the essential humane foundation of all education, in which such scientists as we need must participate, while men like Snow (himself a novelist and man of affairs, although trained in science) demand a fundamentally scientific education which is at the same time humane. Perhaps, you might say, 'the difference between them is only quantitative and since both sides proclaim the virtues of the arts, and since scientists are clearly necessary, let us settle for a broad curriculum containing both arts and sciences. Why all the fuss? In our grammar schools let us have a solution along eclectic lines[4] and let us even extend such mixed curricula to college and university studies. Let us close this discussion.' I think not. I believe that this whole diagnosis of our educational problems, though true in some respects, is dangerously superficial and misleading. I believe this for the following reasons:

1. The relation between the arts and sciences, in particular the nature of their so-called opposition, has been misconceived.
2. The restriction of the arts largely to literary studies neglects a whole fundamental side of man's nature.
3. The conception of science which sees it as a collection of facts, impersonally discovered, and as a fundamentally amoral activity is false, although many scientists themselves seem to subscribe to this view.
4. The omission from the argument of those activities which we may roughly call social projects or studies deprives us of an essential focus in education. I do not here mean subjects like geography* which are unsure whether they are arts or sciences, but rather those activities and projects in which we put the arts and sciences to work for a shared human purpose. Examples are most easily found in our best infant, junior and secondary modern schools. Snow has certainly perceived the moral importance of practical human tasks but he failed to give them any educational role.
5. The assumption that the problem of modern education is essentially one of the curriculum, of a balance of subject matter, and the assumption upon which this first assumption itself depends, that subjects—whether arts or sciences—contain intrinsic values irrespective of how they are taught and learned, and of who teaches them, runs counter to all that we certainly know about the nurture of civilized human beings.

I would hazard the prediction that if we merely diminish specialization at higher levels and insist on a broad curriculum at least up to G.C.E. 'A' level, *and if that is all that we change in the*

* This is not meant as a criticism of geography, which is now becoming a crucial focus for environmental studies—the new frontier in the fight to preserve the biosphere.

present order, then our last state may well be worse than our first. In order to understand the roles of the arts and the sciences in education, and thus to understand our present conflicts, it is necessary to enquire into the fundamental nature of these activities as human achievements, how they are brought into being, and how in our education they enable us to create, sustain and augment our humanity. Let us begin with science.

It is ironical that as science advances from success to success there should appear increasing evidence that in many people's minds its true nature is tending to be lost sight of. The commonest misconception is that science is a collection of facts and of sets of laws. But even a single fact is not at all what it seems—for a fact is nothing but the residue of an act, as the origin of the word should tell us—a human act of observation, and thus in an important sense a discovery. In the beginning every fact was comprised in an imaginative act. Collections of scientific facts constitute the museum or library of science, not the living activity—a point which should be readily perceived by artists who would not confuse, say, a gallery of paintings with the living activity of art. (This is a useful, although I would readily agree a rather limited, analogy.) The dynamism of science which pervades its whole life, or ought to, is the spirit of discovery, and discoveries result from looking at, listening to or treating familiar things in new ways or in new situations, and from arranging familiar things in new patterns or relationships. We may note that this is as true of artistic discovery as it is of scientific. In both cases the discoveries are the acts of *discoverers*.

In a similar way the laws of science are continually misconceived, either by regarding them as somehow like the social laws of say England, which we all obey, or by regarding them as somehow pre-existing and only waiting to be discovered. But scientific laws are merely convenient ways of expressing and summarizing observed regularities and order among facts. For example, we might cite the laws of constant and multiple proportions in classical elementary chemistry, which serve to bring order into a multitude of facts discovered about the ways in which elementary substances combine with one another. The elements do not obey these laws in the sense in which we obey the laws of England. Scientific laws are really hypotheses or guesses about being able to arrange observed phenomena of a certain kind into a pattern. When a new phenomenon falls into the pattern, it does not 'obey' an existing law, it rather confirms the guess or hypothesis made by the scientist.

When it fails to conform to the pattern it falsifies the hypothesis.

New discoveries, whether of single facts or of patterns of facts called laws, result from the activity of the human imagination which, taking the raw material of experience, gives it significant form. But in saying this I might be talking about the work of an artist, in whatever medium, for the essence of what he does is also to give significant form to a particular kind of experience. We say the form is significant because it relates to the purposes of the artist or scientist and to purposes he shares with his fellow men. Thus the indispensable instrument of science and art alike is the creative imagination.

Science is not comprised completely of the discoveries of facts and the formulation of laws—far from it. A science reaches maturity when it can arrange its facts and laws into coherent systems called theories. Theories are themselves further imaginative constructions of the mind; they are systems of concepts or models through which we can exhibit an order and connectedness between the phenomena which the science studies, and in this way they are said to 'explain' the phenomena. Theories are good or bad in science according to the range of phenomena they can include and according to whether they give rise to hypotheses from which new discoveries can be predicted and from which the theories can thus be verified or falsified. An example of a good, and indeed a brilliant and far reaching theory in classical organic chemistry is the one devised by the great chemist Kekulé to account for the known facts about the behaviour of the substance *benzene* and its derivates. Quantitative analysis shows that benzene is a compound of six equivalents of carbon and six of hydrogen, i.e. it has the formula C_6H_6. Kekulé's theory depicts the six carbon atoms of the benzene molecule (occupying positions 1 to 6 in the diagram below) as forming a closed ring, each having one hydrogen atom attached to it, and it requires that these six hydrogen atoms are chemically equivalent to one another. On this theory, if we replace two hydrogen atoms by two atoms of another element, for example bromine, there can be *three* and *only three independent ways* of doing this, as shown in the diagram on p. 42.

With this model there are three and only three possible forms of di-bromo-benzene, namely those in which bromine atoms have replaced hydrogen atoms in positions 1.2, 1.3, and 1.4 respectively as shown in the diagram. Three di-bromo-benzenes are known and only these three have ever been found. This theory has proved its worth in over eighty years of experimental work, and it led directly to the enormous advances which have since taken place in this branch of chemistry.

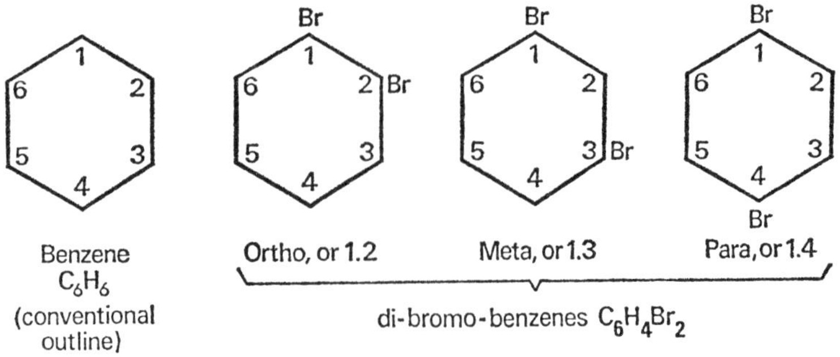

In physics, chemstry, biology, etc., there are many particular theories of this kind and there are also more general theories like those of relativity, of atomic structure and of evolution. Such theories are all the products of a controlled use of the creative and rationally disciplined imagination, and many examples can be given to show how their creators came to formulate them. The one I like best is the story of how Kekulé came to see that some of the complexities of organic compounds could be accounted for by imagining that carbon atoms could form chains among themselves. This concept came to him in a reverie on top of a London bus—a waking dream in which he saw carbon atoms gambolling in space before his eyes and forming links with one another! It was a further development of this chain theory which led to the benzene ring theory discussed above.

The whole point of this account of scientific activity is to give the lie to the idea that science is somehow impersonal, a collection of facts, and that it exists by itself as some kind of entity. Science is a vast co-operative human endeavour in which personal exploration of the world of nature is the beginning. Its theories are simply maps, constructed by the minds of the scientists to enable them to make sense of the world of physical experience. Bronowksi has remarked acidly: 'I have had, of all people, an historian tell me that science is a collection of facts, and his voice had not even the ironic rasp of one filing cabinet reproving another.'

These imaginative constructions of science are an interpretation of reality, just as are the creations of the artist. Again Bronowski says:[5]

> Reality is not an exhibit for man's inspection labelled 'Do not touch.' There are no appearances to be photographed, no experiences to be copied, in which we do not take part. *We re-make nature by the act of discovery*, in the poem or in the theory—

and I would add in the picture or the sculpture.

This idea of science as a human achievement in which the impulse to discover is the prime mover, and the creative imagination the indispensable instrument, does something to give science a claim to being a humane study. But does it do enough? What range of values does science encompass and exhibit, and are these relevant to the nourishment of a civilized conscience? I will choose three major civilized values and will try to show how these are woven into the fabric of science itself—two of them often completely unnoticed. The obvious one is truth. What Bronowski calls the habit of truth—truth to experience—is not only acknowledged by scientists themselves, but the form in which we usually think of truth in most connections we owe largely to science, and to the effect of science on our society since the Middle Ages. This does not require elaboration, but one aspect of it is commonly ignored or denied. Bronowski holds that values arise *explicitly* only when we have learned to ask 'What *should* we do?' In a totalitarian society, whether of the past or of the present, this question does not arise at all, for there are rules of conduct given by authority, or in simpler societies by custom. In our kind of society what we *should* do can only be determined by co-operation between our inner sense of values—of what we conceive of as valuable—and an appeal to experience. Values are not rules to be blindly obeyed. We have to know what works, in order to act wisely in accordance with our ends. These ends themselves which enshrine values are not indifferent to the facts of experience; they arise in experience and can be changed by experience. In helping to shape our values the habit of truth, which we can learn through science, is indispensable, and this is so whether we are concerned with determining the truth of our feelings or the truth of the consequences of an act, although these of course involve very different kinds of mental process. Our capacity to experience values is part of our nature as human beings, but this capacity cannot guide us to acquire particular values in the absence of experience, and the habit of truth is indispensable to the meaningful ordering of experience in a free and civilized world.

But science as a human achievement involves more than this. It involves the habits of co-operation, of sharing and of fellowship. The great edifice of modern science is a monument to free and willing co-operation. Every experiment we carry out and every effort of the imagination we make depends on the work of myriads of others, living and dead. To do our own work in science we have to appreciate that of others, to enter imaginatively and deeply into their minds. If we approach our work in this way we cannot easily escape both a sense of humility and a feeling for human worth and the dignity of man; we are involved in those regions of our being from which human sympathy springs. It is here that as scientists we can perceive, and nourish the perception within us, of the necessity of human freedom—if only for the sake of the continuance of science! Although science may develop and appear to flourish in the absence of certain freedoms—as indeed it can, at least for a time—it cannot outlive the death of all freedom.

Thus the pursuit of science depends in the long run on our valuing truth, co-operation and freedom, and a scientific education is therefore under an obligation to see that these values become manifest in it. This is not to say, of course, that science carries the main responsibility for the maintenance of these values. However, the view of science which sees it as morally neutral is evidently false.

If these things are so, you may ask, why are they not more generally perceived, especially by scientists themselves? You may notice that I have not appealed to the technological usefulness of science in trying to establish its humanity. R. B. Perry, whom I have already quoted, had this to say:

> The humanity of science does not lie in its utility ... In saying this I do not disparage science but protest against its own self-disparagement ... Its humanity lies, on the one hand, in its revelation of the actual world as the environment and source of human life. If it is to fulfil this function of cosmic illumination it must be integrated and assimilated to personal experience, thus enabling men to choose the ends of action in the fullest possible view of nature. Its humanity lies in its illustration of the faculties of men—as a manifestation of reason, imagination, scrupulousness and disinterestedness—in its non-acquisitive enjoyment of truth, and in its alliance with those cultural activities which unite men and contribute to their common heritage.

I substantially agree with Perry here in his main assertion, but not with what he appears to deny. The distinction between 'pure' science and its application is largely false, because at any point it is merely temporary and expedient, and the tone of his comment does no justice to the important moral drive which many scientists who care for humanity find in the application of their work to human welfare.

Perry goes on to say:

> These humanistic functions of natural science do not take care of themselves. The inhumanity of natural science lies in

> the fact that it perpetually dehumanizes itself. Its strength arises from its technique, and its credit from its technology. But scientists may be both strong and famous without humanity. To preserve the humanity of science requires scientists who are so incorrigibly humane as to resist or transcend the influence of their own schooling and the popular applause of their usefulness.

We have here a partial acknowledgment of the charge of the literary humanists that science is inhumane. Perry however admits only the deep tendency to inhumanity which infects science and he clearly points to the source of this tendency. To preserve the humanity of science he says we require scientists who can resist or transcend the *influence of their own schooling*! Here I suggest is a major truth and something of a scandal. The inhumanity of much of science derives from our educational failure sufficiently to nourish in future scientists those humane virtues upon which science itself ultimately depends. In the first place at any rate we may take this charge as being one against our scientific education in the schools, although it is more than this. I will make the charge more precise by saying that our methods of teaching science are all too often antipathetic to its whole spirit.

If I had time I think I could show in detail the truth of this charge, but I will content myself by saying that today science is frequently not approached as a human quest, as a chain of discoveries, as an exercise in the creative imagination, as a vast co-operative human endeavour and achievement, to appreciate which one must to some extent enter into the minds of its creators. It is relatively rare nowadays for the budding scientist to be given much real first-hand insight into the way in which science was created, in the only way in which such insight can be securely gained—by following for himself some at least of the road which scientists of the past have travelled, and by facing for himself the questions and problems that confronted them. On the contrary, science seems to be tending more and more to be taught as received fact, hallowed by authority. The whole emphasis in our teaching is away from personal discovery and towards the impersonal ... 'the facts are ...', away from the persistent asking of questions and towards the receiving of ready-made answers. The science required in our examinations gives the game away, particularly at G.C.E. 'O' level. These requirements and the questions in which they tend to be embodied are a standing demonstration that science is now widely conceived of as a collection of facts and laws, discovered in time past, which the pupils must learn to remember and be able to write down. Pupils may indeed conduct experiments for themselves, which they must later be able to describe in aseptic impersonal prose—experiments from which the established laws can be 'verified', not from which the pupils themselves are invited to make inferences and predict consequences! If true, these charges are exceedingly serious, for they amount to a failure of science in education to exhibit its own true nature.

This failure however is only one of the causes of the persistent tendency of science to dehumanize itself. The second major cause lies in our failure sufficiently to nourish in the growing scientist the kind of imagination through which we come to know and understand one another, an imagination different in kind from that through which we come to know and understand the physical world. Our relations with one another are reciprocal and can grow towards mutuality, and in this they differ profoundly from our relations with non-personal aspects of experience. Mutuality is possible primarily through our power of sympathetic imagination, a power based on the fact of our common humanity and our capacity for awareness of or insight into ourselves. We are able to perceive and understand pain or joy in someone else because we have first-hand knowledge of these feelings. Thus self-knowledge, through imaginative identification with others, becomes the basis of our understanding of them and in turn this understanding of others augments our understanding of ourselves. It is in this way that we come progressively to discover our common humanity and are able increasingly to augment it in the direction of mutuality of purpose. Our conscience, which has its primitive basis in the crude sanctions of what Freud called the super-ego, becomes civilized and refined in proportion as we are able, through imagination, to develop our powers of sympathetic identification. This kind of imagination is capable of being nourished most fully through the arts and perhaps most directly through the literary arts. It is these which are most capable of making us incorrigibly humane—in Perry's phrase—for they can nourish directly our powers of moral discernment and our capacity for sympathy. Literature and history, being about men and women—their vision of nature, the world and life, their hopes, fears, ambitions, loves, hates, predicaments and triumphs—reflect our own passions and speak directly to our condition. So far this part of the popular argument contains an important truth.

I passionately believe that all this can be true of the literary arts, but I fear that often it is not. We come here to a second and even graver scandal, the failure of the literary arts in education to understand their own true nature and function. In many schools poetry and drama, for example, have become in recent years vitalizing experiences, fostered notably by, among others, students of this College; but this is not generally so, and particularly it is not so as external examinations cast longer and longer shadows. Consider the lines:[6]

> A halo flares around my head,
> A sunflower flares across the sun,
> While down the summer's seamless haze
> Such feast of milk and honey run
>
> That lying with my orchid love,
> Whose kiss no frost of age can sever,
> I cannot doubt the cold is dead,
> The gold earth turned to good—forever;

or these perhaps more familiar ones:[7]

> In the highlands, in the country places,
> Where the old plain men have rosy faces
> And the young fair maidens
> quiet eyes;
> Where essential silence cheers and blesses,
> And for ever in the hill-recesses
> Her more lovely music
> Broods and dies.

When we hear them or read them, is our imaginative response quickened or extinguished by being asked to describe in our *own* words the feelings and moods evoked, to explain why we like them, or to contrast the response of the two poets to nature and so on? True, there comes a time when reflection on the achievement of a poet can enhance our appreciation of what a poet has done. But we have to know, love and make the poems our own first. Analysing, paraphrasing and commenting we cannot let a poet speak to our pupils without thrusting ourselves and our opinions between him and them, until it is our commentaries they come to study instead of the poets. In a recent 'O' level paper I found this question: 'The main plot of *Twelfth Night* is not wholly serious, nor is the sub-plot wholly humorous. What is your opinion of this statement?' I know that mine is unprintable. Does this encourage pupils to respond spontaneously to Shakespeare? Reflection upon our experiences there must be, but is this the kind of reflection proper to this stage? Again: 'Describe any two passages from one of the Four Stories which illustrate Conrad's skill in presenting incidents with striking realism.' No doubt there is some place for all this in due season, but will someone please explain to me how this sort of literary study directly enlarges our vision of the world and man's life in it, or augments our understanding of ourselves and of one another? Indirectly it may help to do so—but that is not enough.

In history, which is uncertain whether it is an art or a science, the case appears to be worse still. In what I believe is regarded as a good text I read:

> When the Rump had gone, the soldiers were undisputed masters of England. To clothe the nakedness of their despotism they determined to summon a parliament; and since they could not face the consequences of a free election, they summoned a body representative of orthodox Puritanism.

The author's predilection for anatomical images amuses me as a psychologist—how appropriate too to choose Puritans for clothing nakedness. As an educator however I am not amused. Moreover there are four hundred pages of this sort of thing. Is anyone ever led to ask what is the basis of these statements—what is the evidence from which the historian works to create an image of the actions of men long dead? By what tests can his interpretations of motives be validated? What relevance have these endless intrigues, plots, coups and policies to the enhancing of our understanding of our relations with our fellow-men, to the appreciation of the achievements of our forebears, to an understanding of the political problems of our time? If they have relevance, how can we come to see it? I am told either that this is not what history is for or that I am expecting too much; but I still don't believe that history is nothing but a catalogue of events retold—full of sound and fury but signifying nothing. To fulfil a humane function historical study must engage pupils themselves in an imaginative reconstruction, and this is impossible without some first-hand acquaintance with historical materials. We have in some measure in this sense to communicate directly with the dead and not just through mediums—though these, our teachers of history and writers of good historical novels and texts, are indispensable. Instead, our pupils are expected to respond all the time to somebody else's picture—and usually a second- or third-hand copy at that. And they have to respond mainly by memorizing it.

How far is it true that literary humanism as it is taught in our schools, colleges and universities is failing to exhibit its true nature and thus failing to exert a humane influence on its students? There are those who believe that this failure is seen at its worst in our universities themselves. Professor Mansell Jones, in an essay,

Modern Humanities in the Technological Age, while maintaining that the greatest literature 'offers the most inclusive presentation of the ethos, attitudes, standards, motives, significant myths and psychological types which characterize a civilization' stresses that in order to present such literature in a nourishing sense its students must be led to appreciate it in terms of its essential greatness. He finds instead a pre-occupation with a minute scholarship and erudition which, rather than enhancing the literature, degrades it.

> The humanities [he says] are discredited and rejected. They are being openly attacked *de front*, whilst those who should defend them remain silent and inactive; and they are being undermined from within. The most insidious undermining movement operates through a more or less unconscious abuse of erudition and of the techniques of rational scholarship in the teaching of humane subjects.

He gives examples from French—his own subject—and goes on to say:[8]

> Yet these, alas, are only the pin points of the glaciers of aggressive erudition, on which, if we are not on the sharpest look-out, the teaching of [French] literature ... will founder, and the gulf between a self-centred and a self-defeating scholarship and the true critical approach to a living literature will widen, until Science steps in and claims the lot.*

This picture of our educational problem which I have now drawn is a very different one from that presented at the beginning. The phenomenon of the two cultures, separated by a gulf of incomprehension and mutual distrust (where it does exist, and it is not ubiquitous), is but a symptom of a far deeper malady, the inner decay of two aspects of a single culture. In psychology we are only too familiar with the situation of two individuals or groups who, unable or unwilling to face their own problems, find the causes of their distress or impotence in one another. The atmosphere of mistrust and hostility, and on one side at least jealousy between the arts and the sciences, smells heavily of pathology. It is indeed with the pathology of our educational enterprise that we are dealing, and it is for this reason that simply treating the alleged symptom —the gulf between the 'cultures'—as if it were the disease, by prescribing 'some of each for everybody', will not in itself effect a cure. All our pupils require the arts and the sciences. These

* One might hazard the guess that this myopic and self-destructive pursuit of literary minutiae owes something to a desperate bid to copy science and secure prestige as it *appears* to do through discovering *facts*.

disciplines indeed require one another—but they cannot minister to our humanity, jointly or singly, unless each knows itself for what it truly is. For the literary arts and the sciences to know themselves truly is for them to discover and hold fast to their humane character, and when they do this the opposition—but not the difference—between them vanishes. Moreover it is then easier to perceive that by trying to exclude from the *élite* of the educational company the whole range of other arts and studies, we are arbitrarily excluding from experience activities fundamental to man's nature and thus fundamental to the literary arts and sciences themselves. Sensitivity to beauty in sound, rhythm, texture, line, form, movement and colour may not always be allied with humane feeling, but it is one of its natural allies nevertheless.

Before turning directly to the arts with which most of you are personally concerned, however, I want to enlarge a little on the pathology of our educational enterprise. The idea that our more recalcitrant problems are the expression of a genuine disease is an extremely important one, and is nowhere as yet taken sufficiently seriously. This disease expresses itself not only in mutual distrust and hostility between the literary arts and the sciences but in an obsessional over-evaluation of both of them. You will scarcely deny, I am sure, that in our secondary schools at any rate you, who are to be teachers of the visual and plastic arts and of music, do not enjoy an equal share of the sun. It is part of the diseased condition of the literary arts and the sciences that they should fail to recognize their own state and that each should be so preoccupied with the notion of its own superiority that it cannot admit the claims of others. Specialists in the literary arts and sciences, perhaps indeed *all* specialists, tend to be possessed by their subjects, just as all lovers tend at times to be possessed by those they love. In this condition, not only is the vision of the loved one distorted, but nothing else worth-while exists. It is exceedingly difficult for the zealous specialist genuinely to admit that other subjects are as important as his, when it comes to sharing out the timetable, and to prescribing those subjects which are the *sine qua non* of entrance to the highest levels of our educational system. There is nothing like leather! It is a short step from this to the view that extended study in a certain restricted range of subjects, notably the literary arts and the sciences, is indispensable to an adequate higher education, that is, to a reasonably full humanity.

In pursuit of our specialist obsessions we imprison our children in the grip of an apparatus of coercion which has the effect of debarring many pupils in the most formative period in their lives from adequate participation in activities which are essential to their full humanity, the visual and plastic arts and crafts, the domestic arts and crafts, the arts of movement, of gymnastics, music, dancing, drama and various forms of social study and service. This pathological system of coercion is best exhibited by saying that adults *feel they know in advance* what is best for *all* children. In fact there is a great deal of educational experience to show that different children flourish through the pursuit of radically different things and combinations of different things—things frequently not given much, if any, room in the curriculum. It is common for the claims of the activities I have mentioned to be disallowed on the grounds either that their 'intellectual' content is not high enough or that they are not readily examinable subjects. These turn out to be the same ground, for what is readily examinable is regarded as what can be written down in words or symbols, and it is asserted that what can be so written down is what has genuine 'intellectual' content. 'Intellect' is what matters, and intellect here is equated with what I will call verbality—the diseased and degraded form of the divine gift of language. This enthronement of verbality—which can in no sense be reasonably identified with the creative mind, in all of whose manifestations intellect functions, albeit differently in each—is a complex phenomenon. Complex it may be, but we can certainly see at work here some of the effects of those truly cancerous growths within our educational system—external examinations. Cancers these are, but like other cancers they have to be seen as symptoms of deeper troubles. Our deepest trouble in education is our failure to understand the nature of the enterprise in which we are engaged. We shall have to begin again and we shall have to be prepared to dismiss the criterion of examinability, in the sense in which this is usually meant, as utterly irrelevant, nay fatally dangerous to our genuine purpose. And with this dismissal we shall have to be prepared to sacrifice the utterly insane standards of memorized material—of so-called knowledge—which we at present demand of our young people. Freed from this cross of our own making we could begin to explore how to provide the individual nourishment which each pupil needs to attain and augment his humanity. In this exploration we would also discover the meaning of genuine standards in every kind of work and how these may be assessed for the sake of and as an integral part of the process of learning.

How then should we conceive of education? For me education is an adventure in human mutuality in which persons-in-relation (to use Macmurray's phrase)—in our case younger and older persons—together set out to discover what it means to be human. It is an adventure because this is an end that can never be fully determined in advance. We have to discover our common humanity and how this differs in each of us, a discovery which can only be made by each becoming what he has it within him to be. We can discern very easily in rough outline the scope of the activities through which our humanity grows. All human achievements of good repute fall within this scope. The main clue to the curriculum for even our youngest pupils is to be found in the achievements of civilization. All children, unless suffering from severe organic impairment or psychological maladjustment, want to engage and are capable of engaging in learning to create beauty in sound, clay, paint and movement, and in learning to read, write and count in order to explore the human and natural worlds. Why our own culture has so misconceived the nature of children, and thereby misconceived human nature, as to demand mere literacy and numeracy as the bases of education is a complex sociological problem in which what we may again call pathological features are very evident. But it is a problem which we cannot tackle here. After a great struggle the inherent interests and capabilities of children in music, movement, painting, modelling, poetry and natural discovery have been demonstrated in some at least of our primary schools. I have been in one not far from here in which music is the centre of the life of the school, nourishing and invigorating its work in art, drama and the three Rs. It is not for me to comment further upon these achievements, but we might allow ourselves just one poem by a ten-year-old girl from the book by Marjorie Hourd and Gertrude Cooper called *Coming into their Own*:[9]

THE COCK SO DUMB

The curlew calls,
And salmon jump the waterfalls.
The cat it sprawls in front of a blazing fire
While the cock stands
Silent and still on the top of the church spire.

The deer they run
And the bees they hum;
And every animal has one
Thing which can be done,
Whether it be to call, to swim, or to run
Except the cock who stands silent and dumb.

In modern junior schools of real quality, with which this area is especially blessed, art and science and even the three Rs do not obtrude as such. Experiment and discovery take place in many directions and often in several directions at once in the pursuit of aims meaningful to the children themselves. Artistic activities in many media, and the scientific activities of looking, finding out, asking questions, comparing, naming, classifying and experimenting go on without these fearsome abstractions art and science. Whenever these make an explicit appearance in timetables my heart sinks, for here lies the beginning of those obsessions and pomposities which bedevil our later education. It is where sensitivity to beauty, humane feelings and the spirit of inquiry are fostered together, not in isolation, that the full possibilities of each are best exhibited. Mathematical understanding grows and blossoms too at this stage, if it is not stunted by an enormous, irrelevant and wholly premature burden of calculation. It may well be that one of the most fruitful matrices in which the mathematical mind can have time to grow is one in which arts and crafts play a prominent part—it is fairly certain that the matrix of formal arithmetic as we know it is almost entirely unsuitable for this purpose. Here in these schools the basic humanities—those activities through which we discover what it is to be human—can be observed in their natural and proper relations.

Yet in this vitalizing work, given adequate materials and facilities, everything still depends on how the activities are organized and on the quality and inspiration of the teacher who guides them. What, how and from whom we learn are all inextricably mixed, but in the final analysis the humane value of a subject or an activity largely depends on the humanity of those who teach and learn it. We acquire civilized values primarily by living with and learning from people who are themselves humane. When the activities themselves speak to us and we recognize them as the proper expression of our own nature, it is because our teachers have a deep sense of the humane purposes of those activities. This sense does not have to be capable of being formulated in words—many good teachers are incapable of this—but at every stage of education it is worth while to try to make such formulations. Speaking here only of those arts in which most of you are especially interested, we may distinguish three features which always attend success. First, discovery and learning are personal and meaningful to each child, that is, in a fundamental sense they are creative. Children are, as far as is possible, in action with the whole of themselves; thought, feeling and deed fused together in inseparable unity. Second, there is a sense of co-operation, of participation in an endeavour which eventually reaches out to the past, as well as encompassing the present. Here lie the seeds of that sense of working within a tradition which success in both arts and sciences ultimately demands, and towards which they continually strive. Bernard Leach testifies thus:[10]

> I can still remember vividly how twenty-five years ago I stood before the magnificent examples of the pottery of the Sung dynasty in the Tokyo museum, wondering how an individual potter today could possibly appropriate to himself a beauty so impersonal, so inevitable—the patient unassuming outcome of centuries of tradition ...

Third, the expressive aim of the activity is vividly apparent. This expressiveness is not just a question of 'self expression'—which is involved in all activity, and is a phrase which has had some unfortunate educational consequences—it is a question of meaning and communication achieved through the creation of significant forms. Content and form are inseparable and are relevant to the purpose and stage of development. As Cizek said:[11] 'People make a great mistake in thinking of Child Art merely as a step to adult art. It is a thing in itself ... following its own laws and not the laws of grown up people.' To understand child art we have to understand children, and at all stages, whether in creation or appreciation, art bespeaks a potential communion of minds. Bernard Leach again: 'Pots, like other forms of art, are human expressions: pleasure, pain or indifference before them depends upon their natures, and their natures are inevitably projections of the minds of their creators.' In creation and in communion, then, lies the essential humanity of the arts.* Just one word about music. The problem of what music is, and conveys, is an ancient one. We may content ourselves with Suzanne Langer's dictum that 'music articulates forms which language cannot set forth.' Here the wide-spread tyranny of language breaks down, for divine though language be, it is continually tempted to tyrannize. Music is as indispensable in a humane education as any of the other great human activities. In its highest forms, says Langer, 'music, though clearly a symbolic form, is an unconsummated symbol.'[12] But, we may add, the consummation of the symbol is nevertheless realized; it is realized in the enjoyment of the music itself by its creators and hearers alike.

Is it possible to conceive of the living education found in some infant and junior schools, in which all the humanities not only co-exist but fertilize one another, being carried right through adolescence into higher education? I think it is and I believe that we dare not set our aim lower than this. We can find this life

* This is, necessarily, a relatively superficial statement about the arts. For a profound treatment see Reid.[13]

in some at least of the humanities in some secondary modern schools, in some grammar-school sixth forms and in some colleges and universities—in the latter case, usually in some particular department—but mile upon mile of educational desert surrounds them.

In developing a truly humane education at later stages we must expect gradual differentiation and specialization. For some pupils there is in the end only one narrow path along which maturity lies, for others the path is broad. Arts and sciences represent two different, though related, modes of grasping reality and seizing upon its meaning, and we cannot expect all to be able to discover their humanity equally through both. One thing is certain, that if our education became genuinely free and we gave up our coercive attempts to make children's development conform to *our* preconceived patterns, then the path for any particular child or group of children could not with any certainty be determined in advance. If we recognize this, then we must keep all doors open as long as possible, we must encourage, though not coerce, our pupils to engage in both arts and sciences as long as possible, and above all we must secure that artists and scientists live and work together in a genuine community, in touch with one another in all sorts of ways outside their specialisms. (That is why the new policy of this College seems to me so admirable and full of hope.)

Yet none of this will count unless each particular activity throughout the arts and sciences holds fast to its own vision of itself as a humane study or occupation, and in so doing is ever ready to join with others in pursuit of a common educational purpose. There is nothing wrong with specialization as such, when the time is ripe —and given freedom, that time, let me repeat, can never be decided in advance for any individual. What is wrong is for us to allow our specialisms to possess us instead of seeking to make them the vehicles of our educational purpose. This will never be easy, for as specialists we are naturally prone to be seduced by the particular symbolic world we inhabit, whether of art or science—seduced into behaving as if it were all that there is. It is only in so far as we can resist this seduction that we can become truly free. By resisting we do not become lesser or poorer specialists but truer ones—just as in ceasing to be bewitched by a loved one we may become more truly capable of genuine love. When we are able to see our subject in itself and in its proper relationships with other subjects, we are able to begin to enjoy in company with our fellows the full range of these achievements which represent at once the birthright and the task of humanity.

Originally the eleventh annual foundation lecture delivered at Bretton Hall College of Education, Wakefield, May 1961.

References

1 'Science takes a look at itself', *New Scientist*, 27 April 1961.
2 R. B. Perry in *The Meaning of the Humanities*. Princeton University Press. 1940.
3 C. P. Snow, *The Two Cultures and the Scientific Revolution*. The Rede Lecture, 1959. Cambridge University Press.
4 *Arts and Science Sides in the Sixth Form*. A Report to the Gulbenkian Foundation. Oxford University Press. 1960.
5 J. Bronowski, *Science and Human Values*. Hutchinson. 1961.
6 Laurie Lee, 'Long Summer', from *My Many Coated Man*. André Deutsch. 1955.
7 R. L. Stevenson, 'In the Highlands', from *Poems*. Chatto & Windus. 1906.
8 Mansell Jones, *Modern Humanities in the Technological Age*. Manchester University Press. 1957.
9 Marjorie Hourd and Gertrude Cooper. *Coming into their Own*. Heinemann. 1959.
10 Bernard Leach, *A Potter's Book*. Faber & Faber. 1948.
11 Quoted in W. Viola, *Child Art*. University of London Press. 1942.
12 Suzanne K. Langer, *Philosophy in a New Key*. Harvard University Press. 1942.
13 Louis Arnaud Reid, *Meaning in the Arts*. Allen & Unwin. 1969.

Three

Research for education

Nature and functions

... like a tedious argument
Of insidious intent
To lead you to an overwhelming question ...
Oh, do not ask, 'What is it?'
Let us go and make our visit.

T. S. Eliot, *The Love Song of J. Alfred Prufrock*

Educational research is a controversial subject. In some quarters it commands great respect, in others it is frequently the object of scorn. I think that many arguments about it are misconceived and that both the scorn and the respect are commonly overdone. Its detractors and critics are apt to demand simple and immediate answers to such overwhelming questions as 'What *use* is it?' without giving any evidence that they realize either what a question-begging question that is, or that considerable detailed knowledge is required to answer it and to appreciate the answer. Its champions and devotees on the other hand are apt to protest that only a long and painstakingly technical 'visit' to the scene of research operations can reveal its nature and value, while perhaps rather innocently seeming to deny that overwhelming questions, in the form of presuppositions, continually haunt all its endeavours. Both sides ignore the subtle dialectical relations that exist between a descriptive account of the details of any human activity and the evaluation of its aims and achievements. In attempting to clarify the nature and functions of educational research it may be helpful, as a beginning, to make some comparisons between it and research in other fields.

Educational research necessarily partakes of some of the characteristics of all social science. The most relevant and the most fundamental comparison, therefore, is that between the study of nature and the study of man. Practically no one will be found nowadays in our society to doubt the appropriateness or success of what is called scientific method in the study of nature. But there are still many who not only question but condemn the use of similar methods in the study of man, at any rate in so far as man is conceived to be more than a biological organism. There are both rational and irrational attitudes to this issue. As Freud once pointed out, there exists in many people a tendency to urge certain types of criticism against psychology as a science while refraining from urging similar and equally applicable criticisms against other subjects, for example, astronomy. Stress is laid on its apparent shortcomings and on its inability to provide final and complete answers to important questions. Educational research relying, as it does, very largely on psychology and sociology, is prone to induce similar irrational resistances. First, science is equated, quite wrongly, with measurement. Then it may be allowed that the scientific approach has been shown to have a strictly limited usefulness in relation to the measurable aspects of education, aspects that are regarded as of relatively minor importance. This may then, in turn, be urged as proof that it cannot in principle have anything really important to say about more subtle educational questions, nor about the larger human issues with which education is inextricably involved. What, for example, has it to say about the basis of the good life? The fallacies in this type of argument are of course apparent, and unfortunately for this particular example, both psycho-analysis and comparative studies of child-rearing practices have begun to show many of the ways in which childhood upbringing and education influence adult character. The basis of the good life is being revealed with perhaps unwelcome clarity, for this kind of knowledge is still largely unacceptable to many even among staunch supporters of educational research itself.

But amongst the shadows of such humanly understandable but nevertheless somewhat intellectually disreputable controversies, there lurk some serious and perfectly proper questions. For example, there are many difficult technical problems concerning scientific methods in their application to the human sciences. Moreover, there is the quite fundamental question whether man is only a natural object and if he is more than that, what are the implications of this for the scientific study of his nature and therefore of his education. But rather than attempt a direct answer to these and related questions, let us make some further comparisons between research in the natural sciences and in education, more particularly with regard to the characteristic aims and attitudes of those engaged in such activities.

We have been told that if metallurgical research can, among other things, prevent the distortion of aerofoil blades in jet turbines, petrol-driven cars may well disappear in favour of paraffin-driven ones. Obviously, the practical implications of success in this field of research are considerable, but it does not seem reasonable to expect many metallurgists who may work on relevant aspects of this problem to be preoccupied with, or indeed very much aware of, the possible economic and sociological results of their work. We deem such concern to be primarily the province of others—for example, car manufacturers, oil magnates, politicians and the general public. There are, of course, instances in the natural sciences in which the possible implications of research exert a considerable influence on the researchers themselves, for example, in nuclear physics. But these are limiting cases and we should expect to find, as indeed we do, that with few exceptions technical papers in the natural sciences begin and end with observations confined to issues which lie within the province of these sciences themselves. The physicist can, in the majority of cases, easily separate his role as a scientist from his role as a citizen. The economic, sociological and ethical repercussions of his work do not belong to the study of physics. As a citizen it is clear that he ought to consider the value assumptions on which his work is based and what its results may entail for the welfare of his fellows. He may choose not to consider such things, that is, he may abdicate from his role of citizen in this respect. But he may do so without any necessary detriment to his skill as a physicist.

Is it otherwise in education? Let us take as an example a study of the reading ability of training college students. Here are some excerpts from the summary in the published report.[1] 'The errors in comprehension made by Training College students are sufficiently important and frequent to merit the serious attention of all who are concerned with the selection of students, or with the planning of their English course after entry to a college, or with the education of potential students while they are still at school.' Again: 'Errors of comprehension are likely to occur in students' study of other subjects besides English; therefore the duty of improving students' ability to read is one that must be embraced by the entire staff of a college', and again: 'A considerable part of what has been said ... is probably true of pupils in the upper forms of grammar schools.' The broad view taken of the implications of the results of this inquiry might seem to suggest some fundamental difference between the standpoint of educational research and that, say, of applied physics. But such differences as there are, are mainly implied and not stated. Except for one phrase, the conclusions are entirely instrumental or operational in character—pointing to the need to re-examine the methods of teaching English throughout our educational system and in this general instrumental respect they could certainly be paralleled in physics or chemistry. The real differences lie in the reference to 'duty' and in the obvious, although implicit, assumption throughout that there exists some standard of reading comprehension which students *should* attain and that it is a matter of vital importance that they should be helped to attain it. An educational ideal, a system of educational values, is referred to but without either stating what it is, discussing or criticizing it.

Here lies the real crux of the matter. By implicitly raising but not discussing such questions as 'What level and kind of understanding should students in training as teachers reach in their reading?' and therefore by further implication 'What kind of literature or other written material should such students read?', this piece of research is stopping short at the point where many extremely important *educational* issues arise. Now, I am not criticizing this admirable study for stopping there. What is important is that, although these further issues are obviously ones of 'value', *they do not lie outside education but within it.* The practical repercussions of this piece of educational research rest on assumptions of value which lie within the study of education itself. This is one of the overriding differences between educational research and research in the natural sciences. The full understanding of the nature and functions of research in the natural sciences lies outside the system of these sciences themselves. Ultimately it raises profound philosophical issues. The natural scientist, *qua* natural scientist, may therefore in most cases safely ignore the wider considerations on which his work is based. But the full understanding of the nature and functions of educational research lies within the study of education itself, for education is, whatever else it may also be, ineradicably a philosophical subject. Can those who carry out educational research safely ignore that part of their subject which underlies their own investigations? Although in practice, I should not expect every report on a piece of educational research to raise all the assumptions on which it is based or to touch on all the implications of its results, nevertheless, I think that we ignore this aspect of our work at our peril. For if we do so, we cannot claim to be educationists, but must be content with being a species of laboratory technicians without the right to any expert voice in matters of educational policy. We renounce our professional privileges and responsibilities. In my opinion it is one of the tragedies of current educational research that this view of its status is widely held and is defended even by some of its own practitioners. This is a tragedy, because it is not simply a question of professional prestige. It is a question of professional competence. If we are merely technicians we cannot claim to be able to criticize the educational foundations and implications of our own work. This means quite simply that we cannot claim to know what we are doing.

Now, in taking up this highly critical attitude towards some current conceptions of research in education, I am not denigrating research but rather attempting to show that its current difficulties arise because there prevails an inadequate idea of its nature and functions. I am not attacking individuals or particular research studies. The study I have quoted is a particularly rich and useful one. Within its declared limits it is excellent—that is why I chose to cite it. But I think we are entitled to ask, 'Where is the corpus of educational thought and criticism to which this particular study belongs, and within which its full implications could be realized?' It is precisely because such a corpus of thought and criticism is lacking that educational research tends to be an isolated activity and that its results are so often ignored. It is in fact a familiar lament that research is 'a voice crying in the wilderness'.

In what way, it may be asked, does the example of research quoted stand in need of belonging to a corpus of critical and constructive thought? A perusal of the report shows that failures in comprehension could be analysed into a number of different types. These included: failure to understand a writer's intention; failure to detect irony; failures in vocabulary, particularly in words denoting abstract ideas; inadequate background information; and failure to see how the context influences meaning. At once we are prompted to ask where the origins of these failures are to be found. Is there perhaps something fundamentally wrong with our whole approach to reading and language teaching in the schools? What do we mean by comprehension? By what criterion can we tell that someone has understood in full the thought of a given passage? More fundamentally, however, we should be driven to ask: 'What standard and range of comprehension should we aim at among students training to be teachers? Can we legitimately expect the same standards from all of them? What are these students later expected to teach and to children of what ages? Are we perhaps over-concerned with verbal skills in education? What in fact are the aims of our education?'

It is certainly not my intention to suggest that these questions are not being actively considered at the present time, particularly by training college staffs. But there is little evidence to show that research and the wider study it implies often go hand in hand. Research workers tend to concentrate on techniques and purely instrumental results, while teachers and lecturers search, often in vain, for direct links with their more fundamental problems. There is a wide and widening gap between scientific research and the overall study of education. Unless this gap can be closed by a thoroughgoing revolution in our conception of what the study of education involves, research in education will continue to be judged purely by the instrumental standards of the natural and social sciences. In any such comparison it must suffer, for the good and sufficient reason that education is not a science, although scientific methods are appropriate to the investigation of many of its problems.

The extent to which the study of education is not a science is in itself a source of controversy. Every educational investigation is bound up with questions of value, not incidentally, so that such matters may safely be left to others, but intrinsically in a way which governs our whole understanding of the issues involved. The close connections in education between the questions, 'What is the case?' and 'What should be the case?' cannot be escaped, and it is to be expected that confusion between them will continually arise. There is a double difficulty to contend with. For example, the general question, 'What level of reading comprehension *should* children or students of any given age and ability reach?', cannot be answered solely by reference to any investigation or series of investigations into existing reading standards that could conceivably be carried out. Equally it could not be wisely answered without reference to the results of all such investigations as had been carried out. This is so because the question really means 'What on a considered judgment is a reasonable level of reading comprehension to aim at, bearing in mind the age and ability of the children, the circumstances of their lives, at home and at school, the skill of their teachers, *and the general aims we wish to set for their education as a whole*?' Given the aims, research can tell us what we can reasonably expect under various conditions. It is the aims which hold the key. But our educational aims are implicitly based on judgments of value made either by ourselves personally or, more commonly, collectively by the community. What assumptions underlie these educational value judgments and what circumstances, personal and social, have helped to shape them? What are their practical implications? Surely educational research is also relevant to such questions? We have to face up to the fact that not only are the conditions for our research set by value judgments but that at least some of the foundations of these value judgments may themselves be examined by scientific methods.

It is this involvement of educational research with questions of value that lies at the heart of most of the misunderstanding about its nature and functions.

On the one hand, those who prefer to discuss values without reference to the kinds of facts on which the realization of values depends, or who desire to pursue their own chosen aims without taking facts into account, will have little use for research. They do not wish their judgments to be called into question, or to discover what influences have affected them in arriving at those judgments. On the other hand, those who wish to escape from the responsibility of personal or group decisions among conflicting values will tend to treat 'facts' as if these were absolute and irreducible elements of experience possessed of independent meaning. They will therefore tend to demand from research answers it cannot give. For what those who take up this attitude want is that science, in the form of bare facts, should replace personal or collective responsibility, or, put more fundamentally, they want knowledge to usurp both understanding and judgment.

There are, of course, other important contrasts between educational research and research in the natural sciences. The feelings and rights of metallic alloys do not enter into the considerations of the metallurgist. But educational research is concerned with people, and their relations to one another. It is largely concerned with children and teachers, whose co-operation, and respect for whose dignity and rights, are vital matters. Educational research carries with it a special type of responsibility, and to the problems which this fact raises I will return later. It may well be asked also whether all forms of social research do not carry similar responsibilities. Here I have been concerned to show that educational research cannot, without being untrue to its own nature, allow itself to be wholly identified with science. It must partake of the spirit and must utilize many of the methods of science, but it is not comprehended within what we normally mean by science.

Educational research, properly conceived, has two major and interrelated functions. We may call these its instrumental and critical functions. It has a fairly obvious instrumental function in helping us to do more efficiently what we have decided should be done. It can therefore help to further our chosen aims. It has also a more fundamental function. This is to deepen our understanding of childhood and society, and of how human beings grow and learn. By doing so, it should help to inform our judgments about what we should do, and thus help us to become more sensitively and critically aware of the foundations and implications of the value systems we hold and on which we base our educational actions. It can therefore help us to criticize our aims. Looked at in this way, it appears at once that research is only a special aspect of a more fundamental activity, which we may call critical reflection; in our case it is critical reflection on education as a personal experience and as a social function. Research therefore cannot be separated from the probing, questioning and evaluative attitude which is the basis of all reflective endeavour. If it is so separated it becomes merely a system of technical skills—a technology whose practitioners have no right to claim, and indeed are only too likely to deny, any personal responsibility for the courses of action their work helps to facilitate.

What does the inclusion of research within the larger sphere of critical reflection mean in practice? Like all forms of critical reflection, research has to begin with questions: basic questions to which we want the answers in order that we may educate more effectively and more wisely. Answering such questions always involves asking further questions. Research therefore involves a continuous process of analytic and constructive thought. Through this process we seek to obtain fresh evidence from experience, and to enrich with deeper meaning the experience we already have. It is by approaching educational research in this way, as an intricate web of question and answer, that we may best come to appreciate its nature and value.

The web of question and answer

> 'Why do you sit out here all alone?' said Alice, not wishing to begin an argument.
>
> 'Why, because there's nobody with me!' cried Humpty Dumpty. 'Did you think I didn't know the answer to *that*. Ask another.'
>
> Lewis Carroll, *Through the Looking Glass*

The basis of research, educational or any other kind, is the asking and answering of questions. An adequate understanding of the whole strategy and tactics of question and answer is the indispensable key to the study of education. Of course, we may choose to reject the whole questioning attitude. The harassed teacher, when asked why she is teaching compound proportion to a class of fourteen-year-old girls, may find it difficult indeed to frame any reply which does not savour of Humpty Dumpty, and she may not bother to try. But even when we do think seriously about education we will fail to understand the vital part which research can play in our thinking, unless we are prepared continually to criticize our own questions and the answers we give to them.

Failure to be critical about our own questions may lead us to suppose, for example in relation to curriculum problems, either that research is irrelevant or that it can in principle supply all the answers. If we ask why we teach a given subject, then investigations into its immediate or remote usefulness, and controlled experiments into its general educational (training) value are at least relevant, although the results of such inquiries either singly or jointly may be inadequate by themselves to furnish us with wholly satisfactory answers. The relevance of research perhaps becomes clearer the moment we realize that 'Why teach *x*?' is quite an inadequate sort of question for any practical purpose and that it has to be developed at least into 'Should we teach *x*—if so, what aspects of it should we teach, to whom, when and how?', before any of its implications can be clearly seen.

Thus we may agree in principle that children should have some acquaintance with the mastery of number, not only for its direct usefulness, but also to allow them to glimpse something of the power and beauty of one of the fundamental ways in which men seek to understand and control the world. But such agreement is no more than the tentative flashing of the green light. In fact we have to reserve our judgment as to whether, as we do proceed, the light may change to yellow, or even in some circumstances to red. 'What particular arithmetical and mathematical skills or ideas are useful, or illuminating, and for whom?' 'At what stages in development can they be usefully introduced and by what methods?' Thus the abstract principle concerning the importance of number, which involves making a value judgment, only acquires a specific meaning through discovering the answers to various questions of fact—questions which can only be answered through experience in teaching children and by assessing the results of such teaching by research or with instruments provided by research. On the basis of experience and research, we might eventually be driven to conclude that there are some children who can only achieve a very limited skill with numbers no matter how much time is spent with them or what methods are used. In that case we ought to ask how much of the effort is worth while, and whether much of their time might not be better spent in exploring other avenues of experiences more appropriate to them. Again we will be faced with making a value judgment which in turn will require further experience and research to give it concrete meaning. Some striking initiatives have recently been developed in curriculum studies (stimulated no doubt by the work of Blum and others in the USA), originally by the Nuffield Foundation and subsequently by the Schools Council. Yet it is doubtful whether we have as yet learned to combine in the most fruitful way insightful innovation, careful analysis of objectives, and diagnostic and evaluative techniques.

But failure to be sufficiently critical of the answers to our questions may also lead us into grave errors. Suppose, for example, we ask why some children can learn to read easily by five, while others may not be able to understand even the simplest written material until they are six, seven, eight, or even older. Successfully evading the Humpty Dumpty tautologies in such answers as that the latter children are 'backward' or 'slow learners', we may ascribe such delayed learning to read largely to limitations in 'intelligence' (defined perhaps as the general capacity to profit from education). Now such an answer is true enough, and it is important to stress its truth with the help of precise assessments to support it, but it is, in fact, not very far from being a tautology—just sufficiently far to make it a worth-while answer. If we do not go further than this first answer, then we are begging the whole question of the effect which such factors as inadequate motivation, impoverished human and material environments and inappropriate or inefficient teaching may have, not only on attainments, but on general educable capacity also. Psychologists are far less prone than they were to accept a given child's ascertained intelligence level as a simple and true reflection of innate capacity. Indeed the orthodox view nowadays is that performances on 'ability' tests reflect simply what powers the child is able to deploy at the time as a result of his total life experience to date.

It is evident, therefore, that the value of research lies as much in the further questions it raises as in any direct answer it may give to the question with which it began. Reflection on any important question about education will inevitably lead us sooner or later to 'ask another'. Failure to realize this is responsible for much quite unjustifiable disappointment with the results of research, and such failure always springs from a prior failure to be sufficiently critical in framing our questions and interpreting the answers we give to them. This sort of disappointment might be avoided if it were realized that in research it is always necessary, for our own guidance, to have two quite general questions in mind. The first of these guiding questions is, 'What is the educational problem on which we want research to throw fresh light?' The asking of this question implies that there exists what I have referred to as a corpus of critical and constructive thought about the issue at stake. Where this does not already exist, it is necessary to begin to build it.

This is where, because of inadequate training, the present-day research worker is often at a loss, and where administrators and teachers, because of their direct practical responsibilities, usually feel themselves to be on safe ground. Where the administrator or teacher is weakest, and the research worker is stronger, is in formulating replies to the second guiding question, 'What precise questions relating to the problems in hand could research be expected to find the answer to?' Now the difference in viewpoint between the practical educator and the researcher is notorious. The fact that one is strong where the other is weak and vice versa does not always lead to that fruitful partnership which we might naïvely imagine should be the outcome of collaboration between them. The truth is that unless we are quite at home with both guiding questions, we do not really understand either of them very fully, and we remain ignorant of the subtle dialectical relation which exists between them. It is precisely in this relationship that the crux of any problem is to be found. Only when we can make an adequate statement of the educational problem to which our research is relevant can we claim to know what it is that we are doing. But we cannot make an adequate statement of this problem until we can frame the precise questions that are relevant to what we are doing, and by which alone we can judge whether research is possible, and if possible likely to be valuable.

We may illustrate these points with the aid of an example of research which attracted a great deal of public attention at one time. A debate in the House of Commons on corporal punishment in schools led to the National Foundation being asked to 'undertake an inquiry into the effect on the child of various forms of punishment and reward' and 'to advise the Minister [of Education] in the light of modern scientific knowledge on the most suitable forms of punishment and reward'. After an inquiry lasting some years a report of 430 pages was issued.[2] The answers to the two questions were apparently not simple! In fact neither received a direct answer for the very good reason that neither question was sufficiently precise to admit of one. Moreover, the questions themselves were accompanied by no explicit and reasoned statement of the educational problem to which they were meant to relate. In the report, therefore, an attempt had to be made to criticize the questions at issue and to display what was involved in attempting to answer them. For example, the first question appears to presuppose that a particular form of punishment or reward will affect all children in the same way. Are we also to assume that the circumstances of a particular punishment, and who administers it and in what frame of mind, are irrelevent issues? Moreover, to what extent is it meaningful to investigate rewards and punishments in schools without a full examination of the situations which give rise to them?

Thus analysis showed that the original questions were very superficial indeed and could only be effectively answered by asking more fundamental ones, concerned, among other things, with the factors governing children's behaviour in school and teachers' reactions to it. While many of the factual findings of this particular report were in the nature of confirmations of commonly held opinions about the attitudes of teachers and children, others contradicted popular beliefs, and some were of a more far-reaching kind altogether. One of these latter was that in the opinion of teachers there are a group of children who respond effectively neither to punishments nor rewards. These children are characterized by 'wandering attention; easy distractibility; irresponsibility; work full of careless mistakes; incessant chatter; indifference to failure; enjoyment of aggression (e.g. as shown in bickering and teasing)'. Such children set a problem for educational guidance which cannot be solved in terms of punishments and rewards at all. In this respect the result was to open up a whole set of much more fundamental issues concerning the origin, early diagnosis and treatment of these and other difficulties in development. This particular outcome could be a disappointment, or would seem irrelevant, only to those who had mistakenly supposed that the original questions could receive simple practical answers.

It is worth while following up this particular finding a little further. The existence of maladjusted children of this particular kind was not, of course, a new discovery, but the extent to which teachers recognized their existence and the way in which they regarded them had never been effectively demonstrated before. It would be natural to hope that the research would have revealed at what age such symptoms first appear, where their causes are to be found and what measures, preventive or therapeutic, could be taken to remove or reduce them. As so often happens, these further questions could not be answered, because the research had not been designed to answer them. Actually some further light on the matter had already been shed by a much less ambitious research conducted some years before. This was a study of the emotional disturbances shown by nursery school and infant children over a period of time, and it was intended to show which kinds of disturbance tend to fade out and which kinds persist and grow worse.[3] While it was found that there was a gradual fading out of symptoms of emotional disturbance for the majority of children, an appreciable proportion showed no improvement and, very significantly, excessive day-dreaming and lack of concentration seemed to be particularly resistant to change. Evidently such symptoms appear fairly early and for their causes we must look back into early childhood before school is reached.

Thus we find ourselves entangled in the web of question and answer and having to consider some of the fundamental problems of human development, problems which are often regarded as the province of specialists not directly concerned with education. Following up the matter in this way shows how idle it is to imagine that any one piece of research can by itself deal adequately with any educational issue. We may count ourselves fortunate when any inquiry adds a single clear and unequivocal piece of information to our store of knowledge. Only through carrying out very many interrelated investigations and continually checking and revising their findings can we build up the corpus of thought and criticism which will entitle us to consider education as a fully professional activity.

'Time', Aldous Huxley has suggested, 'must have a stop', and there are many of us who think it reasonable that, in some sense, research also should have a 'stop'. Finding ourselves enmeshed in the web of question and answer, we tend to lose our patience. There is something to be said for this, provided we are genuinely looking for guidance in making a decision. There is nothing to be said for it if we are, quite irrationally, expecting research to perform miracles for us, and are merely expressing anger at our discovery that research is after all not a form of magic, or at any rate not magic which we can command. In fact of the chameleon-like character of educational issues, it is indeed scarcely surprising that research workers themselves are prone to look for problems that seem to invite a direct solution. Are we justified in expecting research to provide direct solutions? Illuminating our understanding of issues is certainly not the only function of research. It has an instrumental function also. But there is still a difficulty to be faced. The two functions are interrelated. Let us consider an example.

The Education Act of 1944 (England and Wales) by making education compulsory and free up to fifteen precipitated a crisis in secondary education. The practical problem appeared to be to find the most reliable, valid and manifestly fair method of filling a relatively limited number of grammar school places from a relatively large number of candidates. Considerable progress was made in determining what sorts of assessments—tests and teachers' judgments—are the most successful predictors of success in grammar schools. Since Sir Godfrey Thomson's pioneer work in this field in the thirties, research had produced for this purpose tests which were highly reliable and gave remarkably accurate forecasts of children's later academic progress.[4] Here research fulfilled an instrumental function. But had the problem been solved? The answer to that depends on one's view of the problem. Certainly to the initial practical problem a solution had been found, but this solution itself created a new range of problems and threw into vivid relief some fundamental educational issues. For example selection itself and the tests used had a generally unwelcome backwash effect on the curriculum of primary schools, tending to force them to concentrate on the narrow immediate examination needs of a small proportion of their pupils. Secondly since selection could never be perfect and there was clearly throughout the country a shortage of grammar school places, questions began to be asked about the assumptions underlying the whole selective system.

The development of selection methods does therefore illustrate an instrumental function for research but at the same time it tends to raise more fundamental issues. By attempting to concentrate on the instrumental it began to be realized that we were in danger of radically misconceiving the real nature of the educational problem at issue. We could not long refrain from asking such questions as 'Can any form of examination ensure complete educational justice?' 'What is the meaning of success in secondary education?' 'Does the kind of criterion chosen not tend to make the argument about the efficiency of selection somewhat circular, and to turn the predictions of the selection tests into self-fulfilling prophecies?' 'In choosing a criterion of success, on what assumptions does the value system underlying the choice depend?' 'To what extent do problems arise in allocating children to different types of secondary school because of the attempt to fit the child to the school, instead of the school to the child?' 'What is the fundamental nature of the educational problem of which the existence of a competitive entrance examination may be regarded as only a symptom?'

With hindsight we can now see that these are among the basic issues and that the last of these questions goes to the heart of the matter. Subsequent decisions to create a comprehensive system of secondary education represent an attempt to deal with fundamental perplexities rather than immediate symptoms. These new developments of course spring from basic trends within our society and were not primarily influenced by research. Nevertheless it is not unfair to suggest that research had a share in impressing upon us the need to look deeper than the instrumental problem. Even so the coming of the new schools has not put an end to attempts to classify children at the secondary stage. As has been cynically said, it has only tended to remove the operation from public gaze. Let us not therefore assume that to solve our problems in secondary education we have only to go ahead boldly and build an adequate comprehensive system without guidance from research as to how these schools might best be organized. To do so would be to repeat the fallacy of supposing that in curriculum reconstruction we require no help from research. Critical thought and genuine innovation in secondary education are still in their infancy.

To sum up, for the moment, it would appear that difficulties in educational research are of two different but related kinds—difficulty in reaching an adequate statement of an educational problem, and difficulty in framing precise questions and answering them. I have here been mainly concerned with the former. Failure to grasp the essential nature of this difficulty is the same thing as failure to understand that education itself is a difficult business. The naïve view that education and the study of it are simple matters seems sometimes to be frighteningly common. Frighteningly? Yes, because is this not exactly where we came in? '"What tremendously easy riddles you ask!" Humpty Dumpty growled out.' Humpty, we may remember, came to a very sad end indeed.

A revised version of two articles originally published in *Journal of Education*, October 1955 and January 1956.

References

1 E. L. Black, 'The difficulties of training college students in understanding what they read', *British Journal of Educational Psychology*, February 1954.
2 *A Survey of Rewards and Punishments in Schools*. Newnes, 1952.
3 J. D. Cummings, *British Journal of Educational Psychology*, November 1946, pp. 163–77.
4 D. A. Pidgeon and A. Yates, *Admission to Grammar Schools*, National Foundation for Educational Research, Newnes, 1957.
5 P. E. Vernon (ed.), *Secondary School Selection*, Methuen, 1957.

Four

Examinations as instruments of educational reform

We are living in a time of tremendous pressure for educational expansion, pressure from the peoples of the various countries in the world and also of drives by governments. The two never seem to match each other. The personal aspirations of the peoples of the world are much higher than they have been and it would seem that either the ability or the will of governments to provide the necessary facilities still lags a long way behind. The result is that there is, and will probably be for a very long time to come, a demand which cannot wholly be satisfied. This inevitably means there will be intense competition for educational opportunity, and what goes along with it, social selection. It is within this situation that public examinations function. I think we have to see that we are part of this kind of situation. There is concern on the part of intending students wanting admission to higher educational institutions, and there is concern on the part of their parents that they should be given these opportunities. There is also quite a lot of concern on the part of those who are responsible for teaching and for the advance of knowledge in higher educational institutions; there is concern about the quality of the students who arrive from the schools and the nature of their previous education. It would be untrue to say that there is complete dissatisfaction at the university level, but that there is a measure of dissatisfaction there can be no question. I think there is also some measure of dissatisfaction among teachers in the schools. We hear it said that students arrive at universities as a result of a 'rat race' in which they tend to be crammed up with facts, and that finding themselves faced with the need for self-directed study and constructive thought they present peculiar and difficult problems of teaching. Must the blame for all this be put on the examination system?

I have brought this question to the forefront because I want to dispose of it now. The examination system is only part of a much larger social situation, and we have to look to the larger social structure for the ultimate sources of those pressures which we all feel. That is to say that examination problems are symptoms rather than primary causes of our troubles.

Nevertheless as factors in the situation it seems possible that according to how they were constructed and used examinations could ease or exacerbate the situation. If the influence that examinations exert at present is harmful, might it still not be the case that this was largely a contingent factor and not a necessary one? Can we think of examinations as potentially presenting an opportunity for bringing about a state of affairs with which we might be rather more satisfied than at present? Is it possible to consider them as instruments of educational reform?

There are two kinds of criticism of existing examinations. The first major kind of criticism is that the examination papers themselves are ineffective and inefficient measuring instruments. This may mean one of two things. It may mean that the examinations are measuring or attempting to measure the wrong things, that is, they are wrongly constructed in relation to the purposes for which we want them. Or we may think that they are rightly constructed in relation to our purpose, but that they do the job badly. A lot of criticism comes into this category.

The second major kind of criticism concerns the effect that current kinds of examination have upon teaching in the schools.

Now these two major criticisms, the inefficiency of orthodox examination papers as measuring instruments and their feed-back effect upon curricula and methods in the schools, are distinct although not entirely separable and they can profitably be looked at separately.

The question of the efficiency of examinations as measuring instruments breaks down, as we have already seen, into two points. The first point is whether examinations are attempting to do the right or the wrong thing. This means that we have got to make up our minds whether in fact they are measuring what we want them to measure. In turn this means that we must make up our minds what it is we want them to measure. I am going to suggest that it is really here that most of the trouble lies. I suggest that we should ask whether in the physical sciences current examinations are measuring what we want them to measure.

The second point about the efficiency of examinations, which I can deal with only briefly, is whether they are doing well or badly whatever job it is that they are doing.

This is the kind of problem dealt with by psychologists who are specialists in mental measurement. It is a highly specialist field, the technology of the measurement of behaviour at the level of the products of thinking. It involves the principles of the construction of measuring instruments—tests and examinations—and their validation. It is a specialism in which Francis Galton, Karl Pearson and Alfred Binet were notable pioneers and it now has quite a long history. Ballard's book *The New Examiner* appeared in 1923 and following the work of the International Examinations Enquiry around 1930 we had Hartog and Rhodes's two well-known books, *The Examination of Examinations* in 1935 and *The Marks of Examiners* in 1936. I find that many people have forgotten how much useful research was done in those days. You may remember that it is a field rich in good stories. I particularly like the one about the college where six professors were examining in history and one of them, the senior professor, constructed model answers to all the questions on the paper and circulated them to his fellow examiners along with the candidates' papers. Unfortunately the papers got mixed up and when he got them back, he found that two of his colleagues had failed him!

Important changes have come about in examination practice in certain parts of the educational system through this type of criticism and through the researches of the psychometric psychologists. Objective tests or new type examinations are familiar to all of us. What is not so well appreciated is that these changes in methods of measurement have brought about changes in what we have been trying to measure. By changing the means of examining the aims have been changed also. Therefore one of the results has been that the aims of teaching have changed. The classic example of course is the eleven-plus examination. Here a great deal of dissatisfaction was felt with methods of examining which involved subjective judgment in marking, particularly essay-type questions, and so there developed the whole of the work on objective tests of English. Instead of getting the children to write essays, they were asked to answer a large number of analytic questions about the use of language, for example, to select from a list of words a word which meant the same as the one they were given or its opposite and so on. Now if you look at what that kind of examination is doing, it is certainly not doing what the essay sets out to do. It is doing something different. Before very long, of course, teachers being concerned for the success of their pupils in the examination began to teach the sorts of things that would help them to pass it. So the primary schools began to be criticized because they were no longer teaching English, but something called 'Moray House English,* and teachers complained that children came into secondary schools with little

* Many of the selection tests used in the eleven-plus examination originate from a test research and production unit in Moray House College of Education, Edinburgh.

ability to write sentences and certainly unable to compose paragraphs and whole essays.

A great deal of effort has been directed to trying to change the methods of examining as an important step in reform, but if you do no more than this you leave to chance the changes in aims which will result from methodological change. That is you will leave to chance the objectives which are going to be created and which teachers will follow. That is what happened in the eleven-plus. Instead of saying 'What do we want children to be able to do with language?', people said, 'Can we construct objective tests in English?' They evaded the basic question of what it is we want our children to be able to do. We must begin with trying to determine what it is we want to teach, that is, what we want children to learn, and then devise ways in which we can assess whether or not they have achieved what we want them to achieve. We must choose our aims and then devise the means to accomplish them. But since ends and means are so closely related, we must in fact study both problems together. Perhaps we can go even further and ask whether, if we achieve a satisfactory and detailed definition of aims, we may not find that in the very process we have solved the problem of finding efficient means of measurement, at least in principle if not in all its technical details. And I think we are then able to address ourselves to the main question. Attempting to answer the question 'What should we teach?' involves us in syllabus construction, and although syllabus construction or revision does not embody a complete definition of objectives it provides an essential step.

Having revised our syllabus as a way to reform, how can we secure that the revised syllabus is taught? More generally, having made up our minds about the kind of things we want children to be able to do, and to understand, and the kind of attitudes we want them to have, how can we get our decisions put into effect?

There are roughly two views, I think, among those who are interested in the reform and development of education. There are the extreme idealists who say, 'You just cannot reform anything unless you abolish examinations entirely.' A more moderate form of idealism with which I have a great deal of sympathy is to say, 'Change the system of examining itself by substituting for external examinations, internal examinations externally moderated, the system which is in fact used by universities themselves.' This is a quite fundamental programme of reform, but for the present I am concerned with more limited matters. There is no opposition between the larger programme of reform and the more limited matters with which I want to deal. On the contrary, the two programmes complement one another, and I shall refer to this again later.

The second major point of view is more realistic in tone. It says in effect that we will never alter teaching until we alter the examinations. We must accept examinations as necessary and not just as necessary evils, but as essential instruments of reform. We must realize that by acceptance of examinations we secure a point of entry into what will otherwise remain a vicious circle. If we want reformed teaching, we must revise our examinations. We must put into our examinations what we want children to learn and to be able to do. If we do that, then teachers will teach these things. It might be thought that this is taking a somewhat cynical view of the dependence of teachers on the external examination system. I would not wish to put it that way. I do not think it is essentially cynical because I think that to some extent even the most strong-minded, gifted and idealistic of teachers are bound to be influenced by the syllabus through which they are preparing their pupils for examination. They may and probably will have aims far beyond such preparation. Most of us who care about our subject, and care about children and young people, have aims well beyond the examinations. Still, responsible teachers at all levels will not be prepared to ignore the examination. It is bound to influence them. I suggest therefore that this second and thoroughly realistic view is one which ought to be taken very seriously indeed. It should not be too difficult a job to enlist teachers in the enterprise of modifying the work of examinations because it touches them so closely. Every subject teacher can concern himself with this and be interested in it. This is not something which belongs to the world of educational generalities. It is a world in which all teachers should feel at home, since it involves them in their own subjects, their own areas of knowledge. However, no matter where our attempts at reform begin, we are inescapably faced with the problem of considering what it is we are setting out to do in teaching.

Let us proceed by way of concrete examples. I have here a couple of volumes of G.C.E. 'A' level examination papers of two of the examining boards in the country. What I have to say should not be construed simply as an attack, because I think this is in the first instance a question of trying to find out what it is that we are trying to do at the present time. We may then pass to the very difficult question of whether we want to do something different, and if so what. I am not at all insensible to the hours of devoted thought and work that has gone into these papers. I take that for granted, but that is not to say that because there is devotion there should be no criticism. As I am not myself a physicist by training, I am not going to comment more than I feel I dare on the actual material of these papers. If we take the first set of papers for Summer 1961, and look at Advanced level Physics, Paper 1, taking $2\frac{1}{2}$ hours, we find that 'Candidates must answer five questions including at least one from Section A'. Section A seems to me to be dealing with the properties of matter. 'B' is electricity. The pattern is a familiar one. Section A begins: 'Explain what is meant by Young's Modulus and Elastic Limit.' This is in italics. Then follows the usual kind of example. Now the point I want to make is this, that any examination paper, any particular question even, embodies an objective of teaching. A question is an embodiment of what the setter of the question considers should be an objective of teaching. So that it ought to be possible to infer, by studying examination questions, what the objectives they embody are. These may not have been conscious objectives on the part of the person who set the questions, but the objectives are there implicitly nevertheless.

Now it would take a long time and a lot of hard logical work really to do this in any detail and I do not propose to attempt this. I am proposing simply to make some general comment on apparent objectives in these papers with which, of course, anyone is entirely at liberty to disagree, if it is thought that I am perhaps being unfair, or that I have been inaccurate in my rather rapid estimate of the state of affairs.

If we take another set of papers from another examining board, we notice that candidates have to answer six questions; at least three from Section I and one from Section II. Question one in Section I is 'Explain what is meant in principle by "The Conservation of Linear Momentum."' And then there follows a numerical example. My feeling would be that you can pass this kind of question and pass very well if, in an old-fashioned phrase, you 'know your book work'. This is essentially what such questions call for from pupils—*reproduction of what has been taught.* Something like half of most of these questions call for obvious reproduction of what has been taught, and the other half seems to be the application of this knowledge to particular circumstances. Now these may be circumstances which none of the candidates has met before but they nevertheless seem to be highly familiar circumstances and to conform to a pattern. For example, numerical values in the examples may not be ones candidates have met but they will probably have solved corresponding problems in the papers for the last eight or ten years! There is running through these papers undoubtedly an important element of application of knowledge but it is mostly something which can be done as a result of having been laboriously taught. The method of dealing with this kind of question depends very largely on being able to reproduce what has been learned. This is not entirely true because there are questions—one has, however, to look for them and they tend to come more in scholarship papers than in the Advanced level papers—which really do call for the application of what the student knows to relatively unfamiliar situations. I would have thought, however, that this is a minor element in most papers. Those who are concerned with scientific education know that it is by no means easy to devise appropriate problems of that kind. It is fairly easy to develop the problem which asks the pupil to work out a numerical example of a principle or law or formula which he has just derived in the first part of his answer. It is much more difficult to devise the kind of situation which is not too difficult and which is not too easy, and which does present something of a challenge, because it takes the pupil into something relatively unfamiliar, but where nevertheless he can use, if he but knows how to do it, the information and the understanding he has already gained.

Physics as it is mainly reflected in the current kind of paper seems to be a subject which could be taught out of books. There can be no doubt that a lot of 'physics' is taught today by means of dictated notes giving pre-digested explanations of phenomena which may never have been actually encountered. The subject becomes a matter of learning formulae. Of such practices we must seriously ask whether it is 'physics' that is being taught at all. I do not want it to be thought that I believe that physics is taught like that in all the schools in the country—I do not think it is. But there must be a strong temptation to teach in this way with this kind of examination, particularly when it is considered that teachers rightly think their duty is to give their pupils a chance of fulfilling their dreams, of getting them through, of getting them high enough marks, so that some university or higher institution will pay attention to them. Every mark is believed to be important.

Whether 'physics' is really being tested at all by this kind of examination may be debatable, but there can be no doubt that more than physics is being tested by it. To a considerable extent, what is being tested is the capacity to use the English language in relation to the subject. There is a verbal component in these papers and I would say its weight is very high. I have not seen a proper psychometric analysis of papers of this kind, but I think there can be no doubt from what we know that the verbal factor would be very high. Now I am not saying that this is entirely wrong. I think we are right to expect students who intend to come to university to be able to express the things they do by way of experiment, the phenomena they encounter and the ideas physics has generated about these, in intelligible English. The question, however, is whether the verbal factor should have as much weight as it almost certainly has. One of these says that 'marks will be deducted for slovenly presentation' and so on. So there is much more than physics being tested.

I think this is not an unfair report of the present situation. The objectives embodied in the examination of physics at 'A' level seem to be concerned largely with the ability to state facts, irrespective of whether these facts have been met with as a matter of direct experience in the laboratory or read about in books. Beyond this the objectives presupposed seem to be the ability to *state* certain general principles and *define* certain general terms, and to be able to *apply* formulae embodying general laws to a rather narrow range of situations. Psychologically speaking the capacity to recall what has been taught, what has been read, seems to be of overriding importance.

By way of contrast, I now wish to consider an entirely different type of science examination. Here are extracted questions from two papers in pre-matriculation physics and chemistry produced for an experiment in a certain university in another part of the world. This was a co-operative experiment between a number of schools, the faculty of science of this university and an educational research institution, in which these people acting in partnership have been concerned to work out a set of experimental papers in these particular subjects. Decisions are not being taken on the basis of these papers at the moment, but the results of the papers are being compared with those in the traditional examinations which are still used in this particular university. One of the main aims of this experiment was to improve methods of selecting university students. But those responsible for the experiment saw that if there was to be any point in having better selection, the instruments of selection would have to be such that they would not merely select the better students irrespective of how they had been taught but would select the better students from among a whole population that had been well taught. It was not only a question of increasing the efficiency of selection but of raising the whole level of performance. Therefore there was a serious attempt to re-define the objectives of teaching in these sciences at pre-matriculation level. As with all examinations, a study of the questions reveals the objectives sought.

The physics paper is in three parts. Part one is called 'Knowledge'. There are forty-seven questions and the time allowed is twenty-five minutes. The second part is called 'Application'. There are twenty-four questions and all the time allowed is twenty-five minutes. Part three is called 'Understanding'—a word that perhaps might not find favour with pedants in this country. In this part there are fifty-five questions and the time allowed is seventy minutes. In passing, it might be noted that there are in all 126 questions and that the total time consumed is two hours. Although this may seem a rather trivial aspect it is not a negligible matter because the analysis of objectives which leads to a large number of specific questions, instead of to a small number of very general questions, is fundamental to the approach to the teaching of the subject which this examination embodies.

We have been helped by the compilers in the first instance by their telling us that they had at least three objectives without subdividing them any further. One they called 'Knowledge', the second they called 'Application', and the third they called 'Understanding'. *Knowledge*, I suppose, would be what most of us refer to as 'facts' —perhaps the most question-begging word in our language. What we all consider as facts are the sort of things that we feel that *pupils must know*. They are the basis of the subject; without the facts we cannot get anywhere at all. *Application* seems not unlike what I have suggested some of the questions in our own examination papers are concerned with. But there are differences. I think it will be found, if we study these questions, that they call for a much more specific, therefore I think more precise, understanding of the issues dealt with, than does the analogous material in our own examination papers. By using the technique of highly specific yet simple examples you get a large number of occasions of testing 'application'. *Understanding* contains questions which attempt to get at the foundations of general principle, and which may call for the application of general principles to situations which may not be at all familiar.

I do not wish to advocate simply that we change our 'A' level examining pattern to this. That is not the point. The point is that we have here two different approaches to examining the same subject at roughly the same level. I think our 'A' level is indeed a bit 'higher' in one particular sense of that term but there is not all that much difference. In these two different approaches are embodied different objectives. In the second approach there has been much more analysis of the subject of physics and of the sorts of things that students should be required to do. As a result of that analysis, I think a rather different weighting of the aims has been achieved. If the paper is looked at as a whole it will be seen that out of 126 questions in physics, 47 are on so-called 'Knowledge', 24 on 'Application' and 55 on 'Understanding'. I think that gives a radically different weighting from what we get in what has become our conventional and orthodox 'A' level type of examination.

The difference between these examinations is not merely, nor even mainly, in their form. The multiplicity of questions of the short answer type is perhaps what strikes one at first. I think to be captivated by that, however, would be to miss the real point of the different approaches to the educational objectives of teaching physics. This experiment arose out of a serious attempt by teachers of physics in schools and universities to get down to what it really was they wanted pupils to know and understand. The method used was to undertake a detailed analysis of physics, and to prepare a large number of questions for testing. These were then tried out to see how well they did discriminate between the abler and the less able pupils. From this point on, the orthodox techniques of mental testing were applied to this material in order to produce a final paper. It will be noticed that the sections contain odd totals of questions. For example, it might be asked, 'Why 47 questions?' The answer to that undoubtedly is that there were 47 items which came well out of the item analysis. There may well have been 130 of that type originally. The main point, however, is that this is not just another objective test of the eleven-plus variety adapted to a more advanced stage. It was not arrived at that way. It was not begun by saying, 'Let us have an objective test in physics.' What was said was, 'What do we want to test in physics?', and having found that out, 'How do we test these things?' So a measuring instrument is obtained, through tackling seriously the aims of teaching.

I have not mentioned the question of the verbal factor in this new type of physics examination. It is obviously low. If we want to test our pupils' capacity to write intelligibly in connected prose about physics, we shall have to do that separately in a different kind of paper. There is nothing to prevent us doing this, and every reason why we should do it.

I will conclude in more general terms. I think our own examinations of the present time lay far too great stress on the acquisition of reproducible knowledge in the form of facts and I think there is far too little stress on the understanding of principles. This introduces the complicated topic of the relation of the learning of facts to the understanding of principles in our teaching. People say, 'You cannot understand principles if you have no facts to go upon. You must begin with facts. Facts are basic.' This is a highly debatable point. It depends entirely on what one means. Undoubtedly the person who is most competent in any subject is the person with the most information at his command with which to think in that subject. It is not that I would rate knowledge low—I do not. The point really is not that sort of point at all. It is a psychological point; it is a point about learning. It is how you come by the facts, and this is frankly where I think the mistake we make lies. You say you cannot understand the principles without facts; therefore teach the facts first. But this is fatal. We surely do not mean that facts can, or have to be, learned first, and then principles arrived at afterwards. The psychology of learning has shown two things quite incontrovertibly. First, that unless learning is imbued with a purpose beyond the mere facts with which it deals, and the search for principles is one such purpose, it is relatively inefficient, and the knowledge acquired is not available in readily usable form. Secondly, where the search for principles is primary, *the relevant knowledge is acquired in this process of search* and, moreover, is acquired in a readily usable form. Seek principles first and facts will be added unto you. At the moment we seem to be doing the exact opposite. The results are not encouraging.

The moral of this whole story is, I think, quite clear: If we are to reform the work of the schools we must begin by reforming the content and form of our examinations, by seeking explicitly to identify our desired objectives in teaching and then embodying these in suitable instruments of assessment.* But can we reach agreement about objectives, in say physics? It is clearly necessary that we should try, in order that we may have some common basis on which to construct syllabuses, but it is more than doubtful whether we need to be wholly successful in this enterprise. It would appear to be desirable that some diversity should occur in the teaching of any subject, leaving room for the genius of individual teachers. Full play for such genius will, however, never be secured until we replace external examinations by internal examinations externally moderated. But such a reform itself makes it more than ever essential that *all* teachers have a clear idea of their own objectives and so can effectively test the progress of their pupils without recourse to external agencies. Hence research into the improvement of teaching through the reform of examinations will be needed in a reformed system of examining, as much as it is required under the present system.

Even if all such reforms were carried through, examination *pressure* and all the ills that flow from it would continue in some measure until we were able to make examinations into qualification tests of fitness for such and such endeavours, instead of their being as at present selective instruments deployed in the interests of a scarce commodity, viz. higher education. When the age of educational abundance dawns, however, we shall still need to assess our pupils' progress and will thus obviously need to see that our instruments of assessment closely mirror the objectives of our teaching.

* Modern thinking about reform of curricula and subject syllabuses owes a great deal to the work of Bloom and associates in Chicago. See B. Bloom, *Taxonomy of Educational Objectives*, Longmans, N.Y., 1956.

To attempt to improve our teaching at the present time of educational scarcity, through the use of examinations as instruments of reform, is therefore not merely to undertake a task made necessary by existing evils but is to contribute directly to the fundamental and long-term improvement of education.

Originally published in the *Bulletin* of the Institute of Physics, August 1964.

Note

The aim of this paper was deliberately limited to the discussion of certain specific problems. There are many issues, for example those concerning the nature of assessment procedures and their relation to conventional 'final' examination papers, which are not dealt with at all. This is also true of more fundamental issues concerning the necessity and validity of any kind of evaluation in education whatsoever. It is probable that, if the whole nature and conception of 'schooling' alters dramatically during the next century, as seems not unlikely, then this will necessarily entail radical alterations in the whole ideology and practice of evaluating the results of schooling.

Five

Guidance as a concept in educational theory

We may describe any educational theory as an attempt to structure educational activity and experience as an intelligible whole, through the constant interplay of critical and constructive thought. Moreover, in the end it should inform our practical judgments and therefore our actions (see chapter 1). If the concept of guidance is to be of use in helping to give an intelligible form to our educational endeavours, we have through critical examination to discover the essential common features of these activities we think of as involving guidance, and through constructive imagination to relate these features to the rest of our thought about education. The crucial questions concerning guidance as a concept in educational thought are those which seek to probe its relationships with the ideal of freedom. In answering these questions it will have to be assumed that there is a generally understood sense of the term freedom. It cannot be defined and adequately discussed here, although much that will be said may be regarded as an implicit definition of it. In its relation to education, freedom has been brilliantly discussed by McCallister (1931). He saw that if it is to serve freedom, education must itself be conceived 'as the embodiment of a principle of freedom'. Is the concept of guidance a natural key to thinking of education in such terms, or does it harbour within it implications quite inimical to freedom? What criteria has guidance to satisfy if its practice is to be in conformity with those components of our educational tradition that stand for freedom. The answer to this question depends on the answer to another. 'What in principle is entailed in the concept of guidance?' The aim of this essay is therefore to offer both a general critique and a particular interpretation of the concept of guidance. The method employed is through discussion of the particular interpretation to reveal the nature of the general issues involved.

Origin and contemporary implications of the concept

The origin of the concept of guidance lies deep in the history of educational thought. 'My father, thou art the guide of my youth', declared Jeremiah, and in a famous passage Plato says (1951, VII, 518), 'there may well be an art whose aim would be to effect this very thing, the conversion of the soul, in the readiest way; not to put the power of sight into the soul's eye, which already has it, but to ensure that, instead of looking in the wrong direction, it is turned the way it ought to be.' Indeed under various guises the concept seems to emerge wherever men have felt compelled to think freshly about education and to attempt to reinterpret its meaning. Some of the basic modern ideas about guidance clearly take their rise within the stream of thought which flows from Vittorino of Feltre with his House of Joy at Mantua early in the fifteenth century, through Montaigne to Rousseau and his successors and on to Dewey at the beginning of the twentieth. Montaigne (1580) was of the opinion that 'the only thing you can do with the appetites and inclinations is to tempt them. Otherwise you only make your pupils into bookish asses.' He was also among the first to assert the fundamental importance of individual differences. Trying to educate 'many minds of different attainments and kinds with the same lesson and the same discipline is bound to fail with all but a few'—an opinion echoed by Rousseau (1761) who observed: 'One nature needs wings, another shackles.' For Dewey with his preoccupation with the social nature of mind, the essence of guidance lay in the skill through which the teacher made it possible for the child to rediscover his social inheritance through personal experience.* 'Basing education upon personal experience may mean more multiplied and more intimate contacts between the mature and the immature than ever existed in the traditional schools, and consequently more, rather than less, guidance by others' (1938). All these ideas are of course fundamentally psychological. They are concerned with a view of mind as an actively growing entity exhibiting spontaneity and individuality and capable of being nourished only through personal experience, and as such they form the core of the child-centred theme in the development of the concept of guidance.

A second theme from which the concept derives much of its meaning is a socio-centric one which is concerned with the social purpose which guidance is meant to serve. In the West, since the

* 'Earlier psychology regarded mind as a purely individual affair in direct and naked contact with an external world. At present the tendency is to conceive individual mind as a function of social life, requiring continual stimulus from social agencies and finding its nutriment in social supplies.' (Dewey, 1900.)

renaissance, this theme has been largely implicit and as a result has often been entirely ignored. We have become used to thinking of society in terms of national cultures which have until recently been developing in the direction of an increasing measure of freedom for the individual in work, conduct and belief. The basic freedom, however, which has been cherished is freedom of judgment and conscience and in educational theory progressively less explicit emphasis has been laid on conformity to tradition. As a matter of historical fact a close connection has existed between freedom of conscience, the disinterested search for objective truth through science and the progressive mastery of nature. From this matrix has developed a degree of technological complexity and continuous social change which has now rendered traditional methods of education and of occupational recruitment inappropriate. Departure from tradition demands the conscious shaping of education and therefore introduces a measure of social planning. Direct social relevance therefore becomes one of the main criteria of what children should learn, a point of view well illustrated in a report of the Council for Curriculum Reform (1945):

> It is obvious that the purpose of education will determine the content of the curriculum, the methods employed, the kind of schools and the amount of education given to children and young persons. This functional relationship is frequently overlooked. Until recently there were many educationalists who thought that education could be discussed without reference to the objectives and values of the community in which it was given ... The purpose of society determines the purpose of the schools; the purpose of the schools determines the content of education.

The opportunities which education offers therefore become structured in terms of society's needs, and educational guidance then inevitably proceeds with the requirements of this structure in mind. Thus the conditions and ideals of freedom which have nourished the child-centred theme are now driving us to accept guidance as an appropriate instrument of our social purpose. The extent to which we can reconcile individual freedom and social purpose, i.e. 'authority', through guidance, depends on how we interpret both freedom and authority. This interpretation forms a third and vital theme in the development of the concept of guidance, and calls for further examination.

Hitherto a substantial part of the educational aim of the West has been to 'provide for growth beyond the type'. This pre-occupation has been possible for us solely because we have been able to take the necessary minimum of social conformity almost completely for granted. As a result, we have tended to lose sight of the fact that the primary function of education in any society whatever is to produce a measure of social conformity among its members sufficient to guarantee the continued existence of the society's culture.* Our disregard for this primary social function in our conscious thinking about education has recently been challenged. Studies in social anthropology have served to remind us of it, with a wealth of illustrative detail, and the appearance again in the world of what Sir Fred Clarke described as 'educative societies' has reminded us of it somewhat more forcibly and painfully. An 'educative society' is one which consciously accepts the primary social function of education and pursues as its overmastering purpose the production of a certain type of citizen. The modern educative society appears to have come to stay and Britain is already in process of becoming such a society (Clarke, 1948). What is to be the overmastering purpose which guidance must serve? Can we reconcile any overmastering purpose with the pursuit of freedom unless freedom itself be that purpose, and how does the way in which we practise guidance affect the prospects of effecting such a reconciliation?

In the past we have in fact concentrated on producing the type of conformity which stressed the virtue of tolerance, particularly in matters of belief, as one of its supreme values, and our psychology has been largely one which has stressed the uniqueness of the individual. In this way we have come to think of guidance as a process of helping individuals through their own efforts to discover and develop their potentialities for personal happiness and social usefulness. By describing its aims as personal happiness and social

* This necessarily implies that the work of guidance (where it exists) has to be carried out within the limits of a given social framework, which offers the individual a finite number of roles from which to choose, exacts standards of conduct which can only be varied within prescribed limits and in subtle ways delimits both the character of the thoughts he is able to think and the values he may hold. For the general effects of social factors on thought, see Karl Mannheim, *Essays on the Sociology of Knowledge*, 1952 (Mannheim does not make the popular mistake of underestimating Marx) and for the influence of language structure in particular see I. A. Richards, *Mencius on the Mind*, 1932, certain essays in *Selected Writings of Edward Sapir*, and B. L. Whorf, 'Science and linguistics' in *Readings and Social Psychology*, Harper, 1947. But there is a danger here of mistaking culture, the societal 'husk', for the 'kernel', the nature of language itself; or more succinctly and accurately, of concentrating entirely on the variety of phenotypes, and ignoring the existence of a genotype. See N. Chomsky, *Language and Mind*, Harcourt Brace, 1968.

efficiency we may tend to obscure the fact that guidance could well pursue such aims in a society which severely restricted freedom of conscience and belief. We are thus in danger of failing to see that guidance is purely a technique, that it is only a means, and that the ends which it serves will be determined both by the cultural tradition within which it operates and by the detailed way in which it interprets that tradition in its modes of operation. While note must therefore be taken of the far-reaching implications for guidance of the social framework within which it takes place, an adequate treatment of this topic would require a lengthy examination of the influence of institutional structures, their flexibility or inflexibility (Richardson, 1967) and the relationship of guidance to social engineering—by itself a wholly amoral technology. It is enough to say here that unless a considerable measure of flexibility can be secured through appropriate organization and the participation of all concerned, guidance itself may easily become an instrument not of freedom, but of bondage.

The essential character of guidance

There is no space here to deal with the influence of what has been called scientific paedagogy, with its stress on individual differences in talents, temperaments and rates of development, on the concept of guidance, nor with the development of guidance as an activity of various kinds of expert concerned with educational backwardness, maladjustment, or vocational placement (Keir, 1952). The influence of the concept on the organization of learning groups in school (Yates, 1966) and on the trend towards the individualizing of instruction (e.g. nowadays through programmed learning) is also a related but separate theme (Smith and Moore, 1962). So too is the inner logic through which the episodic guidance of individuals by experts has developed into a continuous responsibility shared by the educational and other helping professions, by parents and by the community at large. Our concern has to be with a highly generalized form of the concept of guidance.

From this point of view guidance is identical neither with education nor with teaching, nor with giving advice, nor with the treatment of behaviour disorders, although the greater part of all these spheres of action may be approached from the standpoint of guidance. It is both an approach to their problems and a particular kind of activity which may inform all that is done in their name. The idea of guidance as an approach to education, for example, enables us to see the teacher's role as comparable with that of the guide on a long mountaineering expedition. The good guide must know thoroughly his own range of country and he must be quick to assess the strengths and weaknesses of his charge. Within the given purpose of the expedition, the actual objectives, the routes, the stages, the pace and the equipment must all be chosen to suit the climber, and the guide must have at his command a wide variety of skills for use in different conditions. Moreover the expedition should have as one of its aims, that the pupil should gradually become independent of the guide and able to climb unaided.

We have already discussed the scope of responsibility in guidance. The emphasis in this description is on the nature of the responsibility of the guide. Guidance is child-centred, but it also has a social aim which at first the child can neither discern nor interpret for himself, and therefore the key to the whole enterprise lies with the guide. What is the nature of his responsibility? In one sense he is the senior member of a partnership. There is one basic fact about this partnership, however, which must never be forgotten, and that is its inequality, the prolonged inequality of child and adult in our present example, or the inequality of healer and sick in another.* This real inequality can only be prevented from degenerating into exploitation by accepting as the supreme measure of the guide's responsibility the realization of the ideal of mutuality in the partnership. Responsibility of this kind may be exercised through the conception of guidance as mediation.

Mediation

From the most general standpoint, guidance may be conceived as essentially a process of mediating between the growing child, his needs, powers, interests and experience on the one hand, and the needs, responsibilities, opportunities and values of adult life on the other. This definition has the merit of making clear certain fundamental points. If guidance is a matter of mediation this disposes of

* The notion that adults and children can work together as real equals, so far as responsibility is concerned, once fashionable in progressive education circles, is a piece of extremely dangerous self-deception. It was meant to serve the ideal of partnership in education. In fact it is doubtful if it has done anything of the kind. It is dangerous because it marks on the part of the educator a refusal to accept adult responsibility (and therefore may express a wish to remain a child) and perhaps even a deep unconscious hatred of children and a need to exploit them. This need is in fact satisfied when they are saddled with responsibilities for which they are as yet unfitted. Erik Erikson (1964, p. 422) reminds us of the complexities and subtleties of this whole matter when he remarks that 'the prolonged inequality of child and adult is one of the facts of existence which make for exploitability, as well as for technical and cultural virtuosity in human life.'

the question whether it is exercised in the interests of the individual or of society for it has to be exercised equally in the interests of both. The definition also serves to resolve the false antithesis between authority and freedom, for mediation is only possible where common ground exists, and this common ground must be capable of exhibiting the corresponding features on either side, through which reconciliation is possible. Thus the needs of the child as human are not alien but akin to those of the adult, his powers ultimately imply responsibilities, to his interests eventually correspond opportunities, and his experience is a growing fabric within which the values of his society necessarily inhere. If it is objected that these are merely ideal relationships, the objection serves only to emphasize that the function of mediation is to secure that in some measure the ideal will be experienced as real. The extent to which this can be done depends on our capabilities as guides, on our knowledge, insight, integrity and judgment; in a word, on the way in which we discharge our responsibility.

As mediators, we have an essential part to play in the child's attempt to come to terms with what he is and with what he will become, not for the banal reason that we were once children and are now adults, but for two profound reasons. The first is that our childhood lives actively within us; it is the 'real' foundation of our adulthood. The second is that the child's adulthood is burgeoning within him; it is the 'ideal' foundation of his childhood as a human being. We are able to mediate only because the child is still in us and the adult is latent in him. In interpreting the world to the child, we are also interpreting it to ourselves, and helping him to interpret it for himself. We are able to mediate most effectively when we are somehow aware of these facts and the child realizes them implicitly also.

Further, if guidance is essentially mediation, this defines our responsibilities as guides in a flexible way as lying between the total care appropriate for the wholly dependent infant and the detachment required in dealing with the adolescent or young adult adventuring into independence. What the individual can do to help himself and what requires to be done for him is a matter of infinite variability depending on his stage of development and on the complexity of the situation which faces him. The extent of our knowledge of this situation, of our insight into its meaning for the individual and our understanding of the action called for on our part, is a measure of our competence as mediators. Mediation therefore calls for a thorough diagnosis or assessment prior to any action. We have to assess the individual's needs and powers and we have to analyse the situation with which he is faced, be it the task of constructing a proper sentence, of conforming to the rules of conduct of the school, or overcoming anxiety and inhibitions in relationships with his fellows, or of choosing a career. The basis of an assessment is of course information and to help us to secure adequate and accurate information we may have at our command, for example, the techniques and concepts of scientific psychology, our insight into the personalities and problems of children, and our expert knowledge of particular subjects, fields of activity and areas of employment. It is here that we can utilize first-hand observation, or employ appropriate instruments such as tests of ability, attainment and personality functioning, and it is here also that we have recourse to records of the development and experience of the individual and that we can seek to explore the possibilities and difficulties which any particular line of action may hold for him. When we have all the relevant information we must evaluate it for ourselves. This is assessment. It may often be completed in an instant, when all the processes are telescoped in a single intuition, or it may take time and require elaborate analysis and collation of material, but the essential pattern is the same. We are then faced with interpreting what we have learned to the individual. This task of interpretation is the heart of guidance conceived as mediation.

Interpretation

Interpretation lies at the heart of mediation and therefore of guidance because it consists of making what is implicit in a situation explicit. It consists in enabling someone else to see what is indeed there but which they have hitherto been unable to perceive. Thus through interpretation experience acquires new meanings. In this sense it is a term for a general process of learning which by its very nature can never be complete. What is revealed through interpretation may have been hidden because of an individual's lack of knowledge, lack of experience, or lack of opportunity, or it may have been hidden because it formed part of an experience which was never at any time conscious or because although previously known it had become unconscious. The concept therefore applies equally, for example, to rearranging the framework of experience, a process which implicitly provides new meanings, and to revealing unconscious feelings and ideas through the explicit revelation of unperceived relationship among those which are or may be made conscious. But because of the complex interrelations of meanings, interpretation is always in some sense partial and therefore always has its own implicit side.

The best teaching, for example, is always a judicious blend of implicit and explicit interpretation. Thus if we are concerned with children learning mathematics in the primary school, we shall find in the foreground of attention certain problems and tasks, certain operations and relationships on the one hand, and the children's interest, capacities and experience on the other. In the background loom the larger implications of shapes and numbers, their significance for the future life and work of the children and their creative power as symbols with which collectively we mould much of the material fabric of our civilization. The crucial factors in determining the extent to which each child can successfully inhabit, explore and master the world of mathematics are his basic capacities and our skill in interpreting this world to him. If we are freemen of it and it glows for us with infinite possibilities, we can so interpret it that each child can share something of our enjoyment. If we have never assimilated it ourselves and it exists as a dead precipitate of our own childhood within us, it will appear to our pupils as a meaningless and rigid system of rules and routine operations. If this happens, we shall have failed in our task as mediators between our pupils and their social heritage. The crux of interpretation is that it should reveal the social heritage as having definite form and yet as being flexible. The definite form springs in this instance from its own inherent nature as given in the logic of mathematics and the particular conventions in which this has been enshrined in our society. This is an example of the essential discipline or authority of the subject. It is just as sensible, however, and equally important, to talk about the freedom of the subject. This springs from its inherent flexibility which is a function of our capacity to discover from among the infinite variety of relationships which compose it, the particular selection and arrangement of these relationships through which our pupils can best explore it and master its meaning.

The way in which the concepts of mediation and interpretation may be used to redeem such notions as authority and freedom from their usual barren abstractness is one of the marks of dialectical thought. This form of thinking is necessary to any coherent understanding of guidance or of education. For example, to some minds, guidance is essentially directive, even regulative, while to others it is mainly permissive. Thinking dialectically, we can perceive that the aim of interpretation in guidance is, for example, to reveal to a child that as well as being directive, the authority of adult society is also permissive and that these are correlative aspects of the same (ideal) truth. Without the sense of freedom to try his powers and to test out the limits of sanctioned behaviour a child cannot discover his proper place in the world, nor reach an independent view of its meaning. That is to say that without freedom authority becomes tyranny, and that without authority freedom becomes anarchy.

The dialectical relation between the regulative and permissive aspects of guidance is, for example, clearly revealed over the question of standards. Standards are necessary for guidance but in a sense which is somewhat different from the common meaning of the term. They represent intermediate objectives in guidance and therefore they have always to be kept in view. They are defined in part by the purpose of the expedition, but their peculiarity is that they can never be completely known in advance, just as the glittering peak when climbed may turn out to be instead a broad tower of rock or perhaps only a rather formless col. Moreover the routes and the pace by which the objectives are reached have to be adapted to the individual's powers, and frequently the objectives themselves have to be altered as the powers of the climbers and the character of the country into which the expedition is advancing become more fully known. Without such permissiveness the individual cannot discover what is a realizable objective for him, without such flexibility of purpose, disaster awaits the expedition. This is what tends to happen when standards are allowed to ossify, dialectically speaking, into degraded forms of objectives, such as those represented, for example, by most ordinary examinations.* Thus through interpretation the regulative and permissive aspects of guidance are seen to be truly co-relative—one requires the other. This may also be seen when we consider guidance in respect of a choice of course or career. Satisfactory choice demands that certain conditions of knowledge, skill or attitude, for example, have to be met. These are as it were 'regulations', and the function of the guide is to interpret their meaning in terms of the pupil's capacities. But experience shows that this can never be perfectly done, there is never an exact fit between them, and guidance fails unless the requirements or standards can in practice be adapted and modified, i.e. unless through interpretation their permissive character can be discovered. Again, in guidance in remedial or therapeutic work, the individual has to meet the demands of ordinary life in some way. They are regulatory for him and to help him to come to terms with

* These for the most part constitute a rejection of the whole idea of guidance in education. This is so because they are primarily barriers and not gateways; they are competitive and selective processes into which many may be called but as a result of which only relatively few are chosen. A powerful methodological tool, capable of being used in the reformation of curricula and examinations, has been forged by Bloom and his co-workers in Chicago, and already has had considerable influence. B. Bloom, *Taxonomy of Educational Objectives*, Longmans, N.Y., 1956.

them, as best he may, the guide has to interpret them for him in a way which enables him to use them to fashion a life of his own, albeit a life compatible with membership of a given community.

These examples show that the essential function of interpretation as the heart of mediation, and therefore of guidance, is to reveal both the form and flexibility of experience, both the regulative and permissive aspects of life. This revelation clearly always requires some degree of creative re-fashioning of the framework of the individual's experience, and this can only take place within and through the relationship established with him. The first of these requirements for interpretation we may call contrivance, it is what we do for and with the individual, the second, relationship, is what we are to the individual and what he is to us. The first is a process of co-operative action; the second a state of mutual being. The relative roles which these two requirements play in interpretation differ greatly from one instance of guidance to another. The emphasis is on contrivance when we group children for instruction or assist in the restructuring of their circumstances. In psychotherapy the emphasis is always on relationship. In actual teaching and in clinical child guidance there is usually a fairly even balance.

Contrivance

Some form of contrivance is essential to guidance even, for example, in the purest analytic form of psycho-therapy. There the interpretive method and its setting is a form of contrivance. But contrivance plays a more obvious part, in for example the selection and presentation of the materials of learning or in the adjustment of routines of upbringing or of home circumstances or in the arrangement of exploratory periods in different forms of occupation as found in some advanced forms of vocational guidance. The emphasis is on the modification and interpretation of the framework of experience. It may be largely a matter of stage managing the child's experience, of adjusting the demands of life or of creating opportunities for particular experiences appropriate to his powers. In this protective aspect it is essentially a matter of tempering the wind to the shorn lamb. In its creative aspect it is the giving of appropriate opportunities. The demand which contrivance makes on us as guides is therefore a demand on our ingenuity.

Clearly contrivance in guidance is closely linked to social engineering. Creating the conditions in which guidance is possible is often indistinguishable from the contrivance actually involved in giving guidance. Contrivance and social engineering merge into one another. The aim of contrivance may be thought of as being polarized between control and the giving of opportunity. Its aim and its contribution to guidance are to provide opportunities through control. Its danger lies in control becoming an end in itself but this danger is simply the perennial danger attendant on the neutral character of knowledge and power. The balance between control and provision of opportunities depends on the extent to which contrivance can become fully interpretive. The quality of the interpretation given and therefore the nature of the opportunities to which it leads is in its turn dependent on the extent to which it is a contribution to enabling the child to interpret his experience for himself. This is one of the main criteria on which guidance as an instrument of freedom has to be judged. The older the child the more explicitly interpretive in this sense should contrivance and therefore guidance become. The outcome is dependent primarily on the guidance relationship itself.

Relationship

The nature of the guidance relationship is the essential key to the character of guidance and the relationship may be thought of as being polarized between acceptance of the child's dependence and acceptance of his capacities for self-determination. Emphasis on dependence means emphasis on direction and persuasion. Emphasis on self-determination means emphasis on growth towards freedom and explicit mutuality. Again a balance has to be maintained which progressively shifts in the direction of emphasis on the achievement of self-determination. The attitude required from the guide is a balance between concern and detachment. In view of the need for the multiplicity of such balances the role of relationship in guidance is infinitely subtle.

The quality of the relationship obviously depends on the personality of the guide and especially on his insight into the child's motives and feelings and into his own. There has to be an acceptance both of the fact that as guides we necessarily appear as parent substitutes (wherever we are not, in fact, the parent), and that we ourselves react to the child in part in terms of the child within ourselves. We have to realize what we represent to the child and we have to accept the fact that we may appear to him in forms quite different from our own various images of ourselves. It is here that the unconscious forces operating within the child and within us may endanger the outcome of guidance. The possibility of mutual exploitation is an ever-present danger and insight is our only safeguard. We have to learn to recognize and resist not only the child's attempts to exploit and manipulate us but even more to recognize any attempt on our part to exploit him out of our own anxieties, out of our need for affection. The demand which the relationship in guidance makes on us is therefore a demand on our integrity. The extent to which our motives can become wholly other-regarding is another major criterion by which guidance as an instrument of freedom must be judged. It is intimately connected with the aim of self-determination for the individual. The nearest approach which guidance ever makes to the purely permissive is probably to be found in psycho-analysis. 'We do not seek to mould him (the patient) according to our notions of what he should be like, but only to enable him to make his own changes in himself, by understanding his own deeper wishes and counter-wishes. We are not concerned with our own purposes, but with his.' (Isaacs, 1968, p. 119.)

The requirements of contrivance and relationship raise the question of the skills which the guide must command and thus raise the question whether guidance is essentially an art or a science. Contrivance clearly calls for both. We must be artists, that is, we must be able to give the kind of concrete form to our intuition and knowledge which makes them communicable in the readiest way. We must also be able to use and interpret the results of such scientific techniques as are available to us. But as the essence of it lies in the relationships which its practice entails guidance can be neither art nor science although it must depend on both. If guidance were comprised entirely by art or science or both, the relationship in guidance would necessarily be that appropriate to the objects of art and science, that is manipulation. To redeem it from manipulation, guidance has therefore to be thought of as a particular kind of adventure in human mutuality. This requires that as a concept it has to function within a particular kind of educational theory.

Guidance and freedom

We have examined the direction in which the theory and practice of guidance are now developing. We have noted that in our democratic society there is a tendency for guidance to become a continuous and shared responsibility, and we have discovered that whether we can use guidance as an instrument of freedom depends on a number of crucial conditions. There are first two major and interrelated pre-conditions. These are that we can gradually build secure bases both for psychological and social freedom, the one within the personalities of our people, the other within the social structure of our society. Next there are two intermediate or operating conditions, which have to be satisfied in the practice of guidance as mediation. The first is a function of our ingenuity in contriving that our interpretation of experience to the individual shall reveal both its regulative and permissive aspects. The second is that our insight and integrity are sufficient to secure that the guidance relationship is as far as possible free from manipulative and exploitive elements. There is also, however, one final condition. The pursuit of freedom calls not only for the bringing into existence of the appropriate pre-conditions and for the development of the appropriate means, it demands also a rational faith capable of sustaining the effort which the pursuit requires. This faith it is the business of educational theory to render articulate.

Through what view of education can we sustain our faith in human freedom as a realizable end? While there is still a widespread tendency to regard education as simply a social process directed fundamentally and always to securing the continuance of a society's culture, nowadays it is increasingly thought of as guiding the direction of cultural change. On this view the study of education is a branch of applied social science, and guidance a technique, compounded of art and science to be employed for the differing moral ends of particular societies or particular ideological groupings. This is the basis of the actual relativity of educational theories. It offers no fundamental grounds on which freedom can be defended, and its basic weakness is made manifest in the temptation to use guidance for purposes of manipulation and control, a temptation to which scientific methods of guidance are particularly exposed. This is necessarily so because for science man is, and must be, only a part of 'nature', to be studied and controlled like any other natural object. But to treat men as manipulable objects is the supreme denial of human freedom and hence the naturalistic view of education, far from offering grounds for the defence of freedom, contains the seeds of its ultimate betrayal. There is, however, another way of regarding man and his education. In our immediate perception of ourselves and in our deeper perceptions of each other, we do not appear as natural objects, but as beings capable of self-knowledge and of mutuality. It is in this sense, and in this sense alone, that we are persons. (For science we are individuals or 'personalities'.) In Buber's language the I–Thou relation replaces the relation of I–It which is characteristic of science. On this view education is a transaction between the generations, a dialectical process of interaction through which we discover self-hood, otherhood and mutuality, not as matters of abstract knowledge, but as the concrete basis of all experience and all morality. Guidance is then mediation with a single moral aim. This view is the basis of the potential unity of educational theories, in which cultural and ideological differences, in their nature as vehicles of the human spirit, are transcended. Such a view of education forms the ultimate ground for any defence of freedom, because freedom is ultimately expressed by and is only fully attained through the explicit recognition of human mutuality.

Nevertheless the view that the study of education is necessarily bound up with the study of the social sciences is essential to the attainment of freedom. Science is itself one fundamental expression of human rationality and it offers us the possibility of continually deeper insight into the conditions which govern the explicit realization of freedom. It is this very fact of the powerfulness of our developing scientific knowledge which makes a contemporary analysis of guidance such a vital matter. For example, we have now attained a fairly clear idea of the growth and *modus operandi* of the moral function (Rickman, 1951). The important question raised by this discovery is not the meaning of moral order itself but the kind of moral order we wish to have, for it is demonstrable that this depends on the ways in which guidance is exercised. The actual moral ends which are sought and the means employed to attain them through guidance are grounded in the natural history of man and can neither be rationally understood nor rationally influenced without insight into their psycho-social origins. Thus the concept of guidance, in itself ethically neutral, acquires particular moral qualities in ways which are open to scientific understanding. Similarly the achievement of rational freedom within a community of persons requires the critical use of sociological analysis and psychological insight in the exercise of guidance, in order to guarantee that the concrete realization of self-knowledge and mutuality does not remain a sporadic occurrence encountered by a fortunate few. And this argument may be applied, *mutatis mutandis*, to the enormously complex problems of bringing into being a genuine world community, which embraces all mankind.

A revised and shortened version of an article contributed to the *Year Book of Education 1955* (Evans) under the title 'Guidance as a Concept in Educational Philosophy'.

References (omitting those given in footnotes)

Clarke, Sir Fred (1948) *Freedom in the Educative Society*. University of London Press.

Council for Curriculum Reform (1945) *The Content of Education*. University of London Press.

Dewey, John (1900) *School and Society*. University of Chicago Press, 1942.
Dewey, John (1938) *Experience and Education*. Collier-Macmillan, 1963.
Erikson, Erik H. (1964) *Childhood and Society*. Hogarth.
Isaacs, Susan (1968) *Childhood and After*. Routledge & Kegan Paul.
Keir, G. (1952) 'A history of child guidance', *British Journal of Educational Psychology*, vol. 22, part 1, February.
McCallister, W. J. (1931) *The Growth of Freedom in Education*. Constable.
Montaigne, M. de (1580) 'On the upbringing of children' in *Selected Essays* (ed. Tilley and Boase). Manchester University Press, 1954.
Plato (1951) *Republic* (trans. Cornford). Clarendon Press.
Richardson, J. E. (1967) *The Environment of Learning*. Nelson.
Rickman, J. (1951) 'The development of the moral function' in *Year Book of Education 1951*. Evans.
Rousseau, J.-J. (1761) *Julie or the New Eloise* (trans. J. H. McDowell). University of Pennsylvania Press, 1968.
Smith, W. I. and Moore, W. J. (1962) *Programmed Learning*. Van Nostrand/Insight.
Yates, A. (1966) *Grouping in Education* (Report sponsored by the Unesco Institute of Education, Hamburg). Wiley.

Part II

The perspective of the personal

Six

The personal foundations of education

Mental health, maturity and personal identity

Let us start from the perspective that education is an enterprise concerned with the development of persons—with persons growing up. This implies that it is concerned with the care and nourishment in young persons of their distinctively human powers. Inevitably then, considerations of personal maturity, of well-being, of mental health, must enter into discussions of both ends and means in education. Such highly general concepts are not of course easy to define. It would be helpful if we could for example define mental health but it cannot be comprised in a simple formula. Freud gave a minimum but important definition when he said that the healthy person was one who could both work and love. His conjunction of love and work is supremely important, particularly in our type of society. World Health Organization attempts something broader in its idea that 'health is a state of complete physical, mental and social well-being'. Notice that both definitions stress the positive nature of health—it is not merely absence of illness as is so often assumed. This is important for our purpose, since we expect educational aims to enshrine positive values. While it is true that for perhaps the vast majority of mankind, to be free from illness might seem blessing enough, the meaning of health which we are adopting here indicates that man may aspire still higher, to a state of continuous well-being, best characterized perhaps in Whitehead's terms as the union of zest with peace. Mental health thus appears as an attribute of the mature human personality, and equally, as a social value, to be worked for, guarded and maintained through purposeful living. Education for mental health in this sense therefore means education for the enhancement and enrichment of life.

In saying this have we merely cloaked an old educational ideal in modern psychological terminology? We may answer 'yes' but take exception to the phrase 'merely cloaked', for it is to modern psychological thought* that we owe whatever detailed understanding

* To which must now be added, sociological.

we have—and it is as yet limited enough—of the conditions which facilitate or hinder the attainment of our most valued aims. These conditions are intimately related to mental health, for in studying the breakdown of a personality we find we are concerned with the operation of exactly the same kinds of factors as when we are studying the growth of the mature person. How indeed could it be otherwise? The central problem of education is to secure that our children shall cherish and exhibit in their lives the finest values of our civilization. To cherish implies to love and work for. Notice again the conjunction of love and work. To be incapable of love and of work inspired by it, or to be dominated by hate or guilt or indeed the 'love' of evil, is to be mentally ill. Now the whole point of modern psychological thought on this subject is that these considerations are not remote from the classroom with its formal subjects and activities, but intimately concerned with its whole life. When we learn anything truly well, it is usually because there is some love in the learning.* Perhaps, as always, it is when the extreme case arises that we see most clearly the inner nature of what is happening all the time. We recognize the emotional factors at once when a pupil acquires either a distaste or a passion for a subject. We have now to accept the fact that in all learning, in the humble beginnings of reading and counting, for example, a child's feelings are always deeply involved often in ways that are by no means obvious.

The idea of the emotional significance of subjects and activities is not, of course, new, but recently there has been an important shift in the psychologist's vision of the relation of the passions to learning and to cultural achievements like religion, art and science. This shift in viewpoint and its significance for concepts of mental health and education is perhaps most clearly seen in connection with religion. Under the influence of the early Freudian idea of sublimation, school subjects and cultural activities were thought of rather naively as outlets for primitive instincts. Love of God, for example, was merely a socially useful substitute for biological sex satisfaction—a handy safety valve as it were, but of no other significance. Thus in a well-known textbook of the mental hygiene period

* While we shall admit, if we are wise, that fear, pain and sorrow are, in some aspects of growing up, the best, and, I personally think, the inevitable teachers. we now know enough about their detrimental effects to strive to limit their deliberate use to a minimum. Some degree of anxiety appears to be inevitable for the human infant, and the achievement of maturity demands both renunciation and suffering, but these facts are no justification whatever for the deliberate use of fear and other 'negative incentives' when positive incentives are available, as in school they normally should be.

in education (Morgan, 1936), there occurs this sentence: 'Religion serves as one of the best lines of activity for the expression of ungratified desires.' Contrast this with a passage from a modern work (*Personality in the Making*): 'Anthropologists tell us that religion is pragmatically necessary to the individual if he is to overcome his shattering anticipation of death, disaster and destiny. Socially, they say, religion is the core of civilization and the mainspring of moral values, one of the prime integrative forces in society.' Indeed, I think we have to go further than this merely pragmatic evaluation and recognize that the great cultural structures of religion, art and science are not only basic characteristics of the human species from the standpoint of biological science, but that it is only through them that we acquire any experience of the meaning of values, any perception of what human mutuality entails and hence any real self-knowledge.* These achievements all embody as 'components' the

* To Freud, of course, must go the principal credit for discovering the unconscious origins and significance of religious (and other) symbols. In describing religious beliefs as essentially illusions (*The Future of an Illusion*—actually Freud's discussion of this complex matter is extremely modest, fair, and scrupulous), however, he showed how much he was himself bound by the scientific materialism of the nineteenth century which the later influence of his own work has since helped to undermine. His notions of causation and scientific determinism in psychology sprang from the same source and are in fact quite out of keeping with modern developments in the philosophy of science. (Many of these developments are not, of course, essentially new in philosophy itself.) While his professional research forced him into the acceptance of the notion of psychological reality, he continued to believe that the unconsciously generated but concrete symbols erected to explain our experience of value, and to embody our search for meaning in life, are somehow 'illusory' in a way in which the abstract and more consciously formulated constructs, erected to explain the way in which events happen in the 'external' world, are not. While there are indeed important differences between religious and scientific concepts of 'truth', the choice of the term 'illusion', as Freud used it, in this connection betrays the wish to suggest the 'inferiority' of religion to science. It is not a term chosen carefully to designate the logical nature of a system of concepts. I am convinced that in spite of his brilliant discoveries in this field, Freud never understood the full significance of symbolism. Perhaps Jung did, when he said (1921) that analytic understanding was the 'cure for belief and *disbelief*' (my italics). Moreover, with regard to the relations between religious and scientific symbolism, Freud did not face up fully to the fact that what is sauce for the goose is sauce for the gander. The differentiation between scientific and religious modes of thought is of course a late product of social evolution and the recognition of the development observable in both religious and scientific ideas, a still later one. One consequence of the current 'idolatry' of science seems to be that among the educated classes, the 'use' of the pursuit of science as a vehicle for the expression of personal neurosis may be tending to supersede the hitherto not infrequent 'use' of the profession of religion

basic biological urges and are capable, as all human activities are, of a vast variety of pathological expression. This does not mean that religion, art or science are in themselves neurotic activities, nor does it mean that they can be reduced to their psychological components without losing their unique characteristics. It does mean, however, that their social stability and integrative power for the individual depend on specially favourable forms of integration of these same basic biological urges. It is through education in its broadest sense that this integration takes place and the school necessarily carries a great deal of the responsibility. Success in this process spells mental health and educational achievement, failure mental ill-health and educational disaster.* We may say, therefore, that mental health is an important educational aim, or we may equally well say that education and the promotion of mental health are two different aspects, legitimately and importantly different, of one and the same process, the achievement of human maturity. The notion of maturity is itself of course a complex and difficult one. Perhaps the single most significant concept related to the notion of maturity, one which serves to articulate all other related concepts, is that of a secure sense of personal identity achieved through stable and non-exploitive relationships, and through constructive cultural participation. In its modern form this is a psycho-analytic idea, which has been elaborated by Erickson. Its importance is not only in integrating the individual and group aspects of human development but in linking the emotional foundations of personality with the operation of intelligence and reason. Reason can only function as a decisive influence in the wise conduct of life within a personality which is not at the mercy of unconscious anxieties and identifications, but which has achieved a level of integration such that its primitive components no longer function autonomously. Such a person will not be inclined either to exploit his fellows or to be exploited by them and will be immune from compulsive love and hate. These are among the characteristics of a sense of personal identity, and they are the prerequisites for psychological freedom and the reaching of judicious decisions. That is to say they are the marks of the mature and mentally healthy person.

---

for this purpose. The consequences for the mental health of our society of substituting 'science' for Christianity as a 'religion' are not as yet by any means clear.

* Success and failure are of course relative terms. The brilliant but neurotic personality is a case of relative success for which a very heavy price is paid by the individual himself, his family, friends and associates. The fragility and precariousness of the cultural achievement in such cases is clearly to be seen in all intimate studies of such individuals.

How far are these ideas relevant to the classroom situation? Not all of them, of course, are of direct and obvious relevance, but some general understanding of them is important for the teacher who sincerely wishes to understand his pupils and himself, who is concerned to preserve their mental health and his own, and who is eager to provide the kind of educational environment necessary for full human development. The relevance of these ideas for education may eventually be clearer if at this point we try to relate some of them in a systematic way to what is another key psychological concept so far as the notion of maturity is concerned—the concept of normal development.

An outline of normal development

Normal development is a tricky phrase and one requiring some clarification. The word 'normal' has a double meaning. It means first 'socially acceptable' in the cultural sense and in this case may in principle be operationally defined. Normal development also denotes a convenient kind of scientific fiction. In this latter sense it is, if I may use the term, 'a dynamic platonic idea'—the bare 'abstract form' to which no-one's development ever corresponds exactly but which all approximate to or deviate from in varying degrees. In most discussions this 'abstract form' of development is itself culturally relative, and deviations from it may be said to be 'normal' or 'abnormal' in the first sense of the term. For example, in our society a special gift for acting in a boy of fourteen is a 'normal' deviation from the cultural norm, while persistent stealing is an abnormal one, i.e. socially unacceptable. A very reserved child in some American schools might be regarded as bordering on the abnormal, but the same kind of behaviour would probably come well within the ambit of the normal in England. It is, of course, one of the aims of psychology to attain to a generalized 'form' of human development which will not only permit the description of individual differences within one culture, but to which inter-cultural differences themselves may be referred. For example, the Œdipus complex of classical psycho-analysis is an aspect of the 'abstract form' appropriate to the understanding of normal development in western cultures. We may hope that eventually anthropology may provide us with a clear picture of a more generalized form of the 'family constellation' of which Œdipus appears to be only one special variant.

In discussing normal development one has the choice of a number of frames of reference. There is the frame of reference concerned with the development of intellect and skills, the frame concerned with the formation of social attitudes, that concerned with emotional development through personal relationships and so on. All such frames of reference have their own validity and purpose. (Many arguments in psychology are traceable to a confusion of frames of reference, rather than to a conflict of ideas.) To my mind, however, the frame dealing with personal relationships has special claims to primacy. It deals with the integration of psychological processes at the highest level, since it is the one to which the others must be dynamically related, in the sense that the acquisition of knowledge and skill, and the formation of attitudes, is always mediated by, and invariably takes place within, a context of personal relations. Within all other psychological frameworks the human being is described in terms of 'the organism' or of 'processes within the organism', i.e. as less than human. Such other frames of reference are of great scientific importance for the study of component or partial processes, but it is only when we discuss ourselves in terms of personal relationships that we come near some scientific understanding of the conditions under which we achieve the essence of human status, i.e. recognition of our mutuality, one with another. If we admit this we shall see the importance for mental health and education of thinking of development in terms such as the following.

The primary attitude all children develop is one somewhere on the continuum, basic trust—basic mistrust. The foundations of this attitude are formed at birth—with the drawing of the first breath—or perhaps even before birth. This first attitude to the world is, to begin with, mediated through the relationships involved in feeding and tending. Here develops basic security or insecurity (anxiety) and the basic capacity to give and receive which is the biological foundation of human love. The healthy relationship between mother and child in the feeding situation is characterized by reciprocity and mutuality from the very beginning, as Middlemore (1941) has shown, but neither infant nor mother is *absolutely perfectly* equipped for this relationship (apart altogether from interference by other people). Hence some degree of anxiety (i.e. mistrust) and the various reactions to it, including aggressiveness, appear to be inevitable features in human development.* Within the feeding situation, moreover, there is always some degree of frustration, and inevitably some further degree of aggression is generated as a result of this also. Hence conflicting feelings arise—'love' of the person

* Of the innate character of aggressiveness, all that need be said here is that man appears to be equipped with the disposition to behave aggressively in certain situations and these situations, as now understood, are never likely to be absent from his upbringing. Stimulating recent discussions on the nature of aggression will be found in Lorenz (1967) and Storr (1968).

who gives security, nourishment and comfort, and 'hate' of the same person who withholds these things. This is the basic source of that ambivalence, or double feeling, which colours in some degree all our later relationships. One of the outcomes of harbouring destructive feelings against a loved one, under certain conditions at any rate, appears to be a sense of guilt and remorse. Ambivalence is therefore prone to issue in unconscious guilt, and the reaction to it, reparation,* both of which we have some reason to believe are among the foundation stones of our own particular civilization.† So far, and in this schematic way, we may regard the healthy person as one who has acquired sufficient basic trust in the world to counterbalance his own ambivalence, and who has received enough love to give him a feeling of his own goodness sufficient to offset his unconscious sense of guilt.

The rest of the story is one of increasingly complex relations. Briefly, we may note that the child has already begun to develop in phantasy, images of his parents, which are not copies of the real parents but exaggerated personifications of their 'good' and 'bad' qualities—of their gratifying or frustrating attitudes as these appear to him.‡ These unconscious images, or imagos as they are termed,

* These terms, unconscious anxiety, ambivalence, guilt, reparation, etc., are of course all constructs in the sense already described, but their relevance to the understanding of children's behaviour has been well established; see Susan Isaacs (1933).

† The culture of some other societies seems to rest on different foundations. Thus the basis of morality among the Kwakiutl appears to be shame, not guilt—see Kardiner (1949). Extreme caution is necessary here however. Little or nothing seems to be known about the unconscious effects of shaming techniques, and it is *unconscious* guilt which psycho-analysis postulates as one of the basic components of the western super-ego. Moreover such guilt is envisaged as deriving from the earliest stages of infancy, long before techniques, either of shaming or of moral approval or disapproval, are introduced into upbringing (explicitly at any rate), i.e. some degree of unconscious guilt is postulated as the necessary outcome of initial ambivalence and therefore subject to cultural variation only to the same extent that initial ambivalence is so subject. Exactly to what extent this fundamental ambivalence is dependent on cultural variations in feeding, handling, etc., is a matter for further research. The dependence of initial ambivalence on the experience of security and insecurity, and of gratification, and frustration, arising from the same sources, suggests that many items of child rearing showing cultural differences might be important in this respect, e.g. the practice of swaddling, see Gorer and Rickman (1949). Clearly, actual psycho-analytic material from people belonging to widely diverse cultures would be invaluable. For a discussion of the relation between child upbringing and culture see Sprott (1952) and Mead (1948).

‡ In attempting to grasp the meaning of these unconscious processes in the very young child it may be helpful to recall what was said in the opening paragraph of this paper. It may be assumed that these processes have organic correlates, which one day we may know about in detail.

are formed partly by projection of his own feelings on to the real parents and partly from the actual behaviour of the parents. These 'good' and 'bad' figures are introjected by the child—taken into himself in phantasy—in a particular way and with effects which have led to their description as 'internal objects'.* The function of these processes appears to be the double one of enabling the child to control his own feelings towards his parents—already projected on to the parental imagos—and to incorporate some of the parental qualities (or their opposites) into the structure of his own personality. These processes indeed may be postulated as the basis of social inheritance, for it is in this way that a child is provided with the raw materials from which he eventually forms his own character. The double function of control and assimilation is rendered possible by the single process of introjection—the most primitive and the surest way of controlling anything in imagination is to take it inside oneself. It is through such an incorporation or assimilation of parental imagos that both ego and super-ego develop.† The ego is, among other things, the seat of those functions of rational interpretation of the world and of choice which a mature human being is able to exercise. Within the system of the super-ego is to be found the basis of the moral sense or conscience. The super-ego is thus a term used to describe the operation within the personality of representations of the moral standards, sanctions and prohibitions of its particular society as these have been mediated by the parental imagos. It is because these representations or imagos tend to be exaggerated pictures of parental attitudes, particularly disapproving and punishing attitudes, that adults may suffer from over-severe consciences, with results detrimental to their mental health and relaionships with other people. Here are the roots of extreme prudery and vindictive morality of all kinds—characteristics which we know very well are usually associated with mental ill-health.

* The use of this term derives from psycho-pathology—from the observation that mentally ill people sometimes complain that they are 'inhabited' by foreign objects, other personalities (voices etc.). Such hallucinatory experiences have been traced through analysis to the introjected parental or quasi-parental imagos. In mental illness the functioning of these 'internalized figures' is disturbed and the patient is 'possessed' by what are felt to be alien powers—demons, evil spirits, etc.

† The clearest and most stimulating among recent accounts of this process known to me is that by Heimann (1952). In particular I find her treatment of the role of the Œdipus complex in super-ego formation especially illuminating. I have deliberately refrained from dealing with Œdipal aspects of unconscious dynamics because a discussion of them involves technical considerations outside the scope of the present paper. For recent critiques of modern psycho-dynamic theories see Guntripp (1961, etc.).

It is in some such fashion as this that we build our own characters out of what is indeed the only material available for this purpose—the interaction between ourselves and others—to begin with mainly members of our family circle, which involves a gradual accommodation between our feelings and phantasies about our family figures and the actual behaviour of those others as persons in a real world. Thus through creative use of phantasy the child eventually comes to terms with himself and his family as it really is. Any serious disturbance in this whole process of development may produce maladjustment and mental ill-health—and it is easy to see the manifold opportunities for things to go wrong in any process so complicated as this. Probably the most potentially damaging event is prolonged separation from (or 'loss of' in psychological terms) the mother at some crucial period in early life, as Bowlby's work suggests (1951, 1969). There are, of course, many other sources of stress and moreover we are not all equally well equipped by constitution to deal with psychological stress when it comes. The miracle is that things go very badly wrong so seldom and that most of us survive the vicissitudes of development—not unscathed—but able to live satisfying and useful lives. Yet most of us feel that we are fairly far from the goal—the union of zest with peace—the complete sense of personal identity in and through relationships. Perhaps the most important conclusion from these considerations is that they can serve to enhance our sense of rational humility. We are enabled eventually to become mature persons in our own right to the extent that we are, and are able to accept the fact that we are, in our inmost beings, quite literally 'members one of another'.

The picture of development in terms of relationships given here is of course an over-simplified one, and it is a picture of normal development in the strict scientific sense of that term, i.e. it is a purely formal description and one referring particularly to our own type of society.* It would need various modifications to fit any other kind of society, and would need concrete expansion as well as modification to fit any individual within any particular society.

* Among the many obvious omissions, no mention has been made of the bi-sexual nature of personality. The fact that all of us have masculine and feminine components is in part a consequence of the incorporation by a child of both its parent figures. In this way the effects of biological sexuality can be modified, so far as personality is concerned, by social means. The extent to which sex roles differ in different societies and the extent to which different methods of upbringing emphasize or minimize biological masculinity or femininity has now been studied in some detail and is a complicated matter of considerable importance in relation to mental health. See Mead (1949).

Moreover it deals with the child within the family and the major purpose of this paper is to deal with the development and mental health of the child at school. We have yet to establish the relevance of these ideas to the classroom situation. The essential links are relatively simple to describe. Social life demands a wide variety of relationships and in school and elsewhere the child uses the early relationships he has formed within the family as prototypes on which to build others. These prototypic relationships, however, have a special property; they are dynamic structures which enter into and modify their successors. There is a continuity between the kind of patterns established in our early infantile relationships and all subsequent ones, with our teachers, friends, colleagues, marriage partners and children. These past relationships live actively in the present ones—it is not a question of buried and static 'memories' but of dynamic influence in all our behaviour. In serious adult mental illness the early relationships are reinstated and used instead of the current relationships which life demands. In normal functioning they are subtly assimilated into the present and all we can detect of them by ordinary means are their echoes and reverberations.

Nurture and guidance

This description is, of course, abstract and generalized. The actual pattern of development which each child exhibits is determined by his unique constitution and his unique experiences first in home, then in school and community. Although the general bent of his character is shaped before he reaches school, there is a great deal that is still plastic. As we have seen, he has to adapt to a wider social reality through his school experience and he may come well- or ill-prepared for the task, and at the conclusion of each stage in his school career he may be well- or ill-prepared to embark on the next. Here we must remember the cardinal importance for the child of the relation between home and school. One aspect of this is sometimes overlooked. The school often has to compensate for the home in subtle as well as obvious ways and it must be prepared to help some children to complete phases of development which others normally complete at home. Moreover the child needs and in fact uses his two environments in a complementary fashion. For example, the child who is experiencing difficulty in adapting to the demands of his family, or is in doubt as to what the family standards really are, or who is deeply in rivalry with brothers or sisters, can sometimes express in school the hostility he feels towards parents and siblings which he dare not express at home. This sort of situation is one which teachers should understand and be prepared to deal with in an understanding way. But in general the task of the school is always the same. It is within the system of relationships which it provides to *use* its proper educational programme in a flexible way so that the child's confidence and interest are established and constantly maintained. This is the essential meaning of nurture and guidance. The child *needs* to acquire his social inheritance, without it he becomes sub-human. But he has to acquire it in his own way. It cannot be forced upon him without distorting both it and him. The teacher is here the supreme mediator and he has to carry out this task through his own personality, with all its own childhood echoes, and within the limitations which the structure of the school system imposes. Much has already been written about education as nurture and as guidance, and here we need only emphasize a few points which recent psychological thought suggests are of special importance.

Inner security

In discussing development we have stressed the importance of security and the potentially destructive power of anxiety.* It is of course inner, i.e. emotional, security with which we are concerned, and we know that our pupils vary greatly in the security which their early upbringing has given them. Some of the signs of insecurity are well known to us. Excessive and continual aggression and persistent timidity are among them but in many cases so are specific difficulties in learning the basic subjects, and unusual inhibition in play or artistic expression. In what ways can the school contribute most effectively to children's emotional security? We may

* We are again at the frontiers of knowledge. Is anxiety necessarily destructive, or is a certain amount of it necessary to reach certain levels of achievement? It arises in a number of ways, from insecurity or as a reaction to frustration, either directly or via aggression and guilt. If some experience of insecurity and frustration is inevitable for the human infant, it is also a plausible hypothesis that the levels of anxiety and aggression necessary to maintain mental health in a modern community lie between certain limits, which will of course vary somewhat for different individuals. If this is so, we certainly know little of what these levels are. What is reasonably certain is that both over-protection and over-indulgence are as liable to produce mental ill-health as are excessive insecurity and excessive frustration. The kind of inner security here postulated as one of the bases of mental health is the kind which enhances the sense of adventure, which increases the likelihood of advance from a base which has been adequately secured. Adventure which proceeds from an ill-secured base always betrays an element of desperation, or denial and defiance of insecurity. While there may be much to admire in such cases, the risk of breakdown is always high.

suggest three ways which appear to be specially important.

The first of these lies in creating the optimum balance between order and freedom. Where this balance lies varies with circumstances and, of course, with individuals. In general, however, we may say that if there is any other situation as tragic and as fraught with danger for mental health, as that of the class held rigid by fear, it is the class exposed to the anxieties engendered by unlimited or undefined 'freedom'. There is nothing so terrifying to the immature human being as a completely unstructured situation. Children require a recognizable structure and the school has to provide it in educational terms suited to children's capacities and interests. Without it, they feel the teacher has abandoned them—and so he has—to their own impulses, all of which are by no means always constructive. Failure to understand this was the great mistake of some of the early 'progressive' schools.

Second there is the security which resides in being a member of a group. Capacity to accept co-operative roles within a group develops slowly and must not be forced, but the school has an unrivalled opportunity for promoting this development. While the importance of the class group, of forty or even fifty children, should not be minimized, there are special virtues in the small group of six to ten individuals. Modern teachers are making increasing use of group methods of learning—not, of course, if they are wise, as an exclusive device—and in so doing are providing an important source of security as well as helping to develop social adaptation. Apart also from assisting to create a reasonable balance between co-operation and competition and helping individual children to discover satisfying roles for themselves (in itself a source of security), group membership makes available unconscious resources (as well as conscious ones) which no one individual can command.

Third, and basically, there is the role of the teacher. The point to be noted here is that what is vital to the teacher as a giver of security is what he or she really feels about the children. Children know intuitively what we feel about them—in discerning the real feelings of others they are much more perceptive than most adults—and they react accordingly. Here all teachers must seek greater insight and self-knowledge. Children feel secure with adults who are secure—who neither fear nor dislike them. When we can admit to ourselves when we are afraid of children or dislike them, we are half way to overcoming these attitudes. In this sense it could be said that what we *are* is of greater importance in giving security than what we do.

Standards of achievement

The experience of achievement is essential to the healthy growth of the ego, and here perhaps we can throw some light on the recurrent controversies about standards of attainment. There are three important things about standards. The first is that they should exist. This is true however imperfect and approximate our efforts to define them may be, for without them there can be no true guidance. The second is that they should be adapted to the capacities and circumstances of individual children. Unless standards are so adapted they create anxiety and undermine confidence, in ways which lead to cumulative failure, or to slavish intellectual obedience and parrot learning. Such thoroughly unrealistic standards are all too common in our schools and they eventually produce pupils who are not only uneducated but have been rendered practically ineducable, in the deeper meaning of the term. Third, both mental health and education require standards of many different kinds, of social behaviour as well as of knowledge, of skill in expressive activities as well as in the manipulation of verbal or numerical symbols, and of appreciation of beauty as well as in the critical use of intelligence. Nevertheless, while we must not think of standards only in language and number, a mastery of both, commensurate with their capacities, is of the greatest personal importance for all children growing up into a society which utilizes linguistic and numerical skills to the extent ours does. Educational psychologists have shown time and again that retardation is a frequent concomitant of maladjustment, and the ways in which failures in achievement may precipitate or may reinforce behaviour disorders have been for some time common-place knowledge among those engaged in clinical child guidance (Burt, 1935). However, standards can never be fixed and rigid things and we are still far from a complete understanding of how to assess accurately what they should be at a given time for a given child. It is a good beginning to estimate children's general mental ability, apart from special skills in language and number, by means of appropriate tests and then to match achievements against these estimates, but in doing so we are still only at the beginning of educational wisdom. Much further research is still required in this field. I know of one school which has for its motto 'Growth to full stature'. That is realistic idealism. While practical education, like practical politics, is the art of the possible, we are seldom, if ever, in a position to say with regard to any individual child what the ultimate limits of the possible are. But in the interests of mental health, we will be wise always to have proximate limits in mind.

Creative learning

Learning that is healthy is creative and vice-versa. To make every act of learning a spontaneous joyful discovery is the dream of every idealist in education, and perhaps the great majority of teachers have some experience, however infrequent, of the vision becoming reality. It is such experiences that sustain our faith. The whole activity movement in education has this as its aim, although the aim is much much older than this modern movement, and the techniques for inducing creative learning range from the inspiring example, through expressive activity to the subtleties of the art of interrogation. The activity movement has been supported both for its therapeutic possibilities as well as its strictly educational ones, and all I want to do here is to draw attention to an important change of emphasis which newer ideas should bring to our discussions of an old theme. The key lies in the notion of the creative function of phantasy within emotional relationships. So far as therapy is concerned, and from the older standpoint of mental hygiene, activity methods of learning and free expression, through music, drama, visual and plastic arts, were encouraged because they were supposed to give an *outlet* for repressed tendencies. The child was encouraged to express his difficulties in the interests of a rather aimless catharsis. It is now realized that the essentially therapeutic element in play is that through it the child learns to *control* in phantasy, impulses which are as yet difficult for him to control in reality (Balint, 1952). It is often his preferred mode of coming to terms with some aspect of reality which would present insuperable difficulties for a direct approach. In this kind of situation the participation of other children and of the teacher is often a vital factor.

In this view of creative learning the therapeutic and the educational aspects are almost indistinguishable. It is a viewpoint with far-reaching implications for our basic theory of learning, implications which we are only now beginning to explore. It emphasizes that there is a continuity in the child's relationship with things as there is in his relationship with people. Just as our later personal relationships contain echoes from our relations with our parents, so our adult interests in the world of things are impregnated by our infantile interests, for example, our earliest interest in our bodies, the products of our bodies and the bodies of our parents. There is also a continuity of development between the magical omnipotent wish of the child (and the primitive adult) and the controlled imagination of the poet and the reasoned argument of the scientist. We have to see all learning as primarily motivated by unconscious phantasy.* As teachers, however, we do not need any profound grasp of the workings of the deeper levels of mentality either in ourselves or in our pupils, in order to allow creative learning to take place. We must, however, be aware that such emotional undertones always exist, and we have to have sufficient access to our own feelings to be in contact with those of our pupils. The skilful teacher can do much to help children to discover and to come to terms, usually unconsciously, with the hidden meanings which activities and subjects have for them.† Perhaps the essential point for teachers is to realize that although the features of our physical and social environments are indeed peculiarly fitted to be the objects of our interests, it is *we* who invest them with the values which we discover in them. It is an old truth

> we receive but what we give,
> And in our life alone doth Nature live;
> Ours is her wedding garment, ours her shroud.‡

An education which does not permit the constant interplay of the inner and the outer is a violation of our natures and does not provide the nurture essential to healthy growth to maturity. We develop our inner selves through the exploration of the adult world of activities and ideas. As children we invest the world with value and it is the job of education to return our investment—with interest—in due course.

An amended version of certain sections from my 'Mental health in the classroom' in *The Bearings of Recent Advances in Psychology on Educational Problems* (Studies in Education, no. 7), Evans, 1955.

References

Balint, E. (1952) 'The therapeutic value of play in schools', *New Era in Home and School*, vol. 33, no. 10.
Bowlby, J. (1951) *Maternal Care and Mental Health*. WHO, Geneva.
Bowlby, J. (1969) *Attachment and Loss*, vol. 1, *Attachment*. Hogarth.

* For a statement on the nature and function of phantasy, see Isaacs (1952). My point here seems to be very close to what the late Donald Winnicott (1971) emphasized about the psychological origins of culture.

† A brilliant example of this approach to learning will be found in Marjorie Hourd's book (1949).

‡ S. T. Coleridge, 'Dejection'.

Burt, C. (1935) *The Subnormal Mind*. Oxford.
Gorer, G. and Rickman, J. R. (1949) *The People of Great Russia*. Cresset.
Heimann, Paula (1952) in *Developments in Psycho-analysis*, chapter 4. Hogarth.
Hourd, M. L. (1949) *The Education of the Poetic Spirit*. Heinemann.
Isaacs, Susan (1933) *Social Development in Young Children*. Kegan Paul.
Isaacs, Susan (1952) in *Developments in Psycho-analysis*, chapter 3. Hogarth.
Jung, C. G. (1921) *The Psychology of the Unconscious*, chapter 5. Kegan Paul.
Kardiner, A. (1949) *The Individual and his Society*. Columbia.
Mead, M. (1948) 'Social change and cultural surrogates in personality' in C. Kluckholm and H. A. Murray, *Personality in Nature, Society and Culture*, chapter 36. Knopf.
Mead, M. (1949) *Male and Female*. Gollancz.
Middlemore, M. P. (1941) *The Nursing Couple*. Hamish Hamilton.
Morgan, J. J. B. (1936) *The Psychology of the Unadjusted School Child*, chapter 20. Macmillan.
Personality in the Making (Report of Midcentury White House conference on children and youth), chapter 7. Harper.
Sprott, W. J. H. (1952) *Social Psychology*. Methuen.

Additional references

Guntrip, H. (1961) *Personality Structure and Human Interaction*. Hogarth.
Guntrip, H. (1968) *Schizoid Phenomena, Object Relations and the Self*. Hogarth.
Guntrip, H. (1971) *Psychoanalytic Theory, Therapy and the Self*. Hogarth.
Lorenz, K. (1967) *On Aggression*. Methuen.
Storr, A. (1968) *Human Aggression*. Allen Lane.
Winnicott, D. W. (1971) *Play and Reality*. Tavistock.

Seven

Teaching in its interpersonal context

Teachers, pupils and the school

The analysis of teaching, of teachers' behaviour and of the complexities of the conceptualization of teaching roles, has now become a major field of work for sociologists and social psychologists interested in education.[1] Profitable as this sort of development is now proving, there is some of it, probably because of an extreme and out-of-date behaviourist and deterministic bias, which entirely ignores what seem to me to be essential considerations. There is a sense in which, in the final analysis, a teacher is faced with the fact that the fundamental vehicle of teaching is himself, what he is as a person, and what he is able to give to others. He therefore depends for his professional competence largely on the quality of the relationships he is able to develop with his pupils and colleagues, and these in turn depend on the integrity he has been able to develop within himself. The meaning of the learning-teaching transaction, and of the educational enterprise itself, can only be fully grasped when it is seen in this interpersonal context.

What are the major features of this context, both as they inherently are, in the forms in which they are commonly met with, and in the forms they might be enabled to assume?

To begin with teachers need to have some understanding of the fact that in all their dealings with children and young people there is always an aspect of the relationship in which they are treated as parent figures. *They are*, in effect, the mother (and father) who accepts or rejects, gives or withholds, punishes or rewards, and whom the child would like to control, as they control him. This is one reason for the emotionality of the infant room and of inter-generation conflict in secondary schools. *In loco parentis* is not just a legal idea. Moreover, in later childhood and adult life when the distinction between reality and phantasy is much clearer, there are always echoes of the earlier relationships in every current one. Teachers were once children and as adults they carry the active residues of their childhood into their professional work. A teacher therefore necessarily reacts to children in part in terms of the child within himself. This is a key idea and as we shall see is of great importance for our discussion.

These considerations point to certain of the conditions necessary for the achievement of sufficient adult maturity to enable us to play a constructive part in the education of the young. Such a degree of maturity is assured if we are able to deal with the child within us, i.e. our still active unconscious attitudes to our original family figures, in ways which allow us to behave in a fashion consistent with the real requirements of actual adult situations. Our ability to deal successfully with our unconscious attitudes depends on the balance between destructive and constructive impulses achieved in childhood, on the degree of control the ego has gained over these impulses and on the degree of insight we have into their nature. If the balance is on the side of love and constructive impulses then our unconscious attitudes will the more easily reinforce the dictates of reason and adult morality, but without adequate control by the ego we may still behave unwisely. The task of ego control is made easier the more insight we have. Some degree of insight is a prerequisite for rational behaviour, *if* we are insufficiently secure to deal unconsciously in an effective way with our ambivalence, or if we are still unconsciously deeply in rivalry with our parents or siblings, or if the balance of unconscious forces is still on the side of aggressive, retributive or exploiting impulses. When we reflect that few of us achieve a saintly character, and that by no means all of us are so well balanced that we can rely largely on more or less automatic ego control, we shall I think see the value of insight into the child within us, in helping us as adults to regulate our behaviour in accordance with our ideals. Such insight cannot be said to be either an essential condition of maturity, nor is it ever enough by itself to guarantee personal stability. Nevertheless it can be of great value in the service of whatever degree of ego control we have achieved. The conditions under which we achieve maturity are therefore complex and various. There are no simple formulae and mature personalities are not all alike by any means. But as we shall see later there are special reasons connected with learning and with the classroom situation which make personal insight of the greatest value to teachers in their work.

The interpersonal context of teaching is of course exceedingly complex. In school we are not simply dealing with the relations between one teacher and one child. We must take account of group factors, and this means that we have to broaden, and re-interpret the basic notions of, security–insecurity, dependence–independence, ambivalent feeling and sibling rivalry, in terms of the inter-relations of individuals within groups and with relationships between groups. In coming to school for the first time the child is faced with two new sets of demands. He has to form many new relationships, with other children and with teachers, on the basis of the relationships he has already established within his family and immediate community; and he has to explore new experiences, acquire new skills, and has to attempt to conform to the new standards of behaviour and achievement expected of him. Teachers too are members of a special group within the school, they are members also of a profession with a particular status and special duties, and they have private lives as men and women. They have thus to maintain a complex series of relationships and to perform a variety of tasks within a special kind of community which has its own structure of authority and rules of behaviour. The school itself is part of a larger educational structure and is in constant relationship with the rest of the adult community. All these considerations affect the behaviour of teachers, and are thus relevant to the development of their pupils.

The school is itself a community and is made up of groups. There is the staff group, and there are groups of children. There are individuals in leadership roles and there is often a hierarchy of leaders among both staff and children. Some structure of authority is essential for the well-being of any community, but authority may be exercised through a more or less strict authoritarian regime, i.e. in a more or less tyrannical way, or it may be used to create and protect a generally permissive atmosphere in which those invested with it take the lead as required but in which, too, all may contribute to the enrichment of the common life. A good deal is now known about some of the effects on learning and behaviour of different group atmospheres and different kinds of leadership. The issues involved are at the philosophical level those of order and freedom, but in practice and in psychological terms the conditions for ordered freedom concern the minimizing of anxiety and aggression in the exercise of leadership and authority, and the maximizing of security and purposeful participation among the members of the school community. There is no single issue in education which would better repay our schools and other institutions than an honest examination of the relations between their exercise of authority and the well-being and achievements of their members.[2] I would suggest that some of the techniques of group discussions—those which take the acknowledged common problems as topics and in which the therapeutic component is implicit only, not explicit—could very well be utilized by staff groups concerned to make such a self-examination. To be effective, such groups should be led by someone with a deeper understanding than most of the other members, of the issues involved. While this is not, by its nature, a role which head teachers should attempt, there is much to be said for special orientation and training courses for all prospective heads, which would include some experience of quasi-therapeutic group discussion. There should also be a selection of heads on personality grounds. Some teachers are beset by so much anxiety, usually, but not always, of a deeply unconscious kind, that they are quite unable to exercise authority except in an authoritarian way. I would add also that it is here that the real answer to most of the problems of indiscipline and punishment are to be found. In a school where there is an ordered freedom and which is trying to face up to its own internal problems, through the conscious use of its own group resources, and which consequently has a high morale, the majority of acts requiring special and severe punishment are not likely to occur often. There is a close connection between permissive but efficient leadership, high morale, absence of anti-social behaviour and effective achievement.

The school is essentially part of the wider community, even if in some cases the relation may be one of apathy or even of thinly veiled hostility. In this country there is considerable scope for the improvement of school-community relations, whether in the form of parent-teacher co-operation or the interpenetration of school and occupational life. Such developments are difficult, and will be slow, and success will be largely dependent on the degree to which teachers can become aware of and learn to manage successfully the latent anxieties, rivalry and pride which inevitably motivate much of the behaviour shown by both sides in such relationships.*

The personality and role of the teacher

In relation to the teacher's role, Wall (1955) has this to say: 'In the system of personal relationships within which children learn, the teacher is probably, next to members of the immediate family, the most important factor.' This is in line with common sense. Is it borne out by research and what are its implications? Experiments on educational methods almost invariably leave the impression—if they do not actually prove—that efficiency in learning is more a

* The role of the head teacher is a vital one and to those placed in difficult communities, I would recommend a book by a distinguished Australian headmaster—Donald McLean has shown how to apply in practice many of the ideas to which I have already referred, see *Nature's Second Sun*, Heinemann, 1954.

function of the teacher than of the method. Vernon certainly concludes that there is now good scientific evidence that teachers' personalities do affect the personalities and behaviour of their pupils. Clearly there is a close connection between the effectiveness of educational methods and the personalities of their users, and between the personality of the individual teacher and the kind of methods he or she prefers to use. There can be little doubt that complete and slavish dependence on formal didactic methods is a sign of the insecurity and rigidity that characterize authoritarian personalities. Again, activity methods largely reflect permissive attitudes. To this we must add that there is the work by Gardner (1950) and the Eight Years' Study in the USA (*Adventure in American Education*) to show the lasting effect of such methods on pupils' constructiveness, resourcefulness and social behaviour. It is also probably true that formal methods of learning are quite essential for certain purposes at certain stages. Arithmetical facts and spelling, for example, are almost certainly best tackled at some stage—the stage is important—by intelligent drill. But the crux of the whole matter lies less in methods themselves than in the motivation arising from relationships between pupils and teacher within the structure of the particular learning situation. The most carefully designed and fruitful work to date on teachers' attitudes appears to be that of Anderson and his collaborators. He compared what he called dominative and integrative behaviour among teachers of kindergarten and primary classes. He found, with a wealth of illustrative detail, that domination by teachers produced dominative and aggressive behaviour in children and that integrative behaviour by teachers produced co-operative behaviour among children.

What kinds of personalities are to be found among teachers? Is there, for example, a 'type'? The controlled research in this field has been admirably summarized by Vernon (1953). He concludes that 'teachers are as diverse in their psychological traits as any other occupational group'. Teachers may therefore rejoice that the social stereotype by means of which they are often depicted does not correspond to their true personalities. It is of course certain that teaching does attract a small number of abnormal personalities, but it is just as certainly doubtful, as Vernon says, whether the proportion of severely neurotic women or of sadistic and homosexually inclined men—to take two examples dear to critics of our profession—is any greater than in any other profession. In this paper I am concerned with the mental health of the so-called normal—normal children, and normal teachers in normal classrooms. For insight into the dynamics of the normal teaching situation in relation to mental health and into the subtler meanings of the normal teaching role, we have to turn to other sources. First, there have been some important experiments with teachers in therapeutic discussion groups. Some of this work has been published, for example that carried out by Herbert and Trist (1953) and for some years now at Bristol by Richardson (1967). The second source is the collection of thoughtful statements which the New Education Fellowship contributed to the Unesco conference on the mental health of schoolchildren in Europe (Wall, 1955). In what follows I am greatly indebted to all of this work. It will also be observed that the general approach leans heavily on psycho-analytic ideas.

Redl and Wattenberg in their excellent book, *Mental Hygiene in Teaching*, give a long, interesting and stimulating list of roles the teacher is called upon to play. But we may be content perhaps with Wall's brief statement (1955) that the teacher is at once, group leader, the giver and withholder of security and the source of authority, law and order. The emotional implications of these roles however are complex and a study of them shows the specific stresses under which teachers work. These stresses are of two kinds. There is external stress arising from the comparatively poor pay and low status of the profession in most countries. These are added to by the existence of derogatory stereotypes of teachers in the public mind and by the fact that, since the children they teach are not really their children, there is usually some degree of unconscious jealousy and rivalry between teachers and parents. Teachers are also often the targets of public criticism and it would be strange if at times, in face of all this, they did not have a sense of being rejected and exploited. The second kind of stress is internal and arises from the fact that teachers, alone among the professions, spend all their working lives in continual contact with immature human beings. They are therefore peculiarly liable to experience deep reverberations in their own personalities, set in motion by the infantile and immature emotions and behaviour of their charges. Childish behaviour is a constant challenge and stimulus to the child which exists within every adult. The well-adjusted teacher is therefore one who has come to terms with the child in himself and is capable of reacting to immature behaviour with mature attitudes.

It is in the interaction of the external and internal stresses of the teaching situation that the peculiar dangers and psychological risks of the teaching profession lie. The attitudes and emotional reactions liable to be called forth are of great importance in relation to the teacher's own mental health and that of his pupils, and are worthy of some detailed discussion. Let us examine some of the stresses to which he is exposed. The teacher is *in* authority, *vis-à-vis* his pupils, but *under* authority *vis-à-vis* superiors such as head teachers, inspectors and administrators. When in authority he is inevitably tempted to behave as his own parents and teachers behaved towards him. He can, as it were, reverse the situations of his own childhood and gain vicarious victories. When under authority he is tempted again to behave as he himself behaved when a child. He is therefore inevitably involved in a conflict of parental and childish roles and to resolve this conflict constructively calls for a considerable degree of personal maturity. Further there is always some stimulus being given by this situation to his own latent anxieties and aggressiveness. Through unconscious fear of his own latent aggressiveness he may fail to exercise the authority necessary to give security to his pupils and hence to produce orderly behaviour. Alternatively through fear of the aggression he feels to be latent in his pupils (often partly a projection of his own unconscious aggression), he may become a strict disciplinarian incapable of relaxing control for a moment. In dealing with a particular child he may not see him as he really is, but treat him as the child he himself wished or feared to be. As guardians of the morals and behaviour of the young, the teacher is always under some compulsion to make them conform to his own standards. He is unconsciously tempted to try to form his pupils in his own image and in so doing will come up against the needs and strivings of forty-odd personalities quite different from his own. To accept children as they are and not as we would have them be, and at the same time to assist them to grow into mature and independent individuals, each with his own unique sense of personal identity, is the hard task of parents and teachers alike. The teacher also has his problems of love and affection to contend with. Deep personal attachments to particular pupils are dangerous to them and a source of constant frustration to the teacher, for his pupils must always pass on. His love has to be a serene and undemanding affection, both for those he instinctively likes and dislikes, and that, let us admit it, is asking quite a lot.

This description of the psychological stresses under which teachers work may leave us wondering how any of us ever survive and enjoy good mental health. The picture is, of course, an unbalanced one, in that no teacher is continually involved in deep emotional contacts with his pupils, unless he actively contrives to be, as he may do if he is excessively neurotic. For much of the time his contacts are relatively superficial and impersonal, and if he is himself secure, his unconscious reactions to his pupils provide a continuous source of protection both for himself and for them. More than that, the very same situation which potentially exposes him to severe psychological stress also provides him with opportunity for some of the deepest satisfactions in life. The very vulnerability and immaturity of his charges calls forth all the protective and reparative tendencies of the potential or actual parent in him—the constructive and creative residue within his personality of his own parents' love and care for him. Nevertheless it would be foolish to shut our eyes to the fact that teaching is a severe strain on many in the profession. Wall suggests, I think rightly, that teaching is extremely fatiguing work mainly because of unconscious mental strain. Moreover the amount of maladjustment in the population at large makes it imperative that we should seek in every way to improve and safeguard the mental health of teachers, for this is one way in which we may hope to improve the general mental health of successive generations. Since the principles to be followed are the same for the student in training as for the teacher in service, I will deal with them under the general heading of the education of teachers.

The education of teachers

What are the general implications of all I have said for the education and further education of teachers? To begin with our present practice of ensuring a good general academic standard, a mastery of one or two subjects, a bookish knowledge of academic educational and psychological theory and the acquisition of some tricks of the trade is woefully inadequate. But is this a fair description of what we do? Not entirely, perhaps, although I think it is uncomfortably near the mark in many cases. It is certainly true that in a number of our training departments and colleges vigorous attempts are being made to give practical expression to those ideas which recent advances in psychology have brought us. Some accounts of this pioneer work have already been published, notably one by Swainson of Leicester (1952), and in what follows I shall draw to some extent on her experience as well as on other sources. Before doing so, however, I would like to mention once again the close and subtle connections between emotional and intellectual functioning, this time in relation to the need to encourage habits of independent and critical thought among students. A very large proportion of present day students are capable of little more than reproduction of what they have been told, and the attitudes they display, if called upon to reflect for themselves, show how deeply submissive and uncritical they have become under the influence of educational institutions (primary schools, grammar schools and universities), dominated by authoritarian teaching. This teaching has as its real practical aim success in examinations requiring the attainment of high standards of rote learning and of the reproduction of at best second-hand opinions. These standards are a constant cause of anxiety to pupils and teachers alike. But reluctantly I must leave aside this question and concentrate on the emotional aspects of the development of students in training as teachers.

The very first objective of the training course should be to assist students to achieve a satisfactory degree of personal maturity. Teachers in training are by and large either in late adolescence or early adulthood, and the present conduct of our whole educational system results in the majority of students being still very immature persons at the beginning of their course. They are generally well equipped with examination knowledge and as a consequence severely verbally biased. For that very reason their deepest need, although they may at first reject the very idea, is for opportunity to cultivate the under-developed aspects of their personalities through practical and aesthetic activities. It is through attempting creative work that they can first be given freer access to their own, often strongly inhibited, feelings, and so can be prepared for contact with the emotional needs of their pupils. Second, they have to come to terms with themselves when placed in positions of leadership and authority in ways which are conducive to the creation of permissive group situations. Recent psychological work suggests that *there is only one effective way of securing this. The training college or department must itself practise with the students what it wishes them to practise with their pupils.* Wall sums this up neatly in saying that 'it is a revelation to many students to be in a college in which the community is a co-operative group, where the principal deliberately delegates a good deal of authority and where the students study the implications of freedom and responsibility by living them.' Thirdly, students must very early be exposed to the realities of the classroom situation, through teaching practice, but this experience loses much of its value if it does not become the focus of continuous tutorial discussions. Such discussions in small groups should aim at being quasi-therapeutic ones, where the real problems of teaching and of inter-personal relations in school and college can be studied in the light of personal experience. In passing it may be noted also that the personal development of students, as of children, is intimately related to the mastery of practical skills. The acquisition of the wide variety of skills which modern teaching demands—particularly the arts and crafts of the primary school—is the natural complement, and in some cases may be the vehicle, of emotional liberation.

It is of course quite probable that in such an atmosphere a few students may develop quite serious symptoms of personal maladjustment. This must be accepted and it is a potentially constructive outcome, for those with really serious problems will be discovered and may either be induced to give up the idea of teaching or be provided with expert therapeutic help. Clearly the running of a college of this kind will put new and heavy personal and professional demands on Principal, lecturers and tutors. But this is a necessary condition of advance and we shall later discuss some of its implications for the training of the teachers of teachers.

It is against this background of general preparation that the course in psychology must be planned. The aims of the course should be to give students the opportunity of gaining some real knowledge of themselves and of the children they will teach, some theoretical and practical understanding of group psychology, and some insight into the dynamics of inter-personal relationships. The basis of the course should be the intensive study of individual children, of actual classroom situations and of the manifestations of human motivation and personality encountered in everyday life. One effective vehicle for the latter study may be found in biography, poetry, novels, drama, etc. It is within this framework that the necessary minimum of strictly experimental psychology should find its place. This too should be severely practical in the sense of being centred on child development and on those aspects of educational psychology of direct use in the classroom, e.g. the learning of the basic subjects and the simpler techniques of testing (particularly diagnostic techniques) and of remedial teaching.

Now a strong word of caution is necessary in advocating this kind of psychology course. We must guard against trying to make teachers into amateur psychologists and psychiatrists, and must protect them against unnecessarily wounding personal experiences and against unwholesome meddling in their private affairs by tutors. I am also very doubtful of the usefulness or wisdom of trying to teach a great deal about unconscious psycho-dynamics to the *majority* of students through formal lectures and the reading of books on psycho-analysis and psycho-pathology. We ought certainly to offer the future teacher the possibility of acquiring some explicit intellectual understanding of these matters, but detailed study should not be required of the majority. It is indeed not to be recommended any more than a heavy diet of statistical psychology is to be recommended for the majority of intending teachers. But we would be naive indeed if we imagined that the reading of books by itself carried very much danger.

We are, of course, already familiar with the student, teacher or lecturer, who having read some of Freud's works or attended some therapeutic group discussions, or who after a few months' personal analysis behaves as a member of some mysterious elect, in possession of some priceless secret knowledge which he or she is often only too willing to divulge in an aggressive way. Life then becomes a stream of interpretations. Such people are a menace to themselves and to the mental health and happiness of their friends and acquaintances. Perhaps we shall always have to put up with a few of them for the sake of discussing with the majority some of the basic facts about human behaviour and personality. A little learning is not necessarily dangerous and in many fields it is all that most of us will ever be able to have. It is people and the use they make of knowledge who are dangerous, not knowledge in itself, and there may always be a minority whom we shall have to protect against themselves. It must be emphasized that no responsible psychologist ever gives direct personal interpretations of behaviour outside a therapeutic relationship. Teaching is in some respects necessarily a therapeutic relationship, but the therapy required is largely that of spontaneous intuitive understanding. *That* should be the goal of the education of teachers for mental health in the classroom, *not* an extensive academic knowledge of the more intricate parts of dynamic psychology, or a quack skill in discovering unconscious meanings in everyday life.

There is a great deal to be said for a somewhat oblique approach to the central concepts of dynamic psychology, for example through the liberal use of examples drawn from everyday experience and speech, and from literature. The poets are there to teach us. There is no more profound statement of the significance of early mother-child relations than the passage from Wordsworth's *Prelude* which begins 'blest the Babe, nurs'd in his Mother's arms...'.* Is not the very essence of the potentially destructive outcome of infantile ambivalence conveyed in Wilde's famous line?—

Yet each man kills the thing he loves.

None of us needs reminding surely of the storehouse of psychological wisdom contained in Shakespeare. There is a passage in *Julius Caesar* that is particularly relevant to one of the central ideas I have discussed (Act 4, Scene III):

Cassius. Have you not love enough to bear with me,
When that rash humour which my mother gave me
Makes me forgetful?

* With acknowledgments to Professor John Pilley who drew it to my attention.

Brutus. Yes, Cassius, and from henceforth,
When you are over-earnest with your Brutus.
He'll think your mother chides, and leave you so.

No clearer statement of the functioning in adult behaviour of a childhood parental imago can be imagined.* The therapeutic attitude revealed by Brutus should also be noted!

It will be observed that very little has been said about either the ethical implications of theories of mental health, or about the repercussions of psycho-analytic theory on our views of morality. These are large and difficult matters. Nevertheless, discussion of morality is an integral part of any practical course in psychology. The majority of young students in training as teachers are deeply interested in and concerned with problems of personal behaviour, although they are unlikely to reveal this except in a permissive atmosphere. Discussion of these matters in an impersonal setting, and perhaps via children's misdemeanours, presents an admirable opportunity for wise guidance on matters closely connected with mental health. Here also the oblique approach through literature can be a valuable aid in giving personal meaning to discussions while minimizing the risk of wounding exposures. Students will find much to reflect on in such a book as, for example, Robert Louis Stevenson's *Christmas Sermon.* Writing before Freud had published his clinical researches and speaking of people who indulge in militant moralizing and severe criticism of others, he says, 'Ill-temper and envy and revenge, find here an arsenal of pious disguises; this is the playground of inverted lusts.' In helping students to realize that a healthy attitude to life means avoidance alike of the Scylla of a narrow and rigid moral code and the Charybdis of unrestrained gratification of impulse, I commend discussion of the following passage (again from Stevenson): 'Gentleness and cheerfulness, these come before all morality; they are the perfect duties ... If your morals make you dreary, depend upon it they are wrong. I do not say "Give them up", for they may be all you have; but conceal them like a vice, lest they spoil the lives of better and simpler people.' It is important for us to remember, that almost without exception children are better and simpler people than we are. They may yet come to terms with anxiety and aggression in constructive ways, and there is always the hope that we can

* The point is meant to be illustrative. It is unimportant to attempt to decide whether Shakespeare was referring to biological inheritance of a temperamental trait—his use of the term 'humour' might encourage this interpretation—or whether, as the last line suggests, he was intuitively aware of the nature of the developmental factors in character formation.

help them to avoid some of our own troubles. To do this we require deeper insight into our own behaviour towards them.

An intellectual grasp of hypotheses and theories without some practical experience is even of less use in this field than it is in others. What can be done in a practical way to help to raise the general level of insight into our own behaviour that is so desirable in school and college? It seems likely that various forms of group activity will prove helpful. For example, I believe that in a special type of small group discussion we now have a practical technique of considerable value. This kind of technique has evolved in England primarily from Bion's experiments (1963) in discussion with neurotic patients,[3] but the actual procedure varies with the aim of the particular group (Jaques, 1951). A form of it which retains the vital features of Bion's methods adapted for use with non-patient groups has been found by experience to be of considerable value as a training device for teachers and other students of the social sciences, in heightening their awareness of their own feelings and deepening the perception of the motives and feelings of others. One learns from an experience of this kind to listen to and to understand some of the 'music behind the words' of every-day intercourse.* Although the development of this work has been guided throughout by psycho-analytic experience and concepts, the form of the technique evolved for use with non-patient groups of professional people interested in acquiring deeper insight into behaviour is not even remotely the equivalent of a psycho-analysis. It does demand of participants, however, that they make an attempt to see themselves as others see them. In practice this technique may resemble intimate discussion of common problems among friends, but it goes further and is distinct from such discourse in that it requires the guidance of someone with special skill. The spread of this technique will necessarily be gradual, because it depends on the availability of suitably trained people to act as group leaders and at the present time opportunities for training these leaders themselves are rather few. In the meantime much more use could be made of simple free discussion than has yet been attempted.†

* See Richardson (1967) and n. 3 of this chapter.

† What kind of skill and how much of it is needed to guide such discussion groups and how can such skill be obtained? There are at least three quite distinct levels of skill. The central source of skill is the qualified psycho-analyst with group experience, or alternatively, the analysed person who has made a special practical study of groups or the naturally intuitive person who has had intensive training in group methods. Such a person can undertake the training of group leaders. It must again be made clear that this training is in no sense a psycho-analysis—but such persons will be capable of guiding quasi-therapeutic group discussions among

The importance of such developments may be clearer if we consider what alternative methods exist to help us to come to passable terms with our unconscious selves. We must first be frank and admit that the dynamic unconscious is big magic, but that it is also neutral magic, the source alike of creation and destruction. We have to come to terms with it in creative ways if we are to improve the mental health and education of our community. Now those who can become qualified magicians are, and always will be, few in number—initiation is long, arduous, painful and costly. Again the number of people who can obtain direct therapeutic help through individual analysis will always be severely limited. We have therefore no real alternative so far as adults are concerned* but to make use of the new group techniques of discussion and activity, allying them with a more adequate use and understanding of the age-old pursuits through which men have harnessed unconscious forces to create and sustain civilization—the pursuits of games, entertainment, the arts and crafts, the sciences and religion. It is precisely in guiding children into healthy participation in these pursuits that our task as educationists consists, and already there are those who can testify from experience how an approach to these traditional activities through the new group techniques can help us to re-vitalize ourselves for our task.†

Much of what has been said bears closely and inevitably on the

---

teachers and other professional groups. Their competence in this respect represents the second level of skill. The third level is one which many of us possess without perhaps being really aware of it. It is a combination of sensitiveness and social competence which allows certain developments to take place in a group of which we are members, which do not take place when we are absent. Those of us who possess this skill are natural 'leaders' of permissive and so-called 'leaderless' group discussions. No special training is needed to begin. It is by utilizing as much of this skill as exists that we could achieve substantial advances in developing teacher training along the lines indicated. This sort of discussion is something that could be developed in every educational institution in the country, where there are one or two people with the courage to make a beginning. It is already being increasingly used in educational conferences. The purposes of groups of this kind are various and may include intellectual clarification and the reaching of executive decisions, but their emphasis, unlike that of a committee, is on the exploration of the barriers preventing adequate mutual understanding and common action.

* It may be said that in the long run it is in more enlightened ways of rearing and educating children that we must place our hopes, but since it is adults who educate, the very fact of the cycle of the generations makes the continual re-education of teachers and parents a vital matter.

† The World Education Fellowship has been particularly concerned in promoting this kind of development.

role and training of the teacher of teachers. It may be thought that the argument developed here implies a severe criticism of present training, particularly in psychology. This is of course true, but the criticism is entirely impersonal. Any generation of teachers and lecturers has to work within the framework of thought and feeling in which it was brought up. Few teachers of psychology have had any opportunity to acquire first-hand experience in the field of the exploration of unconscious motivation and reproaches on this account are entirely out of place. The ideas discussed here are only now beginning to bear practical fruit and there is an immense amount still to be learned about them and their application to education; it ill becomes anyone to pose as an infallible authority on such matters. Reflection on our own behaviour and on that of others, whether in life or literature, is open to all. Children's play is an inexhaustible source of revelation, if we will but dare to see and hear. Objective study of our own behaviour is difficult, but within quite a wide compass very valuable. Permissive group discussion is an instrument to hand for those who have the courage to begin, and opportunities for therapeutic group experience as a deliberate form of training are likely to increase. We may also look forward to the time—it is still quite a long way ahead—when every training department has on its staff one psychologist who has had a personal analysis. It would be the duty of such a person to teach about the unconscious aspects of motivation and to provide appropriate group experience for those advanced students in the area who were preparing for responsible positions in teacher training.

The central thesis developed here is that recent advances in the study of unconscious motivation and of group behaviour throw a great deal of light on education in relation to the work of the schools and the attitudes of teachers. A major factor in advance will be the extent to which teachers are able to recognize and come to terms with the child within themselves, and it is suggested that certain forms of group activity could be of great assistance in teacher training. The reduction of anxiety and consequently of aggression, the tolerance of frustration and the management of ambivalence, are seen as crucial matters in the development of a healthy human personality able to sustain and create a civilized culture. They are central to effective teaching when it is seen in its interpersonal context.

An amended version of certain sections from my 'Mental Health in the Classroom' in *The Bearings of Recent Advances in Psychology on Educational Problems* (Studies in Education, no. 7), Evans, 1955.

Notes

1 My colleagues Eric Hoyle (1969) and Philip Gammage (1971) have recently made valuable contributions to the literature of this field.

2 A report of a notable pioneer achievement of this kind will be available shortly, by my colleague Elizabeth Richardson, under the title 'The Teacher, The School, and the Task of Management'.

3 Bion's work at the Tavistock Institute of Human Relations has been the inspiration of most of the psycho-analytically oriented group work in the U.K. I had the good fortune to be among Bion's first students there (see 'How does a group learn to work together' in *How and Why De We Learn*, Niblett (ed.), Faber, 1965.

References

Adventure in American Education (5 vols). New York, Harper, 1942; London, Methuen, 1950.

Anderson, H. H. (1945–6) 'Studies of Teachers' Classroom Personalities', *Applied Psychology Monographs*, nos 6, 8, 11.

Bion, W. R. (1963) *Experiences in Groups*. Tavistock.

Gammage, P. (1971) *Teacher and Pupil*. Routledge & Kegan Paul.

Gardner, D. E. M. (1950) *Long-term Results of Infant School Methods*. Methuen.

Herbert, E. L. and Trist, E. L. (1953) 'The institution of an absent leader by a students' discussion group', *Human Relations*, vol. 6, no. 3.

Hoyle, H. (1969) *The Role of the Teacher*. Routledge & Kegan Paul.

Jaques, E. (1951) *The Changing Culture of a Factory*. Tavistock.

Morris, B. S. (1965) 'How does a group learn to work together?' in W. R. Niblett (ed.), *How and Why Do We Learn?* Faber.

Redl, F. and Wattenberg, W. W. (1951) *Mental Hygiene in Teaching*. Harcourt Brace.

Richardson, J. E. (1967) *Group Study for Teachers*. Routledge & Kegan Paul.

Richardson, J. E. (to be published) 'The Teacher, the School and the Task of Management'.

Swainson, M. (1952) 'The training of teachers and their mental health', *New Era in Home and School*, vol. 33, no. 10.

Vernon, P. E. (1953) in *Year Book of Education 1953*, chapter 3. Evans.

Wall, W. D. (1955) *Education and Mental Health*. Unesco.

Eight

Personality study for students of education

The educational context

To discuss the aims of any kind of teaching is to discuss a problem in educational philosophy. Therefore, whatever is taught to students regarding the development of human personality has to be considered not only in terms of psychological concepts and insights, but also in relation to the whole of the training students of education receive, and to the purpose of that training. Any statements of aims in an activity is fraught with difficulties, for there are unconscious as well as conscious aims, implicit as well as explicit ones, ultimate and also proximate ones, ambitious ones and humble ones. Also, aims in teaching are inextricably interwoven with methods, nowhere is the subtle relation between ends and means better exemplified. Moreover, whose aims are we considering, ours as teachers, or our students' aims in coming to learn from us? Can we assume an identity between their aims and ours, at both conscious and unconscious levels?

Intending teachers are looking for practical skills. *They* want us to teach them how to do the job. *We* hope, perhaps, that gradually we may bring them to see that the use they will be able to make of techniques of teaching depends primarily on their relationship with their pupils, that this in turn depends not only on their understanding of the nature and development of children, and of the materials of learning (subjects), *but on their understanding of themselves and their own aims in helping to educate others.*

It has been a commonplace assumption for many years that to teach John mathematics (or Latin, if you prefer the original) it is necessary to know both mathematics and *John*. Can this assumption be justified, and what is implied in its justification? There are commonly thought to be two approaches to this question. The first involves knowing John in the sense of having a sort of psychological inventory about him, including his feelings, struggles and intellectual gifts and limitations, and in relation to this knowledge of

John, knowing mathematics in such a way that his interest in it can be easily awakened. From this point of view, what is involved in knowing John is in principle in no way different from what is involved in 'knowing' a machine or a chemical reaction. The teacher himself in relation to John does not appear in this approach save as a *deus ex machina*. Teaching then becomes a case of 'Bunty pulls the strings'—a very sophisticated kind of puppetry. An element of this approach may be necessary in all teaching, but it is nevertheless at bottom an approach which is based in principle on the manipulation of others as if they were only machines or complex systems of chemical reactions, that is on a view which sees education as essentially doing things *to* others, e.g. training them, rather than doing things *for* and *with* them.

But is this view of the way in which we come to know others true? It can be argued that to have genuine knowledge of John in the sense of understanding him, even on the basis of a psychological inventory, involves being able to relate John's experiences in learning and development to our own. This springs from the fact that we can be said to understand the behaviour (and experience) of others (in the usual sense of the word understand) only in so far as their behaviour awakens in us sympathetic echoes of our own experience. For example, we understand anxiety in others only because we ourselves have experience of it. Freud made clear the implications of this view of understanding, and the difficulties that flow from it when he said: 'Only someone who can feel his way into the minds of children can be capable of educating them; and we grown-up people cannot understand children because we no longer understand our own childhood.'[1] Therefore coming to understand John in relation to his learning mathematics involves understanding ourselves in relation to our own learning and to our teaching of John. This implies coming to understand that there is a valid common purpose between John and ourselves, that that purpose is John's development as a person, that is, as a being progressively able to have an important say in his own development. To this end his learning of mathematics may be a means. Manipulation may then in principle be replaced by mutuality of purpose. The search for, and discovery of, this mutuality, which alone can redeem his work from degenerating into mere manipulation, is an essential task for the educator.

This view of learning and teaching points to a particular view of what it means to be a teacher. Since our students, for the most part, come to us bent primarily on becoming purveyors of knowledge (as so many of their teachers were to them) through the acquisition of skills which have a strong, if perhaps only implicitly manipulative, component, it follows that we seek to bring about in our students a change of attitude to the work of teaching, a transformation of their own self-image as teachers. In Bristol we have become accustomed to indicate the transformation we desire in the question formulated by Professor Roger Wilson: *'The Teacher, Instructor or Educator?'*[2] Some sort of idea of what we mean by the distinction between 'instruction' and 'education' will be clear from the above discussion, but a fuller conception of it must be left to emerge from the rest of this paper. It will be clear that personality study conducted in such a context becomes, whatever method of teaching is used, of necessity charged with personal implications. The extent to which individual students will consciously perceive these implications will however depend on the methods used. It is necessary at this point to draw attention to the fact that in speaking of our work with students in this way, we are making some very definite and far-reaching presuppositions.

Our work is of course based on the obvious assumption that the kind of attitude change or self-development we desire in our students is in fact possible through the means we employ. These means are essentially theoretical study involving reading and discussion, coupled with observation of children and experience of schools and of teaching. We are therefore assuming that through means, which are apparently largely intellectual, we may bring about changes in feelings and in ideas, and in the organization of feelings around ideas. There is no conclusive evidence that in our circumstances this assumption is justified, but in the University Department of Education at Bristol we are now beginning to take steps to find out what sort of developments, if any, graduate students experience in themselves during their training year. However, we can scarcely expect that the fruits of this aspect of our work with our students would show to any large extent during training, but we hope that these will become manifest later in their teaching careers.

Our other presuppositions are essentially moral ones. We are committed to assuming that (a) we have a moral right to aim at a particular kind of development for our students, and (b) we know what this kind of development is and can defend it rationally. Personally I accept the first of these assumptions because I believe that acceptance of it is inescapable for the educator. It is impossible to educate at all without claiming this right. What is crucial is the kind of development envisaged for others and the way in which the means used accord with the end desired.[3] In our kind of society we are committed in principle, by our aim of freedom, to educate our children and our students so that they may progressively discover for themselves what they have it in them to become, and may thus be helped to choose for themselves their own values and allegiances. Although our methods are, in their explicit form, quite different, our aims are here very close indeed to those of psychoanalysis as defined by Susan Isaacs: 'We do not seek to mould him (the patient) according to our notions of what he should be like, but only to enable him to make his own changes in himself by understanding his own deeper wishes and counter-wishes. We are not concerned with our own purposes but with his.'[4] We therefore claim the right—I would say the duty also—to help to make it possible for our students to come to grips with themselves as persons, and as teachers, and with problems of human values, more clearly than they might otherwise have done, and in a form in which they can wrestle with the issues without undue risk to their personal stability and integrity. Some students reject this opportunity outright, some reject it in the form of personality study. Such rejection must always be accepted and we find it possible to do this through offering alternative avenues of educational study.

To my mind, the heart of the matter, morally speaking, centres round our own intentions, and more particularly perhaps our unconscious intentions. We have to search our own hearts regarding the motives of our teaching. If we require self-knowledge of our students how much more must we require it of ourselves! This means, for example, purging our teaching, so far as we can, of aggressive elements. It is indeed notorious that it is only too easy for attempts to enlighten others to become assaults on their modes of behaviour, and on their cherished beliefs.

In what I have said there already have appeared some of the arguments whereby the second assumption may be justified also—that we know the kind of development we are aiming at for our students, and that we can defend it rationally. Its further justification is to be found in what we try to teach—dealt with later in this paper. I think it also a moral duty for us to define our aims to ourselves and to our students as best we may, that is to avow our purpose. We have to acknowledge a purpose for education as we see it and pursue it—children's, students' and our own—and we have to invite our students to seek and define the purposes to which they will devote their teaching lives.

These general considerations have a considerable bearing on our approach to the form personality study should take for students of education. Pre-eminently the approach to the study of the human person must be one which accords with what we believe about man and the purpose of his education. *The aims of the study must therefore ultimately be expressed in educational terms* (*i.e. valuative terms), not in neutral psychological, (i.e. scientific) terms.* Secondly, our general aims should accord with those of our other colleagues approaching the study of education from different view-points. Our teaching about personality has to contribute to the aims of a course which includes much else besides. Thirdly, the study must whenever possible be clearly based upon and remain close to students' experience of children, teachers, and of themselves. While it must be subject at all times, as far as possible in this field, to the discipline of scientific observation, logic and experiment, it must avail itself at need of the accumulated wisdom to be found in literature and in ordinary experience. Finally, students must be given opportunity to become aware of, and follow up if they wish, other approaches to the study of personality.

With these criteria in mind I have distinguished what seem to me to be five of the paramount aims of personality study for students of education. These aims are not put in any pedagogical order—I would reject the very notion of such an order in this connection—and must not on any account be taken as the contents of a syllabus. The pursuit of these aims will necessarily involve the student in explorations in feelings, in exercises in the construction and understanding of scientific concepts, and in the effort to achieve a conception of the human person and his development which will be practically effective in his own life and in his own teaching. The design of a practicable course based on these aims is another matter, and the possibilities have to be sharply and realistically assessed in relation to the calibre of the students and to the time available. On the one hand we have to cater for university graduates—of very varying capacities and backgrounds—whom we have with us for one session—seventeen weeks of academic study—and on the other for training college students fresh from school who are with us at present for two years—soon to be three—and for some of whom an ambitious intellectual programme is quite inappropriate. It is obvious that students will develop differently with respect to the aims of personality study as regards starting points, pace, emphasis and achievements.

Aims

In scope these aims envisage changes in students' feelings in the direction of wider sympathies and deeper insights into themselves and others, the emergence in their minds of some system of working concepts with which to think about what they are experiencing and doing, and with the aid of awakened feeling and fresh ideas, an opportunity to make a personal attempt to re-assess their own experience, to re-interpret education and to achieve a working philosophy of educational action.

This aim is centred around helping students to develop a clearer awareness of themselves and others, in particular of the distinction between 'self' and the 'other'. In part this means widening their conception of human nature through achieving deliverance in some measure from both ego-centricity and ethno-centricity. All studies which help to emphasize the variety of human beings, of human societies, and of personalities, while at the same time re-affirming fundamental human identity and which therefore work towards a catholicity of outlook and a sympathetic understanding of human affairs, assist in the process of self-realization and self-liberation. While *tout comprendre est tout pardonner* indicates an extreme position, and one which if unqualified by personal adherence to a set of moral values is indefensible, nevertheless, without considerable development in this direction, the teacher is severely limited in his approach to his professional task. Joyce Carey, in the preface to his novel *Charley is My Darling*, brings the point home: 'And it has always seemed to me that every ordinary child is by nature a delinquent, that the only difference between us as children was the extent of our delinquency, whether we were found out in it and how we were punished for it.'

Here is the beginning of wisdom, and of that extension of it which grasps how easily we condemn in others things which we are unwilling to admit about ourselves, and how equally easily we attribute to them qualities which we treasure in ourselves or treasured in those whom we loved in infancy, and which we want to believe they possess. Some recognition of the ubiquitous nature, subtlety and power of projection is a necessary pre-requisite for the discovery of the 'other'. Without some such awareness, the lover cannot progress from a narcissistic attachment to a projected self image, or escape from the compulsive power of the bonds which united him with a loved parent, to a real concern for another person. Without such awareness the teacher cannot come to terms with children as they really are, as distinct from a variety of versions of his own childhood.

With such a view goes also the beginnings of the realization of the complexity of each human being, of the limitations of a shallow rational view of behaviour which sees only the surface personality —the persona or mask. The quickening of the imagination about others, about children, not only leads to the clearer recognition of an inner world of our own, by virtue of which alone the outer world is able to clothe itself with value for us, but also points to those deeper recesses of feeling and thought, to hidden intentions, to purposes but half avowed or perhaps never consciously admitted. Here our aim cannot but be to awaken in the student some awareness of the existence of the vast unconscious dimension of his own personality, and to help him towards some degree of acceptance of those aspects of himself from which his consciousness may recoil in fear and revulsion.

There is much common experience which lies to hand to help the student thus to enlarge his vision of himself. He is aware of the 'I' which may struggle against impulses which appear to lie outside it and to emanate from a region of his being which may be felt as alien to him. He is aware too of the 'voice of conscience' which the 'I' may obey or disregard. From this awareness he may be led to increasing candour with himself about the existence of his own passions, often strenuously denied, his anxieties, hates and loves, and to the conflict among them, and between them and his conscious ideals. He may be helped, too, towards an increasing tolerance of these divisions within himself, and to the discovery that through tolerance comes the possibility of further integration. It is thus that his insight into and sympathy for children's struggles and difficulties may be enhanced, and thus too that he may come to understand the folly of trying to work against the grain, and the educational wisdom which advocates patience and the search for means whereby he may ally his efforts with that part of the child's growing self which wants to learn, to love and master the world. The child's conflicts and his own difficulties can thus be illumined by a growing realization that such struggles stem from emotional conflicts in the past which are still potent influences in the present, that they are activated now by the present situation and that they point to the future. In such terms the student can begin to glimpse the importance of early infantile experience, can try to make sense of the behaviour of young children and of adolescents, and by relating his own past to his present self may receive an intimation of the meaning and possibility of future personal maturity.

For personal growth to take place, feeling and thought have to work in intimate collaboration, and increasing insight should whenever possible be stabilized and given communicable form through the growth of appropriate concepts. On what these should be there is no doubt room for a considerable divergence of view and the intellectual capacity of individual students will demand a considerable flexibility of approach. The teacher in charge of personality study, however, requires some reasonably adequate and self consistent scheme of his own from which to work. The scheme with which I work myself is very roughly as follows:

Dimensions in which the human being may be studied

I distinguish the biological, the social and the personal dimensions, each with its own super-ordinating concept—respectively those of organism, culture, and personality. Each of these concepts is of vital importance to an understanding of childhood and so are the ways in which they are interdependent, and the way in which they are hierarchically related, so that for example the concept of personality pre-supposes those of culture and of organism.

Personality as a dynamic structure

This emphasizes a cross-sectional view of personality which embraces the conscious and unconscious levels of functioning, and stresses the larger dynamic structures of 'instinct' (id), ego, and moral function (super ego), each with its unconscious as well as its conscious aspect, and each part of the total self.[5]

Personality as a developing structure

This introduces the longitudinal or developmental view, and the dependence of the growth of the self and its moral function on the emotional aspects of early experience. On the quality of this experience depends the balance between security and anxiety, and the effect of this balance on the development of the basic passions of love and hate provides a foundation for the understanding of the concepts of introjection and projection and those of conflict, ambivalence, guilt and reparation. There is explicit reliance on the principle of genetic continuity as exemplified by the way in which early relationships are prototypic of later ones. Particular emphasis is laid upon the rôle of parents and, later on, of teachers, in supplying through their attitudes and behaviour the 'material' through which the self and its moral function are nourished. Education is thus regarded as personal from the start and the idea that 'we are members one of another' is given psychological substance. It is in this context that the early identifications, the Œdipal tensions and the development of psychological sex identity are placed. Finally this whole system of concepts is related to the vicissitudes of development, to the learning and behaviour problems of home and school, and to the gradual emergence of a rational self enjoying a degree of autonomy.

Goals of maturity

These are conceived in terms of a progressive integration of the personality around and eventually through the activity of a central ego. The mature Self is thought of as being characterized by an adequate degree of conscious self-control, of personal insight and of foresight into the consequences of action, by the capacity for objectification (dispassionate thought), for making value judgments of an informed kind and of acting on them, for fellowship and for concern for others. At this level sexuality is truly genital and expresses itself equally in love and work. Freud's criterion—a capacity to give love greater than one's need to obtain love—is regarded as the hall-mark of emotional maturity, and indeed as the essential basis of rationality and therefore of freedom.

The approach to personality study described obviously invites the student to undertake a re-assessment of his experience, of his beliefs, his values, and his own learning. This is for our students an opportunity, not an obligation, but any genuine effort to grapple in this way with his own and other people's behaviour cannot but begin to throw new light on beliefs, values, and the purpose of education. He becomes sensitized to the concept of psychological or inner reality, and to the way in which projections of inner experience are endowed with outer reality. It is in this region that great resistance is encountered, and this is true whether the student comes with a background of quite naïve and uncriticized beliefs, for example, religious beliefs, or with one of an equally naïve rationalism, in which, again for example, religious statements have been taken as having literal meaning, and have therefore been dismissed as nonsense. Precisely because the study of personality may challenge students' deepest convictions is, however, no argument against the duty of the teacher in this field to point out how such study enables a fresh approach to be made to the whole life of the imagination, to the difference between 'scientific' truth and 'poetic' and 'religious' truth and to the problems of symbolism in general. It is of course likely that this is a challenge which only the bolder spirits will be able to accept.

In a very similar way an understanding of how the moral function develops provides an important basis for a critique of conduct, and such a critique, if applied in a realistic fashion to the everyday situations of the classroom, may put the problems of teacher-pupil relations, of authority and freedom and hence of discipline in a completely new light. A grasp of the dual basis of morality, that is, its internal embodiment in the moral function or super-ego, and its external embodiment in cultural norms, and of the inter-relation of the internal and the external, paves the way for the re-valuation of many of the dictates of conscience and of the obligations of conventional mores. This may lead to a realization of how it is that much of what has been and still is accepted as moral law, is an expression of hate rather than of love, and of how it is that fear, hate, and envy have at their command what Robert Louis Stevenson called 'an arsenal of pious disguises'. From this a clear distinction may be drawn between the compulsive operations of a primitive super-ego and the deliberations of what, following Sir Fred Clarke, may be regarded as 'an instructed conscience'.

It is, however, through initiating a re-assessment of his own learning, his stock in trade of knowledge and skill, that personality study may most directly lead the student to a re-interpretation of education. Through realizing that the bonds which tie us to things, to ideas and to technical activities, are expressions of the same fundamental energy which unites us with other human beings, the way is opened to see the materials of learning, the so-called 'subjects' for what they are, that is, as forms of human achievement, and, as such, among the proper means or vehicles of personal development. Intellectual development is then no longer opposed to 'personal' or 'emotional' development, but represents one of the most important means through which maturity is reached. Our search for truth, and our skill in creating beauty, become as William James put it 'extensions of personality'.

It is against such a background that the significance of the contrast between 'instruction' and 'education' may be more fully grasped. Personality study begins to fulfil its wider function of enabling the student to re-consider what he is doing in education when by means of it he can sense the implications of the *difference between imparting techniques and releasing powers*, powers which are the common possession of his pupils and himself and which form the basis of his relationship with them. Thus his understanding may be deepened by his coming to conceive of learning not as a mechanical mastery of the so-called impersonal aspects of experience, but as an activity through which, what may appear impersonal, is revealed as personal in the way in which it is created and sustained by the co-operative effort of human beings.

Finally, it is through a consideration of the nature of this co-operative effort, in the light of personality study, that he may be led to a new view of his own rôle as a teacher in furthering the development of his pupils. Such study can reveal for him both the nature of the unconscious relationship in which he stands to his pupils, and the conscious means which he can adopt to help them gradually to take hold of the common birthright of human freedom. It is in this way that it may become meaningful for him to think of education as an adventure in mutuality.

The ultimate aim of personality study for the student of education is the same as that of all his other studies, namely to provide him with the means of deepening his understanding of what he is doing as a member of the educational enterprise. In seeking to illumine for him the behaviour and development of his pupils, it provides him with a means of acquiring a better understanding of himself, and hence of fashioning for himself an effective critique of his own educational actions.

The aims of personality study for students of education which I have outlined may thus appear ambitious in the extreme, even grandiose. If so, this is only because they are *aims*, because they represent explicitly what it seems to me is implicit in our work with our students. None of us needs to be reminded of the gap between such aims and what in fact we would claim to be able to achieve, and any attempt to clarify aims must certainly be judged in terms of the extent to which it helps us to criticize and improve our methods of teaching.

Originally published in *Sociological Review Monograph* no. I, University of North Staffordshire, 1958.

References

1 S. Freud, *The Claims of Psycho-analysis to Scientific Interest—The Educational Interest* (vol. 13 of Standard Edition, 1913), p. 189.

2 Lyndale House Papers, Bristol University Institute of Education, January 1954.

3 Some of the problems presented for education, when it is seen as guidance in this sense, are discussed by the author in the *Year Book of Education 1955*, Evans, chapter 6, pp. 121–40.

4 S. Isaacs, *Childhood and After*, Routledge & Kegan Paul, 1948, p. 119.

5 This simple, virtually descriptive phenomenal scheme is close to Freud's original psycho-biological concepts. Later, students are introduced to more sophisticated, modern and *personal* models. See J. D. Sutherland, 'Object Relations Theory and the Conceptual Model of Psychoanalysis', *B.J. Med. Psych.*, vol. xxxvi (1963), pt 2, pp. 109-24.

Nine

Personal growth through professional education

A critique of theory and practice

All forms of education, general and professional, are concerned with the healthy development of persons living and working together in communities. To think of education in terms of personal growth is therefore to think of it in terms which are close to the aims of mental health programmes. Central to any programme for the improvement of the mental health of human beings is the education of those who will work professionally in the mental health field. The main thesis of this paper is therefore that such education must itself be considered in terms of the personal growth of the students while in training. In this context, personal growth will be expected to take a particular direction.

Limiting discussion to professional education in the mental health field still leaves its scope very wide. It is possible to discuss all the varieties of training at one and the same time only by concentrating exclusively on the essential core of mental health work and leaving aside the highly specialized knowledge and skill appropriate to the different professions. My own experience has been in clinical and social psychology and in teacher education, mainly the last, but I will try to present a generalized image of the essentials while drawing examples from various fields.

Is there a central core in all mental health work? I assume that there is, and that it is concerned with the understanding of man, in health and in illness, with the understanding of the human situation, its blessings and its vicissitudes. This entails an active understanding of the problems of growing up, of maturity, and of growing old. This understanding has to be active because what is required is an effective personal capacity (as distinct from mere knowledge or purely technical skill) to help forward, to support and to alleviate distress. The central and major concern of all professional education in this field is therefore to promote the growth of this basic understanding of oneself and others in ways which can ultimately find expression through the special skills of each particular profession. An adequate critique will therefore concern itself with the common aims of professional studies, and with the impact of such studies on students and their tutors, including within this a discussion of tutors' responsibilities in the guidance of their students' development.

The common aims of professional studies in the mental health field

The educational objectives common to all forms of work in this field may be briefly described as the development of (a) adequate powers of objective sympathy, i.e. detached identification, (b) a usable conceptual framework of theoretical ideas, and (c) a repertoire of relevant skills. For personal growth to take place development in all three directions must occur, not necessarily simultaneously, but certainly in relation to one another. There is little use in the future psychiatrist or child care officer acquiring an intellectual command of what Halmos has called 'the shibboleths of psychodynamics' if the student himself remains insensitive or defensive towards a large range of human feelings.[1] Likewise the teacher who possesses only an untutored sympathy is inadequately equipped to comprehend the complexities of child development and behaviour. Feeling and thought have to come to work in intimate collaboration, and increasing insight should whenever possible be stabilized and given communicable form through the growth of appropriate concepts and skills.[2]

It is however on the first of these aims that I want to concentrate, the growth of sympathetic powers, those powers through which we may come to possess what Bruno Bettelheim has called 'an informed heart'.[3] I have already referred to this as a kind of 'detached identification', for such sympathetic powers are always, *au fond*, based on identification, but this term is so frequently used to denote simply *unconscious* forms of identification, particularly 'projective identification' in Melanie Klein's sense, that the use of it here could easily cause confusion. It is precisely with the development of insight into our own identification that I am here concerned, and the phrase detached sympathy seems the one best suited to describe the powers we wish to cultivate. I am speaking here then of a heightening and deepening of sensitivity to feeling in ourselves and in others, of an extension of sympathy not only to those with whom we immediately feel akin, which ought to be relatively easy, but more importantly to those who appear alien to us in character or culture or both. This latter feat of the sympathetic imagination is difficult.* It requires the discovery of and a coming to terms with those latent anxieties and hostilities in ourselves whose unrecognized existence interferes with the perception of the problems of others. It is the recognition of these elements in ourselves which is essential. How essential it is may be seen in some of the problems encountered in training. For example, Lewis[4] cites the case of a social work student who had mastered difficulties of dependence in her own adolescence through denial of them in a prematurely assumed independence and sense of responsibility, and who had consequently grave difficulty in dealing sympathetically with an adolescent in the throes of self-pity.

The development of this power of detached sympathy in professional education requires stressing since it appears to be rather imperfectly nourished at the present time in both general and professional studies. For example, I have on several occasions set the following statement by the novelist Joyce Cary as the basis of an essay or examination question for graduate students of education:[5] 'It has always seemed to me that every ordinary child is by nature a delinquent, that the only difference between us as children was the extent of our delinquency, whether we were found out in it and how we were punished for it.' The majority of students react defensively, either through arguments about the definition of delinquency, and its causes and cures when considered in the legalistic sense, or by pouring scorn upon the statement, attributing it to some old-fashioned believer in original sin. Only a minority interpret it as meaning 'There but for the grace of God go I?'

In professional studies themselves there also exist tendencies either to stress intellectual understanding and practical skills and to assume that the feeling component will look after itself, or to believe that insight into feelings and motives can only be significantly deepened through personal analysis. Without in any way denying the inestimable value of a personal analysis for students who can get one, I regard this latter view as clearly not only a gospel of despair but a *reductio ad absurdum*. The basic fact is that it is primarily with what is common in our humanity, as commonly experienced, that we have to work in educating our students for the mental health profession. Some power of detached sympathy is common to all, and it is this which forms the indispensable basis upon which, with the aid of scientific discoveries in all the human sciences—from biochemistry through ethology and cultural anthro-

* Margaret Mead has pointed out to me the particular complexities and difficulties involved in the development of detached sympathy between the sexes.

pology to psycho-analysis—and with the lessons of accumulating practical experience to guide us, we seek to enlarge our own and our students' understanding of what it means to be human.

The impact of professional studies

There are certain difficulties in professional education in the mental health field which are not found in general education, at any rate not in the same form, and not to the same degree. These difficulties relate to certain misconceptions, students being prone to some, their teachers to others; to the relation between content and process in learning; to the problems of giving and gaining insight; and to the fact that success in these studies is ultimately to be assessed in terms of student growth towards maturity. While a consideration of these difficulties always looms large in any discussion of this form of professional education, it is of the first importance to realize that it is these very difficulties, and the opportunities within the training course for surmounting them, that constitute the means to personal growth.

Misconceptions of students and teachers

One obvious source of difficulty is that the student is apt to see his task simply in terms of the acquisition of certain practical skills. It is the action point that matters to him. It is here that he feels on trial—here he must succeed. To the student in training as a teacher faced with a class of forty children his problem appears to be one of keeping order and 'putting across' the required knowledge. To the social work student faced with a complex family situation what is required may appear to be the alteration of certain circumstances or arrangements such as moving a young married couple away from their in-laws or the husband taking another job which does not involve a night-shift, or having a stepdaughter go to stay with her maternal grandfather and so on.

The student's spontaneous misconception of his role is strongly reinforced both by the need to simplify his task and by his desire to help. He longs for the security of simple general rules which can be applied in a variety of situations. When these are not forthcoming he is apt to be made anxious or to feel frustrated. His frustration is increased by his urge, as a member of a helping profession, to do things to or for people. To learn that, physical methods of treatment apart, people can only be significantly helped by enabling them to help themselves, brings with it the realization that in helping others he has imaginatively to enter into their situation and that this makes demands on him as a person which removes his role altogether from that of manipulator or arranger. This insight is at first resisted and can come only as a personal discovery.

The initial urge to action and the need for certainty reveal that students' apparent misconception of their professional role is itself based upon anxiety. Students feel challenged by the problems they have to face and by clients who come to them for help, but since the real source of the challenge is unconscious, its nature is at first misconceived and it is transmuted into the need for action. Here unconscious anxiety reinforces purely conscious and rational concern to succeed in action. As it becomes apparent that the simple actions envisaged are not the required solutions, and as their tutors continue to insist on the need to try to understand what they are doing, a secondary source of anxiety is added to the first. Their tutors are or ought to be aware of all this, aware that for a student to acquire the necessary skills, far-reaching changes in thought and feeling have to take place within him. Their main task as tutors is to facilitate these changes, a task going altogether beyond merely imparting information or demonstrating skills. In carrying out this task they are in much the same position *vis-à-vis* their students as the students are *vis-à-vis* their clients, with the essential and important difference that they, the tutors, should be fully aware of this.

The means at the tutors' disposal are primarily the professional content of the course, and it is in relation to this content that misconceptions are apt to arise on the part of the tutors. The most potent misconception is one based upon anxiety lest they fail to furnish their students with all that is generally considered essential to their education in the way of knowledge and the opportunity for practical experience under supervision. The temptation is to conceive of their task as that of turning out the 'finished article'. To succumb to this temptation is to fail altogether to understand both the nature of education as personal growth and the nature of professional work. The professional person is one with a capacity for understanding what he is doing, and the education of such a person entails primarily enabling him to acquire this capacity. It cannot provide him in advance with all the knowledge and experience required to solve the problems he will meet in the future.

The relation of content and process in learning

The professional knowledge required in mental health work is drawn, on its theoretical side, from all the human sciences—biological, sociological and psychological. If the student is to find his way in this vast territory he needs expert guidance, and to be persuaded of the relevance of theory to practice. These must interlock for him. Hence well thought out syllabuses and graded practical experience are essential, but they are far from being enough. Teaching and learning are never simply articulated to one another. Students hear and read much which has no effect on them at the time, although it may later bring illumination, and what they do learn at any point may not be what the tutor is focusing upon. Moreover there are great individual differences among students in their approach to learning.

Hence the syllabus can be nothing but a rough guide for the tutor. He has to be constantly aware of, and responsive to, the actual process of learning. What appears at first to be the firm ground of the syllabus turns out to be shifting sand. What have the students understood or misunderstood; what has been rejected or over-valued; to what extent is emotional response keeping pace with intellectual clarity; what links are the students forming with their own experience and with their practical work? Clearly, to follow and to assist student progress, adequate discussion is essential at all stages, among students themselves and between tutors and students in both individual and group tutorial situations.

In general terms this is what all good education entails, but in the mental health field there are once again special difficulties to be considered. These arise from the gaps, uncertainties and rival theories which flourish in the human sciences, and from the personal reference which much of the material is bound to carry, since it deals with human beings, their passions, vicissitudes and problems. It is for example necessary to guard against playing into the hands of defensive scepticism or of too eager belief. Yet for theory to be educative, there must be on the one hand a reasonably coherent system of concepts, based on well-attested observation, which does justice to the total complexity of human beings; and on the other there must be a willingness to reveal gaps and uncertainties and to entertain alternative hypotheses. Provided the student learns to think dispassionately and to respect scientific method and established fact there is much to be said for encouraging speculation. The understanding of any particular situation, problem or case always calls for an imaginative reconstruction which can be tested against the facts.

It is of course notorious that the materials of study in this field themselves militate against rational thought and that for this reason the tutor requires special skill in mediating it to students. It is in coming to grips with psychodynamic concepts that the heart of the difficulty lies, for here is the major source of anxiety in education for mental health work. The central concepts with which the student has to come to terms might perhaps be reduced to four—viz., the ubiquitous nature of unconscious processes; the persistent effects of previous, particularly early, experiences on later life; the co-existence and dominating influence of impulses of love and hate; and the protean character of the defensive manoeuvres that the ego can call to its aid. The implications of these ideas for his own stability and beliefs, as well as for his professional competence, are so far-reaching that it may take many years for a student to come to reasonable terms with them. It is however the tutor's task to see that significant gains in this respect are achieved during training.

Gaining and giving insight

Students should early be accustomed to the implicit self-reference of their studies. Group work at the very beginning usually gains enormously from the use of a 'mutual introduction' technique, all students (and the tutor) revealing as much of themselves and their history as they feel inclined. I have also found that these early sessions, coupled with a short essay on 'Formative Influences in my Life', provide admirable material for discussion with individual students. This kind of approach which draws directly on the student's own life and personal experience of family situations creates an atmosphere into which discussions of observation of children or problem situations, reading (both literary and scientific accounts of human problems), lectures and practical work can all be geared.[6] At this stage there usually emerges some realization of the multifarious forms which the transfer of affection and hostility can take and some inkling of the existence within each of our more or less mature selves of an immature part—the child within. The major contribution of this type of discussion is to provide a secure setting in which later more serious issues can be discussed and deeper insights gained.

Some students can go much faster and further than others, and this may have little to do with their intellectual capacity. To some, much of the material discussed may appear not only as a threat to their conscious values and beliefs, but may be felt as undermining the deeper foundations of their personality, as when in discussions of child-rearing some students may feel that their own parents' standards are being attacked. The work of the tutor here is in one important respect analogous to that of the psycho-analyst. He has to seek ways, usually indirect, in which through discussion, reading and practical work such resistances may be lessened without needlessly endangering the student's stability.[7]

This aspect of his work raises an important issue for him. What is his responsibility with regard to the interference with a student's personality which studies in this field necessarily entail? He has to ensure that his activity is not in fact an attack upon the student's feelings and beliefs, although the student may at times construe it as such, but that it is always directed to enabling the student to make such changes in himself as he safely can. There is always the risk that a student may require psycho-therapeutic help, and it is essential that this help should both be readily available and wholly removed from the teaching situation. It goes almost without saying that the tutor himself should be thoroughly aware not only of the ego strengths and weaknesses of individual students, and their needs for dependence and independence in different ways and at different times, but aware also of his own counter-transference to these needs. Ideally tutors charged with this particular responsibility should have experience of personal analysis.

Conditions and signs of growth

What are the essential considerations to be borne in mind if the anxieties and difficulties of learning to undertake work in the mental health field are to be used to promote personal growth? What are the signs of such growth? I would emphasize two major sets of considerations. The first concerns the teaching programme in which four points stand out:

1. Student growth is facilitated more through working from their strengths and giving them confidence than by dwelling on their weaknesses, although sometimes a weakness may have to be tackled directly.
2. In an educational context changes in feeling have to be brought about by what are overtly mainly intellectual means.
3. It is reassuring for students to realize from their personal experience on the course that current situations as well as past events influence behaviour. They are thus helped to see that in learning they are growing and re-making themselves.
4. Emphasis is best kept firmly on the objective problems being studied, the self-reference being there but implicit rather than explicit; the students should wherever possible be allowed to draw the morals for themselves. Sometimes it may be possible and valuable to go beyond this. It depends on the students and the skill of tutors. The use of 'therapeutic' group discussion gives opportunities for rather more direct comment and interpretation.[8]

The second major set of considerations relate to staff attitudes and the atmosphere of the training institution. All depends here on the creation of a secure atmosphere in which challenges can be safely accepted, on having a teaching team united in spirit and purpose, but without concealment of genuine differences, and on an endeavour by the whole staff to exemplify in their relations with students the attitudes they wish their students to acquire in relation to their clients.

What can we look for as signs of a maturing self in a student? Charlotte Towle has described these in detail.[9] I will here content myself with suggesting five key directions in which growth should be evident:

1. a recognition and tolerance of personal difficulties and weaknesses and a consciousness of genuine strengths and competences
2. a capacity to understand the problems of others in terms of his own strengths and weaknesses
3. a capacity to objectify relations with others so that hostility can be tolerated and love accepted
4. recognition that we cannot do things to or for people but only with them, i.e. that all educative and therapeutic work implies a mutuality of purpose
5. a reformulation of personal beliefs and values in accordance with a deeper perception of life.

In conclusion, the theme of this paper could be summarized by saying that in all mental health work it is the self which is the main instrument, and that therefore the major purpose of professional education in this field is to secure growth towards a degree of personal maturity adequate to the tasks involved.[10]

Originally published in *Excerpta Medica*, no. 45, Proceedings of the IVth International Congress on Mental Health, Paris, 1961.

References

1 Paul Halmos. Personal Involvement in Learning About Personality.
2 Ben Morris. Personality Study: Its Aims and Implications for Students of Education.
3 Bruno Bettelheim. *The Informed Heart*. Thames & Hudson, 1960.
4 K. M. Lewis. The Impact of a Course in Personality Development on Individual Students.
5 Joyce Cary. Preface to *Charley is My Darling*. Michael Joseph, 1940.
6 Edna Oakeshott. Means by which Students of Education May Learn About Personality Development.
7 F. E. Waldron. Observations on Teaching Methods for Courses in Personality Development.

8 W. R. Bion. *Experiences in Groups, and other papers,* Tavistock Publications, 1961; also J. E. Richardson. *Group Study for Teachers.* Routledge & Kegan Paul, 1967.

9 Charlotte Towle. *The Learner in Education for the Professions.* University of Chicago Press, 1954.

10 Michael Balint. *The Doctor, His Patient and The Illness.* Pitman, 1957.

Articles 1, 2, 4, 6, 7 are printed in *Sociological Review Monograph* no. 1: 'Papers on The Teaching of Personality Development', University College of North Staffordshire, 1958.

Ten

Education and mental health

During this century it has gradually become obvious to us that there is much common ground between the educational profession on the one hand and other social professions, notably child care, social work and medicine, particularly child health, and psychological medicine on the other. As in other instances, however, the area in question seems more frequently to be viewed as disputed territory rather than as common ground. Myths and mystiques grow fast on this fertile soil and entrenched defensive positions are rapidly taken up. These have served very greatly, as is the nature of jungle growths, to obscure the actual features of the territory itself, and there remain still today some fairly genuine puzzles as to what is at stake. I do not intend to spend time on the myths and entrenched positions save to remark that it seems to me that during my professional lifetime, medical omnipotence on the one hand, and educational paranoia on the other, have both notably diminished—a sign of a more healthy state of affairs.

Friendly and genuine co-operation is now much more the order of the day, but progress is still hindered by misconceptions on all sides, which although they ultimately have defensive roots do seem to some extent to be amenable to rational analysis. Thus many professional mental health workers, particularly medical ones, see education as essentially an affair of intellectual development, leaving emotional development in their care. Equally there are many educators who take essentially the same view. It is a highly convenient view for it appears to eliminate disputed territory. By the same token however it tends to eliminate common ground. A view which seems to me much more adequate in relation to all we know about human development is one which sees the concerns of mental health and education as having very substantial common interests.

Attempts to establish a middle position are common among those who are often styled 'progressive' educators and many of them would claim the mental health of their pupils among their educational aims. This position is however often attacked from both sides, a common charge being that it confuses the roles of therapist and teacher. Other charges are that insufficient attention is in fact being given to mental health requirements or that 'true' education is being neglected. Instructive examples of current educational arguments will be found in the writings of some modern educational thinkers, notably G. H. Bantock (1967), Richard Peters (1959, 1964) and John Wilson (1968). Professor Richard Peters, let it be said, is himself notably friendly to, interested in, and knowledgeable about dynamic theories in psychology. One of Peters's major contributions has been to clarify the notion of 'aims' in education by reaffirming the dependence of ends on means. By way of general illustration of this thesis he remarks: 'The Puritan and the Catholic both thought they were promoting God's Kingdom, but they thought it had to be promoted in a different manner. And the different manner made it quite a different Kingdom' (Peters, 1959). His work has served to remind educators, and we constantly need to be reminded of this, that it is our educational practices which in fact define our educational values. Incidentally this sauce for the educational goose is also sauce for the gander of mental health, and we might profit by examining what values are implied in current mental health practices.

Peters is interested in mental health but has some highly critical comments to make on the notion of 'mental health' as an educational aim, chiefly on the ground that it confuses the roles of therapist and teacher and reaffirms what he regards as the obnoxious notion that education must have an end beyond itself. Many of his remarks here are very apposite but in the end I think he fails to follow his own prescriptions in relating ends to means and he does so primarily because he seems to me to underestimate the extent to which intellectual achievement and the very possibility of rationality itself (which he rightly regards as a cardinal human virtue) are intimately bound up with the ordering of the emotional life. For example, he thinks it important to remind teachers from time to time that their pupils have emotions to control, a love life to lead and a living to be earned. But he thinks this is better done by speaking of these things in terms of vocational training and of the training of the emotions and character, rather than in terms of mental health, which he sees as the province of the therapist. He regards it as a fact, and one to be deprecated, that a stress on mental health implies that 'children are to be treated as patients who have to be weaned in a kindly way to nibble at the raw meat of the modern world'. Since Peters is, in my opinion, the most knowledgeable and the most incisive critic, and since his position is in many ways typical of an important current trend in educational thought, I propose to quote him at some length.

> It is unnecessary and misleading to saddle the teacher with a remedial function by saying that 'mental health' should be one of his aims when what is covered by this term can be referred to in more traditional ways which do not carry the implication that the teacher is a special sort of doctor. This is not, of course, to say that there should not be experts readily available to whom the teacher can refer cases of breakdown; there are school doctors after all, and school dentists, so why not school psychiatrists? It is only to say that 'mental health' should not be regarded as an aim of an educator.
>
> The cynic, of course, might reply that schools for many adolescents are in such a sorry state that there is little more that can be done than to have policemen in to stop riots, caretakers to keep the place clean, doctors and dentists to look after physical health and psychiatrically trained 'teachers' to care for the 'mental health' of the inmates. For the conditions of schooling and the attitudes of the inmates make any talk of 'education' as out of place as a fashion parade would be on a dung-hill. But the cynic here concedes the main point which I am trying to make; and it is questionable whether his counsel of despair is justified in the light of examples of what can be done by imaginative teachers with the most unlikely material in appalling circumstances. Education is so much a matter of confidence, of imagination, and of enthusiasm; and it has not got to take the form of initiating farmworkers into a love for Shakespeare and symphony concerts. The emphasis on 'mental health' reflects, among other things, a failure of nerve on the part of educators, a retreat from the positive.*

From this it seems to me that Peters has to make the distinctions he makes because he is using what I regard as inadequate concepts of mental health and of education.

It will now be apparent I think why I said that the attempt rigidly to separate the concerns of education and mental health is so convenient. It is convenient for educators since it allows them to continue to treat human development as if it could be neatly divided into more or less independent segments; on the one hand the growth of intellect, on the other the training of the emotions and character.† Any casualties which result from adopting such a

* I think it is very difficult indeed to maintain that there is any 'retreat from the positive' to be found for example in the writings of W. D. Wall (1955, 1959) on the general theme of education and mental health.

† The writers I have mentioned explicitly deny that they make this dichotomy, but the whole tenor of their arguments is to suggest that feeling is not *intrinsic* to thought. It is my contention that it is.

view can then be handed over to the therapist. This has also been extremely convenient for, at any rate, the organization of mental health work in education. It leads to confining activity to the treatment of the casualties of the educational system and doing little about prevention. For what precisely would prevention really mean? Would it not mean in fact the re-designing of education in a way which allowed for the growth of persons as a whole; so might *some* of the casualties at any rate be prevented, those in which treating children as disembodied intellects or minds without passion and desires (or at any rate hopelessly underestimating the role of the latter in human functioning) had played a large part. Of course the mental health professions have had numbers of pioneers who have seen the truth of all this and have tried to influence education in a radical way—just as there have been pioneers among educators who have tried to do much the same thing. But I think it not unfair to suggest that by and large, this neat separation of tasks has served as a defensive device against more radical approaches. It has allowed the teacher to remain in his classroom undisturbed by radical doubts and has allowed diagnosticians and therapists to get on with their specifically clinical work. Some of my pioneering friends in child psychiatry and in educational psychology are likely to protest that this is unfair and that the real resistance to more radical approaches is in the schools. There is plenty of resistance there of course, but does it only exist there?

This discussion raises the question of the nature of modern concepts of mental health and of education and whether the major values implicit in these concepts are ones which can be shared. We are now I think growing out of the notion of mental health as implying the absence of conflict within the personality. This was once quite widely regarded as its most important internal criterion. Correlative with this was the notion that mental health implied '*adjustment*' to the social *mores* by means of conformity to them. Modern ideas I think centre on two rather different notions. Health is first of all demonstrated by a developed capacity to deal with both internal conflict and external stress, through containing these, and growing through them and by means of them. It is thus demonstrated in the capacity, as Freud put it, to both love and work effectively, in the widest senses of these terms, and this would I think include all that Peters wants to safeguard within education itself.

Second, to love and work effectively implies the capacity of the individual to come to terms with social demands in a way which means he is not simply a conforming victim of social pressures but can make his own distinctive contribution to society however small. Implicit in these newer conceptions is the idea of human beings as persons, each enjoying some degree of autonomy, an autonomy expressed in terms of internal integration and limited by the similar autonomy of others. The relative nature of this conception of mental health is obvious, but we are by no means lacking in practical criteria by which we may say that persons enjoy good or poor mental health!

What about our conceptions of education? I also see the roles of educator and therapist as distinct and as conditioned by their different settings and skills, but I also see them as closely related and as needing to influence one another. To have a clear conception of each it is necessary to have an understanding of what they have in common as well as of what makes them different. It is the communality with which I am here concerned. Foremost among the things they have in common is a concern for the effective functioning of human beings as persons in a civilized community. To be concerned with this as educators is not, in my view, to subscribe uncritically to what is often pejoratively labelled (particularly now in the USA) as 'soft pedagogy'. On the contrary it demands an understanding of both the delicacy and complexity, *and* of the robustness and simplicity of human functioning, and an understanding of the intimate relations between emotional and intellectual growth and between the personal and the impersonal aspects of experience. Moreover such understanding has to issue in procedures which take account of stabilities and instabilities, of weaknesses and strengths, and of the conditions for, and implications of, success and failure in learning. The essential common task of educator and therapist is one I think we may define as promoting both personal and social well-being and such well-being is at present impossible for most people in our kind of society without achievements in the sphere of both love and work.

We may conclude then by asserting that educators and mental health workers have vital interests in common in nourishing stability in the young and in making possible genuine personal achievements. But to do this teachers must often be concerned to reduce and if possible eliminate sources of unnecessary conflict in the lives of children and young people. To talk of 'unnecessary' conflicts is of course to beg a number of very large and important questions, but examples of what I mean are easily found. To demand of children the successful accomplishment of tasks which are quite beyond them in terms of their experience, resources and situation at any given time is to subject them to quite unnecessary and often highly damaging conflicts. And our educational institutions continually make such demands on very large numbers of children.

Yet more is required of teachers than the reduction of unnecessary conflicts and tensions and in attempting to do this, what is crucial is the quality of their relationships with their pupils. The notion of discipline, so dear to the heart of teachers, is one which at once enshrines and obscures the essential character of productive relations between teachers and taught. The discipline which matters is one which is directed towards the growth of internal controls in the young, which will sustain them in conflicts of feeling, while not demanding crippling sacrifices in the expression of natural desires, interests and talents.

How can this be done effectively within institutions which are based on quite other notions of discipline? Clearly, only by a significant change in the whole *ethos* and *eidos* of most schools. Since such changes can only be brought about by teachers themselves, it is clear that the task is essentially one which lies within the education and re-education of teachers. It is, of course, an immense task. How could it be otherwise? But to gain a wider acceptance of the way in which concepts of personal well-being can enrich our view of education, and so enable education to play a fuller part in promoting a healthier, more humane and more creatively fulfilling society, would be in itself an important advance. I see no reason for despair. In sombre moments one sometimes entertains Samuel Beckett's wry comment that 'life is a syndrome which admits of no palliation', but despite its kernel of seeming wisdom, one knows this to be untrue. One has only to visit some of the pioneering schools within our state system and participate with the children in their activities to know that not only is a great deal of palliation possible, but to feel that one essential clue to the redemption of much of human life lies here. I therefore prefer Edwin Muir's vision (1960) to Samuel Beckett's.

One foot in Eden still, I stand
And look across the other land.
The world's great day is growing late,
Yet strange these fields that we have planted
So long with crops of love and hate.
Time's handiworks by time are haunted,
And nothing now can separate
The corn and tares compactly grown.
The armorial weed in stillness bound
About the stalk; these are our own.
Evil and good stand thick around
In the fields of charity and sin
Where we shall lead our harvest in.
Yet still from Eden springs the root
As clean as on the starting day.

Yet this important truth is still only a partial one. Since education must always be a transaction between the generations, there is never a wholly fresh start. Muir continues:

> Time takes the foliage and the fruit
> And burns the archtypal leaf
> To shapes of terror and of grief
> Scattered along the winter way.

But not necessarily. The transaction between the generations need not wholly cancel out the fresh start. We are gradually coming to understand the intricacies of developmental processes and also the subtleties of those human relationships which lie at the heart of the educational enterprise. Such increased understanding should in time do much to render otiose current border-zone disputes between educators and workers in the mental health professions.

This is a shortened and amended version of a paper read before the Royal Medico-Psychological Association (Psycho-therapy section), London, 1968.

References

Bantock, G. H. (1967) *Education, Culture and the Emotions.* Faber.
Muir, Edwin (1960) *Collected Poems.* Faber & Faber.
Peters, R. S. (1959) *Authority, Responsibility and Education.* Allen & Unwin, p. 95.
Peters, R. S. (1964) 'Mental health as an educational aim' in *Studies in Philosophy and Education*, vol. 3, no. 2, p. 197.
Wall, W. D. (1955) *Education and Mental Health.* UNESCO.
Wall, W. D. (1959) *Child of our Times.* Convocation lecture, National Children's Home.
Wilson, John (1968) *Education and the Concept of Mental Health.* Routledge & Kegan Paul.

Eleven

The revolt of youth[1]

Protest and social change

Future historians of Western education may eventually label the second half of the twentieth century as the era of the revolt of youth. How appropriate would such a description be? How far should the changes in behaviour patterns of young people be construed as something essentially pertaining to a particular age group? Would it not be more in accordance with all the facts to see youthful protest as a symptom of far reaching changes in the nature of society? Should we perhaps see at least some aspects of the world of modern youth as a harbinger of a new culture, one in conflict over many issues of value with the still dominant older culture, and one actually demanding a transformation of education in line with its emergent values?

Certainly there now exists a crisis of confidence in the educational systems of the Western world. In many countries there is at least some degree of conflict between a notable proportion of youth and the educational system—in some countries the conflict has become very severe indeed, and is marked by protests and disturbances, sometimes violent, by the young, and by authoritarian, repressive and in some cases brutal responses on the part of their elders. Moreover, as well as causing their elders trouble within educational institutions, youth is also in conflict with adult society over a wide front, over appearance, dress, sex, drugs, amusements, attitudes to work, politics and social values generally. It is clear that the ultimate sources of current conflicts lie beyond the bounds of educational systems, i.e. they arise from the nature of modern societies themselves (Wall, 1968), but it is clear also that these systems contribute significantly to the crisis because of their failure to adapt to social change.

Is it legitimate to generalize about a whole age group irrespective, for example, of class, and to some extent irrespective of nationality or culture? Many commentators assume that it is, for example Hawkins (1970).

> It is possible and desirable to discern a distinctive youth sub-culture, capable of encompassing disparate groups, some openly in conflict with others but sharing several basic characteristics. First there is a sense of overall identity with other young people; secondly, a sense of confrontation—at times of conflict—with the older generations; thirdly, an avidity for new experience; fourthly, an attitude of intransigence and inflexibility; and finally involvement in specific art forms.

In considering what may be done about youth in conflict with society it is natural for many people to look to education and educational institutions for help. I suspect that for the most part this takes the implicit form of saying in effect, 'Help us to find some means of enabling the youth of today to adjust to society—to adjust to life, to social demands and to social reality.' Perhaps I should make it clear, that I have little sympathy with this point of view. It is of course a natural and understandable response from an older generation which has failed to understand the significance of the revolt of youth. And this failure to understand is part of the larger failure to create a society in which youth can feel at home. Clearly, however, blaming the elders will not help matters, for we ourselves have been caught up in conflict, in change, and in crises, which by and large we have had little chance of understanding, and where we have understood, have been virtually powerless to act. Nevertheless it is necessary to take issue sharply with those who want to help the young to 'adjust'. Adjust to what? Is it proposed that we should help them to adjust to the miseries and injustices which exist in the world, to hunger and poverty in the midst of plenty, to race conflict, to the 'participation' of the great powers in wars like those in Nigeria, the Middle East and Vietnam? Are we to ask them to adjust to a world which has become potentially genocidal, whether in terms of atomic or biological warfare, or simply from a total pollution of the environment?

Conflict of values with the adult world however goes further than current issues concerning the major evils of the times and extends to the adult vision of 'the good life'. Some not uncharacteristic youthful criticism tends to run like this. Within our so-called affluent societies there are obvious trends towards what is perhaps best described as an increasing 'embourgeoisment'. This is a trend towards what is conceived of as a nice comfortable state of society epitomized by a white collar job, a house in suburbia, a car, a television and a spouse and two children. While the desirability of such trends themselves is arguable, they have also to be seen in both the national and international contexts which make them at present realizable aims for only a very small section of mankind. Moreover, the criticism runs on to say that those who realize these aims, of a comparatively *dolce vita*, do so at the price of their moral and spiritual freedom, that they are in fact, the passive and 'adjusted' captives of the modern state, the great industrial empires and the military blocs. The very facelessness and impersonality of these latter bureaucratic structures is also seen as rendering them impervious to reasoned criticism. This in itself is an incitement to radical and perhaps violent action. Moreover to counter disaffection these leviathans may tend to use their power and the power of the mass media, which they can influence, to manipulate the values and aspirations of the people of the world towards the preservation of the *status quo*.[2]

The general nature of the charges hurled by the radical sections of modern youth against society as a whole tend to reappear again in the criticisms made of educational institutions in the West.[3] These, because of the general expansion of educational provision, tend to become larger and larger. Individuals tend to be lost sight of. What is learned and how it is to be learned are laid down from above. Moreover the prescriptions offered are commonly felt to have little relevance to life, as even the majority of educated people know it today. Much of education, particularly at the secondary stage, appears to be conceived in terms of the 'rat race', the survival of the academically 'fittest', on whom adult society will later bestow its rewards in return for adherence to the *status quo*. Moreover a benign paternalism and chaperonage by institutions is substituted for parental care, in order that the adult world's professed moral values may be preserved, at least in appearances. One consequence is that youth tends to reject the conception of *in loco parentis* which still tends to dominate higher educational systems and to reject, too, a narrowly conceived and purely intellectual education. There is a call for reform and for participation by youth in shaping those aspects of their lives which most closely concern them and this includes both curricula of educational institutions and rules of life. While many of the criticisms do tend to be overstated there can be little doubt that there is a case to be heard. Indeed, contrasting the spectacle of widespread human misery with the direction in which the powerful and wealthy Western societies seem to be moving, may in some of us encourage the thought that in these circumstances perhaps we all ought to be either activist protesters or drop-outs. Certainly the contrast prompts the question: 'Who is sick—the protesting young, or the social order against which they are protesting?'

But just as it does not help to castigate the elders, neither is it sensible to glorify and worship youth as if they were the saviours of mankind. The revolt of youth in all its manifestations is not something wholly to be approved of. Clearly, of course, some of their arguments and their ideals are naive, but this is surely to be expected. These confrontations with youth are properly part, and an important part, of their and our education. But what is serious is that there are certainly within the youthful protest movements some highly destructive elements—severely psychologically disturbed young people who get on the band-wagon of any movement and may easily find themselves in leadership positions. They are of course matched by the severely psychologically disturbed adults who feel outraged and rigidly oppose them, those whose immaturities and insecurities make them take refuge in 'law and order' battle cries and reactionary and repressive attitudes. These are among the basic truths about all revolutions—necessary reforms, and the opposition to them, become the vehicles for the destructive behaviour of the severely disturbed.

Can social change come about in any other way? To think that it cannot, is surely a gospel of despair and one which ignores our increasing insight into the dynamics of social systems. What is true however is that those in authority, in educational institutions particularly, often have a desperately difficult task in promoting necessary reforms while preventing violence and destruction. The separation of destructive elements among youth and elders from well-intentioned radicals and moderate reformists is never easy. Obviously there is still a great deal which is worth while preserving in modern societies and their educational institutions and which could be the basis for further advance. We must then strive to find some way of preserving what is worth while, and yet help young people who are eager to improve the state of the world and who are eager for a say in things to find useful and workable means of realizing their aims. And this remains true even when it is realized that the issues chosen as battle-grounds by youth may not be the crucial issues at all, but may be functioning as symptoms of more deeply seated troubles. Indeed to understand the revolt of youth at all, it is necessary to see many of the details of their behaviour as quite patently symbolic, even if at times the exact meaning of the symbolism may be hard to grasp. Put another way, the protests of the young must be seen, in part, as symptomatic of social disease. Our problem is to attempt to understand the conditions which give rise to the symptoms.[4]

To look at the matter in this way implies as a major pre-supposition that the so-called revolt of youth is incomprehensible except in the context of the problems of particular societies each taken as a whole, and in the context too of a world of peoples with divergent needs and at very different stages of development. It is part of this context that governments seem incapable of acting in accordance with the long evident fact that the welfare of any particular human group is now intimately bound up with the welfare of all. As a species, man is rent by internal strife, strife increasingly marked by racial intolerances and focused on issues of privilege and deprivation. Within developed industrial societies the breakdown of the old order is symbolized by the occurrence of a group of apparently unrelated phenomena, which nevertheless may be complexly inter-related. For example and to name but a few of the more significant items, there is a narrowing of the scope of political freedom, a decrease in genuine participation in social process, a heavy emphasis on sexual 'freedom', all alongside widespread apparently meaningless violence, a vast growth in bureaucratic control, and a significant increase in the arbitrary exercise of power by those in authority. The context of these phenomena is the priority accorded to technological achievement over human feeling, to competitive practices and ideologies over co-operative ones, and to activity and 'busy-ness' over reflection and meditation.

The widespread conflicts within and between societies do however reveal constructive developments as well as destructive ones. There are now those, particularly in the USA, who see definite evidence of the emergence of a 'new' or 'counter' culture which seeks to operate on different principles and values from the old (Slater, 1970; Reich, 1970; Roszak, 1970) and there are those who seek to identify the 'new' with 'youth'. This is clearly a mistake, however, for while the divisions over essential issues of value may show a preponderance of younger over older people in favour of the new, not all young people think and feel in this way by any means, and there is a not inconsiderable number of older people whose allegiance is on many matters with the new culture.

Moreover it is also a mistake to suppose that the new culture offers solutions to all problems or that there are not severe conflicts within it. In his penetrating and enlightening study of the USA today, Slater for example points out (1970, pp. 103–4) a basic schism in the ranks of the new culture.

> The core of the old culture is scarcity ... The key flaw in the old culture is of course, the fact that the scarcity is spurious, man made in the case of bodily gratifications and man-allowed or man-maintained in the case of material goods ... The new culture is based on the assumption that important human needs are easily satisfied and that the resources for doing so are

> plentiful. Competition is unnecessary and the only dangers to humans is human aggression ... that a certain amount of work is required to release the bounty that exists from the restraints under which it is now placed. Whereas the flaw in the old culture has caused it to begin to decompose, the flaw in new culture has produced a profound schism in its ranks—a schism between activist and drop-out approaches to the culture as it now exists.

With these considerations as background the full complexities of the issues begin to appear.[5] While however it is clearly a mistake to see the revolt of youth as a single phenomenon on its own, it is equally mistaken to suppose that youth does not have, and does not see itself as having, a distinct and important role to play in the transformation of world culture. Too much or too little may be made of the different perspectives of younger and older people today, and the term 'generation gap' may in certain ways be misleading. But that there is a unique and important difference in kind, not just in degree, between the perspective of successive generations now and in the recent past, is ably argued by Margaret Mead in her study, *Culture and Commitment*. She categorizes cultures as 'post-figurative' (characterized by well-known forebears); 'co-figurative' (characterized by familiar peers) and 'pre-figurative' (characterized by unknown children). Her basic point is that no one now over the age of forty has any experience of what it is like to be young in the electronic age, with all its technological and social implications. This is why an unprecedented generation gap must be acknowledged by old and young alike before communication can begin. It is not necessary to agree entirely with Mead's approach or arguments to accept the point that social well-being depends on the development of an adequate dialogue between the generations. For education this is absolutely crucial. For the adults it would seem essential also to have some grasp of the salient biological and social context of growing up today, in order to understand why the events which often agitate them are taking place just now.

The new context of growing up

This is a very complex matter indeed but it seems possible to point to a number of major bio-social conditions which would appear to be relevant. They may perhaps be summarized as follows:

1. The extension of educational opportunity into adolescence for the majority of youth in industrialized societies, and the conse-

quential prolongation of their social childhood far beyond puberty, is a new phenomenon with which as yet educators have failed to come to terms (Gorer, 1961). It is particularly noticeable at secondary level in both the UK and USA and now at college level in the USA Hawkins (1970) comments:

> As society becomes more complex and the development of skills and techniques require young people to remain longer in tutelage, puberty is reached well before they can become full members of adult society. This produces characteristically the rumbustious apprentice of guild society, the youth between sixteen and twenty-three, of whom Shakespeare wrote, 'There is nothing in the between but getting wenches with child, wronging the ancientry, stealing, fighting' (*Winter's Tale*, III. iii). This is the gap that pop culture tries to fill—and its mission is serious and important. But youth is serious also in another sense and is rapidly becoming politicized.

2. The educational movement to prolong schooling has been accompanied, and its dissonant effects reinforced, by a striking tendency for the time of adolescence to become earlier—the secular trend towards earlier maturity—as manifested by the increase in body size in relation to age and (in Western Europe) the steady decline in the age of girls at menarche (Tanner, 1961).

3. Widespread changes have occurred in patterns of child-rearing—in the general but vague direction of what is called permissiveness, without the pubertal and post-pubertal consequences having been understood and provided for (Newsom, 1965). It may also be the case that disturbances due to wars, migrations, separations, divorces, and work patterns involving mothers of young children, have undermined the family's function as a psychological security system on a larger scale than ever before, producing more fundamentally disturbed individuals only too ready to be drawn into and to catalyse situations which always contain both constructive and destructive possibilities. This speculation may be considered a legitimate extension to the family as a whole of the work of Bowlby and others on maternal care (Bowlby, 1952).

4. The inclusion of an increasing proportion of children from lower-middle-class and working-class families in the higher reaches of educational systems, which were originally evolved to meet the needs of upper- and upper-middle-class families, produces conflicts of aims and values which in the short term can be highly destructive in their effect (Jackson & Marsden, 1966).

5. Increasing dissonance between interlocking biological and social patterns of development, coupled with the sheer complexity

of modern societies, tends to produce an intolerable postponement of those initiations into adult life which lie at the root of effective human personal identity in modern societies, notably in the spheres of sexual and productive service roles, i.e. Freud's 'love and work'.* Moreover the tensions and dissatisfactions found in much family life and marriage, together with marked changes within adult society regarding sexual *mores*, have also helped to draw young people in an active way into the so-called sexual revolution.

6. Beyond the struggle to achieve adulthood, particularly in the sphere of sexuality, lurks what may be a more ultimate threat. What use, in fact, do our modern technological societies have for the young, after their prolonged tutelage? Might it be that not only many of the roles offered, the young reject, but that there is a growing suspicion that there are no real roles for them at all? Bettelheim (1969) believes this to be the case. 'I refer to their feeling that "youth has no future", because modern technology has made them obsolete and that they have become socially irrelevant and, as persons insignificant ... If a young man does not feel it is he who will be building the future, and is genuinely needed to bring it about, then the feeling is that he has none.' And again quoting Jerry Rubin, the yippie organizer: 'Who the hell wants to "make it" in America any more? The American economy no longer needs young whites and blacks. We are waste material. We fulfil our destiny in life by rejecting a system which rejects us.' Certainly in the case of college youth there is a growing sense of aimlessness and alienation. Among Harvard seniors one in five do not know what they are going to do (Todd, 1970).

All these conditions help to produce a prolonged period of confusion and doubt for young people, doubt about who they are, and about what they are for, that is, about personal identity in Erikson's sense (1968). Erikson's own conception of the psychosocial moratorium which he thinks modern youth requires before being able to embrace adult identity, valuable as it is, may turn out to be based on an insufficiently radical diagnosis of the modern dilemma. The necessary moratorium may turn out to be very long indeed for some sections of youth. For them, faced with old

* 'Freud was once asked what he thought a normal person should be able to do well. The questioner probably expected a complicated "deep" answer. But Freud simply said, "*Lieben und arbeiten*" ("to love and to work"). It pays to ponder on this simple formula; it grows deeper as you think about it. For when Freud said "love" he meant the generosity of intimacy as well as genital love; when he said love and work, he meant a general work productiveness which would not preoccupy the individual to the extent that he might lose his right or capacity to be a sexual and a loving being' (E. H. Erikson, 1968).

culture identities which have lost their appeal, and a new culture which does not provide ready-made identities, the result may well be a profound loss of a sense of personal identity which has to be compensated for by a massive emphasis on the importance of the 'group', and the 'commune' and the 'underground' or alternative society.

Youthful solidarity certainly seems to be in part an attempt to counterbalance this sense of loss of identity. A character in a student novel about the Harvard uprising of the spring of 1969 (Todd, 1970) says:

> What was most euphoric, however, was us, and what we were to each other. For these few hours we *were* brothers and sisters. We did reach out and hold onto each other. You could be flip about it. 'I haven't seen so many of my friends together in two years,' one girl said. But you had to realize whatever your politics and whatever your tactics—that we were very beautiful in University Hall, we were very human and we were very together....

This solidarity is also expressed in a specific rejection of the declared and ostensible adult value systems surrounding sex and love and also work and social ambitions. If there is a single target for the hostility of youth, apart from adult authority itself and hence the 'system' as a whole, it might be said to be the particular interpretation which our Western societies, under the influence of capitalism and of some aspects of Christian tradition (more particularly the Puritan tradition), have put upon the nature of sexuality and love and upon work and its relation to social functioning. In fact important sections of youth have openly rejected prolonged postponement of adult sex satisfaction and are producing their own patterns and moral codes, which however are themselves by no means free from conflict and distress.* Similarly, attitudes to work, to earning a living and to the owning of personal property have undergone significant changes.

Faced with the phenomena of the revolt of youth in the context of vast technological and social changes, can one reasonably expect educational systems to adapt sufficiently fully and sufficiently quickly to the new situations? These systems originated under

* Youthful sexuality has of course always existed, in some degree and in some form or another, but in modern societies it has until recently been forced underground, and 'respectable' parents and teachers have tended to act as if it didn't exist. Nowhere was this attitude so clearly marked as in single-sex schools, particularly but not only in boarding schools, in England.

A useful study of the contemporary scene is given by Schofield (1968).

totally different conditions from those which now obtain, and are largely staffed by people who were young in a wholly different age. The transformation required is momentous. Some things seem cardinal. What is permanently valuable in the old culture must be preserved or technological civilization and the tradition of rationality itself may disappear. But can it be preserved in a form which guarantees the necessary flexibility of mind demanded by continually changing social needs? Can scope be found for the claims of the life of feeling without diminishing the quality of intellectual effort? Can schools as institutions so transform themselves that they offer not only an appropriately protective environment but meaningful social roles as well? Can teachers as a profession so alter their attitudes to their task and to the young that what they offer is dialogue and partnership instead of instruction and tutelage? The changes suggested here are in general of the kind which pioneer schools today and in the recent past have tried to offer (Neill, 1915, 1962), but from now on a leavening of pioneer schools, valuable as these will always be, simply will not meet the case. The majority of schools and the publicly maintained educational systems of our modern societies now have to face the challenge of radical change.

Towards a transformation of education[6]

What potentialities exist in our educational systems for changes of a sufficiently radical character to measure up to the challenge of evident present ills and to the protests of youth? It would be folly to be sanguine despite the signs that an educational revolution is afoot, and that a new culture, that of post-industrial society, is coming into being. There are huge resistances to change in all societies and a built-in slowness of response to innovation seems to be part of the very nature of the educational enterprise as we have hitherto known it. The traditional view of education as the transmission of knowledge, or of the heritage of ideas, skills and values, with its necessary interpretation of the teaching–learning relationship as one of dominance–submission, still maintains its sway, despite considerable modification. A newer view of education as a meaningful transaction between the generations through which society is changed and redefined, implying a teaching–learning relationship of partnership and discovery, is only slowly gaining ground (Morris, 1966, 1967). Yet as knowledge grows, and the burden of memorization and reproduction of pre-digested information swells, the untenability of the older conception becomes ever more visible. Even enlightened teaching of intellectual discipline cannot redeem it.

Accompanying the increasing weight of knowledge and the lengthening of formal education is an adherence to examination systems which embody the older conceptions of education, perpetuate the rigid orthodox classification of persons by 'intellectual' criteria (increasingly mistrusted by youth as valid only for the self-fulfilling criteria of the academics) and which glorify ordeal by memorization or intellectual productivity within narrow time limits. Again, only slowly are newer conceptions of the assessment of human talents gaining ground (Morris, 1964). Methods of learning and teaching are of course profoundly affected by conceptions of educational objectives and the nature of the tests used to assess these. As a consequence of the considerations advanced above, learning situations are still rarely structured in terms of the ascertainable needs of individuals and groups, although there are many hopeful signs and innovations. See for example Anderson (1966); Kaye & Rogers (1968); Lovell (1967); Richmond (1967); Taylor (1971). Even so, the implications of the pioneer work to be found in some primary schools in England and of recent general ideas on learning, particularly those of Piaget and Vygotsky as developed by Bruner (1966), have not been fully worked out in relation to the educational provision for youth as a whole, and their effects on this stage of education are therefore at present small.

Moreover much of this work emphasizes almost exclusively the cognitive aspects of learning. Unless these are integrated within a motivational context which relates directly to young people's interests and aspirations and hence can capture their imaginations, they will remain powerless to produce profound changes in achievements and attitudes. It is here that the relevance of the current revolution in a section of primary schools in England may be of cardinal significance. In the best of these schools, the whole ethos is being changed (Plowden, 1967). A new way of life is developing in which the traditionally tightly structured institution with its rigidly separate classrooms, grades and groupings, and its equally rigid classification and separation of subjects and activities, is giving way to a more flexible kind of structure in which all the resources within the school and in its environment can be utilized in an attempt to base learning on intrinsic interests (Marsh, 1970; Razzell, 1968). This represents a reliance on ego-based activities, rather than on superego ones.

Doubtless the particular devices employed would need to be altered for adaptation to the secondary and college level and, as young people developed into Piaget's formal reasoning stage, more *explicit* use of 'structure' in learning situations in Bruner's sense would be required. There is plenty of 'structure' of course in the good pioneer primary school, but it is largely implicit as far as the pupils are concerned, as it should be.

Given these modifications, what would be critical would be a change in *ethos* at the secondary and tertiary levels corresponding to the change taking place in the primary. It is to such a change that we should look for a new basis for education in personal relationships and the development of creative attitudes to work. At present the majority of schools and colleges are still dominated by the assumption that children and young people do not have sufficient capacity for self-direction to be trusted to work out educational programmes and life patterns in genuine collaboration with their elders. Instead, the elders tend to believe unquestioningly (in terms of their behaviour) in the need to subject the young to an almost *wholly* external authority and discipline, until the time comes for them to have developed (by magic, presumably) the necessary degree of self-discipline. Unfortunately this time does not appear to come until they have left the educational system ... they are *never quite ready* for freedom and responsibility ... just like colonies and subject nations at a political level.[7] It is time that this self-fulfilling and self-perpetuating system of ideas was given a very thorough analysis, and the built-in feed-back systems exposed along with the unconscious attitudes which they mirror. All these factors contribute to the feelings of irrelevance which many educational procedures induce in a fair proportion of adolescents. If large numbers of young people still conform, this may be less a testimony to their good judgment than to their lack of initiative. This feeling of irrelevance is accentuated by the nature of the academic and vocational choices which appear to be open to them. Moreover, the increasing irreversibility of these decisions and therefore their apparent fatefulness are apt to exercise an oppressive effect.

It is notable in large schools particularly, which are apt of course to be hierarchical in structure, that not only pupils but junior staff also tend to be treated as though not worthy of trust or initiative. Yet liberalizing tendencies do exist, and within the system of maintained schools new approaches to the problem of changing a school as a whole are being tried (Richardson, 1967, 1971). The conception of trying to bring about changes in the very nature of the school itself has of course been at the heart of the progressive independent school movement ever since John Dewey pioneered this conception in Chicago at the turn of the last century (1899). And we might go back further still. One question insistently raised by these reflections is whether indeed schooling as we know it, which is still having to be fought for as a basic human right all over the world, may not have outlived its usefulness. There already exists a movement for 'non-schools' (Robertson, 1968). What sorts of places would these be?*

A modern infant or primary school in England staffed by teachers who *believe* in this educational way of life (Lunn, 1970) points the way forward. The work of James (1968) and even more fundamentally of the Nuffield 'Resources for Learning' project (Taylor, 1971) give promising leads at the secondary level, but the changes required are more fundamental here than in the primary school and the problems of and resistance to change very much higher (Hannam, Smyth & Stephenson, 1971). Youth needs opportunities to discover its powers through meaningful and socially productive activities and within a relationship of partnership with adults. One of the basic changes necessary is to modify the use of education as simply a social classifying device based almost entirely on intellectual talent. This means that a wide range of relevant human talents and individual gifts are ignored. At present even those with well-developed intellectual interests are becoming disenchanted. They are coming to regard education as they know it as merely a sort of academic game; that is, as an activity which is fundamentally irrelevant to the realities of living.† It is in these circumstances that the demand for partnership and for a partnership which will bring about changes is being made. While many of the more extreme elements among youth appear virtually to be asking the adults to abdicate their responsibilities, in fact this is often coupled with quite obvious dependence on the adult community. The more thoughtful and the more mature among youth do not wish for abdication on the part of adults; what they want is a genuine

* A fascinating pupils'-eye view of the current situation and of desirable change is given by Blishen (1966). One fifteen-year-old girl said: 'Schools usually have one thing in common—they are institutions of today, run on the principles of yesterday.' See also n. 6, p. 179.

† A 'game', in its traditional sense, is not merely a contest in which the rules can be spelled out, but one in which the deepest and most important aspects of oneself and others are either not involved, or are denied expression. It is symptomatic of our times that inter-personal relationships (and in particular sexual relationships; see chapter 12) are now often treated in this way (Berne, 1968), and that 'war games' have become an intellectual pursuit for some people. Conversely, many pastimes and sports, hitherto treated as 'games', have now become so professionalized that the name is no longer appropriate in its original sense. Aspects of life which were once treated as vital and serious, like the affections (love and hate), are now trivialized (i.e. the deeper implications of sex and aggression are denied), while what were formerly playful activities have become deadly serious. Such trends, of course, have always existed, as witness such phrases as 'the game of love' and 'jousting with death'.

partnership. This however argues a basic re-orientation of our relationships in education, and from the very beginning. Erikson (1963) has made the point brilliantly and memorably: 'in our time man must decide whether he can afford to continue the exploitation of childhood as an arsenal of irrational fears, or whether the relationship of adult and child, like other inequalities, can be raised to a position of *partnership in a more reasonable order of things.*'

Although the young are not clear what to substitute in detail for what they reject, they are at least clear in asserting their right to be treated as responsible beings, in asserting the claims of the feeling life as of equal value to those of abstract intellect, and in asserting the need to 'be' as well as the need to 'do'. In much of what is obviously important and useful protest there is also, however, an implicit calling in question of the very presuppositions of the kind of abstract thought on which modern science and technology and therefore modern societies depend, and which has also apparently led to the creation of an impersonal genocidal world in which people are reduced to computerizable data or to functions interchangeable at will by remote *fiats.* The dangers of a flight from such a menacing and insane social order into an equally irrational abandonment of reason and abstract thought are inherent in such an attitude, but the questioning itself is crucial and is wholly justified.[8]

How can schools and educational systems generally be made more relevant to the needs of modern youth in respect of human values and of a worth-while future life? If major changes have to be made, what sorts of problems does this involve for us as adults, in particular for those of us who are teachers and parents? We have, I think, to face a number of rather serious questions, and those of us concerned with teacher education are no less involved than those who carry the primary burdens in the schools.

1. How are we going to allay anxieties about children's 'progress', traditionally conceived of in terms of measurable achievement in traditional skills and knowledge, while educational practices focus more and more on processes of development over the whole range of human activities?

2. How are we going to meet the growing and increasingly vocal and active hostility of those sections of society who are either hostile to 'education', or who have no fundamental understanding of its nature? (although they may be making their living out of it!).

3. How are we going to deal with our own insistent impulses to direct, control and manipulate others, i.e. our need to make the young obey us and *our* rules at all costs? Such impulses seem to be part of the irrational belief that we adults have found the answers to the major problems of life! Is it not time that we stopped taking

refuge from the truth about our own impulses in the belief that since we are older, we are necessarily wiser?

4. How are we going to deal with our own sexual jealousy of the current freedom of the young? What kind of personal and sexual education can we give in view of fairly widespread adult failures in love and marriage and of our conflicts about the relationship between sex and love, particularly in a world in which contraceptives are becoming increasingly freely available?

5. How are we going to deal with our own anxiety, guilt and envy about youthful experiments with drugs when we ourselves consume drugs in such large quantities that in fact to a large extent we might be regarded as running our education and welfare services off the profits of the drug industries?

6. In face of the massive tendency to conformity of institutions and in particular of the school, can we discover ways in which we might make the school something other than what it is rapidly becoming—an institution which exists for its own sake rather than for the sake of the growth of persons?

This last question is crucial, but it is not the end of the matter. Obviously changes in the school, in the direction of making it a place more suited to the growth of young people towards participation in a more fully human community, will by no means solve all the problems of youth or of society. Nor can such changes be brought about on any large scale merely by acting within the school system itself. The school is part of and is an instrument of society, and therefore society at large not only shapes but has an inescapable responsibility towards the purposes which schools seek to fulfil. It is for this reason of course that, at this level, educational issues necessarily become political issues. We are concerned with the basic conditions of human life.

One of the main effects of modern communication systems is to ensure that the basic conditions of human life everywhere are more readily grasped by more and more people. Among the results appears to be an increased knowledge of human deprivation, inequality and misery, and a clearer grasp by youth of the seamier and more destructive sides of so-called civilized life, often previously obscured by hypocritical conventions. While continued exposure to evil, human misery, brutality, selfishness and inefficiency may tend to produce a callousness or somewhat helpless indifference, there seems also to be an increasing awareness that things need not be as they are—they could be changed, different and possibly better. The net result of the *élan* of youth and of the problems and the temper of the times is apt to create impossible demands for instant change. This sometimes takes the form of demanding paradise now.* However, the irrationality of this demand is apt to be matched by the irrationality of some of the elders who deny the possibility of a better world. Faced with this situation, responsible adults need to ask less about the problems of youth, and more about how they themselves can sufficiently alter their perspectives to be capable of working alongside youth—in educational institutions and elsewhere—to create a better world, one more fitted to realize human creative potentialities.

To hope and work for such an end is not necessarily to be misled by unrealistic dreams of the perfectibility of man. Rather it is to hope that if men and women can come to understand themselves more fully, and begin to act on that understanding, their powers of love and reason may yet hold in check their powers of hate and unreason. Indeed, in the long run this is the only hope there is that man may come to act more constructively as an agent of his own destiny. The alternative is likely to be the final silence.

Notes

1 I once referred to 'the revolt of youth' as the 'inkblot of the world', meaning, that it is a series of ambiguous events on to which we all project our own preconceptions.
2 There are a number of variants of this analysis of 'bourgeois ideology'. See Blackburn (1969).
3 For a sympathetic and perceptive philosophical discussion of student criticism in relation to authority, see Reddiford (1971).
4 For two extremely valuable analyses, see Curle (1971) on the 1969 troubles at Harvard and Silver (1969) on the crisis at Columbia in 1968.
5 See also Keniston (1965, 1968) and Morse (1965).

* This is the title of a brilliant, provocative and acutely argued article by Passmore (1970), concerning neo-mystical and perfectibilistic cults. While being in basic agreement with much of his analysis, although by no means all of his evaluative judgments, I feel that the article is unbalanced in two ways. It is over-concerned with an evaluative diagnosis and therefore fails to reveal sufficiently clearly those features of modern societies which form the soil on which such cults grow. It does not therefore provide much positive guidance to those who work for the reform of society. Moreover, it is unfair to some of the new movements in not sufficiently appreciating the positive and necessary role of the *non-rational* (as distinct from the irrational) element in human life. To take but one example, it makes no mention of those movements which advocate and practise the art of meditation and so provide a constructive matrix for the life of many modern people who find orthodox religions uncongenial to them. [*Note.* I have now seen Passmore's book from which the *Encounter* article was taken, and I think that the criticism I have made still stands.]

6 This whole chapter was written before the extreme radical trends in education in the Americas crystallized into a 'movement' and adopted in the name of 'de-schooling'. Its prophet is Ivan Illich (1971); see also Riemer (1971). The argument of this study and indeed of this whole book is not for 'de-schooling', but for radical transformations in school and society. (See also Curle, *Education for Liberation*).
In this immense task, new conceptions of institutions, systems and their administration will need to be developed. See Baron and Taylor (1969).
7 The idea of children and young people as a subject social group, aspiring to freedom, has recently been elaborated in France by Mendel (1971).
8 A balanced interpretation of the positive and negative aspects of the revolt of youth and of the counter-culture is extremely difficult to achieve. Even the judgments of the most respected commentators sometimes seem to lack vision. See for example Riesman (1969).

References

Anderson, R. H. (1966) *Teaching in a World of Change.* Harcourt Brace.
Baron, G. and Taylor, W. (1969) *Educational Administration and the Social Sciences.* Athlone.
Berne, E. (1968) *Games People Play.* Penguin.
Bettelheim, Bruno (1969) 'Obsolete Youth'. *Encounter,* September 1969.
Blackburn, H. (1969) 'A brief guide to bourgeois ideology' in Cockburn and Blackburn, *Student Power.* Penguin.
Blishen, Edward (ed.) (1966) *The School that I'd Like.* Penguin.
Bowlby, J. (1952) *Maternal Care and Mental Health.* Geneva (World Health Organization; Monograph Series no. 2, 2nd ed.).
Bruner, J. S. (1966) *Toward a Theory of Instruction.* Harvard University Press.
Curle, Adam (1971) *Making Peace.* Tavistock.
Curle, Adam (to be published) 'Education for Liberation'.
Dewey, J. (1899) *The School and Society.* University of Chicago Press. (The Laboratory School was founded in 1896 and Dewey lectured on it three years later.)
Erikson, E. H. (1963) *Childhood and Society.* Norton.
Erikson, E. H. (1968) *Identity, Youth and Crisis.* Faber.
Gorer, G. (1961) in *Teenage Morals.* Councils and Education Press.
Hannam, C., Smyth, P. and Stephenson, N. (1971) *Young Teachers and Reluctant Learners.* Penguin.
Hawkins, J. R. (1970) 'Attitudes of Young People to Society', *Journal* of the Royal Society of Health, May–June 1970.
Illich, Ivan (1971) *De-Schooling Society.* Caldar & Boyars.
Jackson, B. & Marsden, D. (1966) *Education and the Working Class.* Pelican.

James, Charity (1968) *Young Lives at Stake.* Collins.
Kaye, B. & Rogers, I. (1968) *Group Work in Secondary Schools.* Oxford University Press.
Keniston, Kenneth (1965) *The Uncommitted.* Harcourt, Brace & World.
Keniston, Kenneth (1968) *The Young Radicals.* Harcourt, Brace & World.
Lovell, K. (1967) *Team Teaching.* University of Leeds Institute of Education.
Lunn, J. Barker (1970) *Streaming in the Primary School.* National Foundation for Educational Research in England & Wales.
Marsh, Leonard (1970) *Alongside the Child.* Black.
Mead, Margaret (1970) *Culture and Commitment.* Doubleday.
Mendel, G. (1971) *Pour Decoloniser L'Enfant.* Payot, Paris.
Morris, B. S. (1964) 'Examinations as instruments of educational reform', *Bulletin of the Institute of Physics and the Physical Society*, 15, 8.
Morris, B. S. (1966) in Tibble, J. W. (ed.) *The Study of Education.* Routledge & Kegan Paul, pp. 133–79.
Morris, B. S. (1967) in *The Educational Implications of Social and Economic Change.* Schools Council Working Paper no. 12. HMSO.
Morse, Mary (1965) *The Unattached.* Penguin.
Neill, A. S. (1915) *A Dominie's Log.* Jenkins.
Neill, A. S. (1962) *Summerhill.* Gollancz.
Newsom, J. & E. (1965) *Patterns of Infant Care.* Pelican.
Passmore, J. (1970) 'Paradise Now', *Encounter.*
Passmore, J. (1970) *The Perfectibility of Man.* Duckworth.
Plowden, Lady B. (1967) *Children in Their Primary Schools.* HMSO.
Razzell, A. (1968) *Juniors: A Postscript to Plowden.* Penguin.
Reddiford, G. (1971) 'Authority, education and student power', *Ed. Phil, and Theory*, vol. 3, pp. 113–26.
Reich, C. A. (1970) *The Greening of America.* Random House.
Richardson, J. E. (1967a) *Group Study for Teachers.* Routledge & Kegan Paul.
Richardson, J. E. (1967b) *The Environment of Learning,* Nelson.
Richardson, J. E. (to be published) 'The Teacher, the School and the Task of Management'.
Richmond, W. K. (1967) *The Teaching Revolution.* Methuen.
Riemer, Everett (1971) *School is Dead.* Penguin.
Riesman, David (1969) 'The young are captives of each other', *Psychology Today*, October, pp. 28–31, 63–7.
Robertson, S. (1968) 'A serious proposal for setting-up non-schools', *New Era*, vol. 48, no. 3.
Roszak. Theodore (1970) *The Making of a Counter Culture.* Faber.
Sanford, N. (1967) *Where Colleges Fail.* Jossey-Bass.
Schofield, M. (1968) *Sexual Behaviour in Young People.* Penguin.
Silver, Allan (1969) 'Who cares for Columbia?' *New York Review of Books*, 30 January.

Slater, P. (1970) *The Pursuit of Loneliness.* Beacon.
Tanner, J. M. (1961) *Education and Physical Growth.* University of London Press.
Taylor, L. C. (1971) *Resources for Learning.* Penguin.
Todd, R. (1970) 'Voices of Harvard '70', *New York Times* Magazine. 7 June 1970.
Wall, W. D. (1968) *Adolescents in School and Society.* National Foundation for Educational Research.

Twelve

The life and death of Eros

'The varieties of love, like those of error, seem infinite, and not worth classifying.' (Anon.)
'Where love stops, power begins, and violence and terror.' (C. J. Jung, *The Undiscovered Self*, Routledge & Kegan Paul, 1958, pp. 105-6.)

The sexual revolution

An avalanche of publications, films, stage shows, television programmes, advertising material and pop songs has descended on us of recent years, seeking to celebrate, clarify, articulate, justify, condemn and, in general, cash in on the sexual revolution of our time. Amidst the chaos of opinion and the confusions of behaviour, should the educator remain silent and inactive? Wouldn't it be wise to do so, since the revolution involves all of us, and the risks of making asses of ourselves, or of being caught *sans culottes*, are obviously very high? So-called sex education (the very name is question-begging) operates in a kind of no man's (or no woman's) land, between 'simple biology' (is any 'biology' 'simple'?) on the one hand, and highly 'spiritualized' personal relationships on the other. It is a delicate plant, always in danger of being killed off by adult 'do-gooders', adolescent anxiety and/or contempt and peer-group pressures, or of being choked by the surrounding jungle of pornography, advertising, 'frank' magazines, novels, films and stage shows, high-minded treatises and 'how to do it' manuals. Amid the din of controversy over nudity on stage and in films, homosexuality, prostitution, abortion, contraception, venereal disease, pre-marital and extra-marital sex, loveless sex, 'shacking up', marriage, divorce, 'swinging' (partner-swapping), pornographic literature and sex shops, the still, small, good-humoured voices of love and reason can scarcely be heard. They are drowned by the jungle cacophony; the braying of the moralizers and the screams of the 'liberators' mingling in a less than inspired jam session.

To what extent does the sexual revolution represent a genuine change in behaviour patterns, as distinct from being merely a phenomenon of the mass media? In one sense there is nothing new at all. All forms of sexual expression (and repression) are very 'old hat' indeed. But a number of very important things have in fact happened. First, many veils of hypocrisy have been torn aside and the realities of sexual life widely exposed and admitted. Second, while behaviour may have altered less than attitudes, circumstantial evidence suggests that full and frequent sexual experience among the younger age groups (15-21) is now commoner than it was in some social groups.[1] Third, the emancipation of women has really begun, and the 'double standard' of sexual morality, inseparable from male dominance, is beginning to be abandoned. One concomitant has been important changes in marriage patterns, and in attitudes to marriage as an institution (Gorer, 1971a).

There has been, and still is, a good deal of resistance to these changes. The moralizers, however, are certainly on the defensive, and the liberators are celebrating an apparently famous victory. Yet many young and older people alike are caught in a confusion of liberated euphoria and questioning doubt, of casual encounters and subsequent depressions (often disguised by a tough cynical 'line') of romantic exhilaration and eventual disenchantment. No reasonable person could deny that much of the revolution has been entirely beneficial, a clean wind sweeping away needless shams and hypocrisy. Yet it is not unreasonable to wonder whether the very vehemence of the more extreme wing of the revolution, the inverted prudery of its shrill insistence on total freedom and frankness, do not serve to conceal a genuine crisis in potency, a kind of desperation (particularly in urbanized white industrial society), an incapacity for forming relationships other than casual or manipulative or destructive ones, and indeed, *au fond*, a fear and therefore a hatred of sexuality and its deeper implications. Are we hopelessly confused by the subtleties of the relationship between sex, fear and aggression? Are we celebrating the liberation or the death of Eros?

May it not be the case that on the one hand the widespread fear of darker-skinned people (usually a socially exploited or underdeveloped group) and on the other the acknowledged sexual attractiveness of the darker (more 'primitive') group are both, in part at least, manifestations of a feeling of diminished general potency, which is always closely allied to genital potency?* Closely con-

* The existence of the counter-attraction, the appeal to the darker-skinned person of a lighter-skinned sexual partner suggests, of course, that the matter is more complex than this, as indeed it probably is. But it is at least arguable that the lighter-skinned partner is less of a sexually valuable object than a socially valuable one, that such a choice has more of a status basis (unconscious) than an erotic one.[2] The status factor may not be absent from the opposite situation either. Apart from the (presumed) extra sexual potency, to have a darker-skinned partner may serve as a symbol of 'unconventionality' and 'broadmindedness'. None of these considerations of course means that there may not be genuine individual attraction as well.

nected also with the sexual revolution are the unisex and the women's liberation movements. While the freedom of appearance and dress among the young, and the sexual similarity, is often very appealing and has much to commend it, may we not also detect here a subtle over-compensation for former highly artificial and over-emphasized sex differences? Do we not always face a major difficulty in at one and the same time acknowledging difference *and* equality? If so, similarity represents an obviously safe compromise.[3] Be it noted, however, that it is usually boys who make themselves look like girls rather than, on the whole, the other way round. On the part of both, however, it is a gesture of comradeship. Liberation of the female half of the human race from the age-old tyranny and dominance by the male half is by far the most profound revolution in human affairs at present in sight, but no one can surely pretend that female tyranny and dominance would be any better for human welfare than its male counterpart has been. The more extreme among women's liberation movements, e.g. SCUM (the Society for Cutting Up Men), do not at all conceal that their motive is revenge (hate), and that their objective is not equal partnership, but the elimination of men (through the sperm bank).

These reflections ought to make us cautious about some aspects of the sexual revolution and of the permissive society. Whether in some respects we are not celebrating the death of Eros, rather than his liberation or coming of age, may turn out to be rather a crucial question, for the realm of Eros runs far beyond the confines of overt sexuality and embraces many of the sources of our creativity, and of our capacity for reason, order, work, foresight and endurance. That it would be unwise to study the sexual revolution in isolation is strongly supported by all that we have learned from psycho-analysis and is further reinforced by a whole range of social phenomena which are certainly concomitant with and are probably connected to our much vaunted new sexual freedom. Here we ought to list the spread of meaningless violence, the increasing tendency of the young to 'drop out' of orthodox adult society and to despise 'work', the general erosion of privacy and the constantly diminishing sphere of political freedom, i.e. of liberty. Very little attention indeed seems to have been paid to the possible interrelation of these phenomena. Education, as at present institutionally conceived, at any rate at secondary and tertiary levels, may appear to have little to contribute to such a discussion. But no one engaged in education, who believes that it is about life and for life and that its major concern is with human well-being, can neglect these issues, particularly as they relate to what appears at the biological level as sex, fear and hostility and at the personal level as love, anxiety and hate.

There are many advantages in discussing the implications of the sexual revolution in this broad context. It allows attention to be focused on central issues within society as a whole, and prevents it being diverted on to defensively motivated studies of, for example, the sexual behaviour of the young. It also ensures that issues which properly belong together are not arbitrarily (and defensively) split off from each other. The difficulties of any such discussion are equally obvious. Sexual behaviour alone, without any of the concomitant issues, is a complex and confusing subject. This area of human experience is profoundly affected by cultural differences. Its subtleties are so many, and its certainties so few, that moralizing about it is not only futile but potentially damaging. Yet so long as we admit that health is better than illness, that happiness is better than misery, that kindness is better than cruelty, that love and respect are better than hate and manipulation, that civilized order is better than barbarism, we cannot eschew value-judgments. This means that we cannot refrain from regarding some forms of human sexual relationships as more 'mature' and more desirable than others. And that is the central difficulty. Who is to choose; how far is 'choice' possible in a realm so dominated by feeling and impulse, so open to social influence; and on what criteria can value-judgments be made? It may well be that no definitive answers can be given to such questions, but it is nevertheless vital to discuss them. The conversations rather than the conclusions may be what matter most, and it is to the credit of the sexual revolution that it has created a climate in which it is very much easier than it ever has been for such conversations to take place.

Sex and the varieties of love

Despite the sexual revolution, there is today widespread confusion and disagreement about the role of sex and its relation to love in our Western societies. According to a recent commentator, 'We all have our sexual ideologies, even if we haven't worked them out very fully; that sex is degrading, or that it is the main root to ecstasy, or even that it is a bore' (Wright, 1970). Whatever else it is, it has become a major obsession. Illustrative of the nature of the obsession are the evident paradoxes which now beset the whole matter. These have been insightfully described by Rollo May (1969). The first of these is that 'enlightenment has not solved the sexual problems of our culture.' Anxiety and guilt have taken new forms. Now they are about sexual attractiveness and competence.

Thus arises an emphasis on sex technique, and mutual orgasm becomes the standard below which no one must fall. It is a new form of tyranny. The second paradox is that 'the new emphasis on technique backfires.' The more concern there is with 'performance', the less feeling enters into the affair—'We went to bed and made love, but I didn't feel anything.' Third, there is the paradox that 'our highly vaunted sexual freedom has turned out to be a new form of puritanism.' In illustration, May aptly remarks that what *Playboy* has really succeeded in doing is 'to move the fig-leaf from the genitals to the face', and again: 'Our dogmatic enlightenment is self-defeating; it ends up by destroying the very sexual passion it set out to protect.' There is here clearly a threat to the life of Eros.

It is helpful here, as in other matters, to begin at the beginning. Sexuality* at the human level is at once a biological, a social and a personal function, but the extent to which these functions are felt to be fruitfully separable from one another, or requiring to be integrated for the full expression of each, is a matter of both cultural and individual differences. Likewise the relative emphasis placed on each varies widely. Yet there is, despite widespread behavioural variation, a persistent belief in Western societies that unless sexuality ultimately finds expression in mutual love and concern it has somehow fallen short of its built-in possibilities. In a word, we think that love is what sexuality among humans is fundamentally about, and sexuality is at its most meaningful when experienced at a fully personalized level. But what is meant by 'love' in this context? Again we turn to Rollo May:

> There are four kinds of love in western tradition. One is *sex*, or what we call lust, libido. The second is *eros*, the drive of love to procreate or create—the urge, as the Greeks put it, towards higher forms of being and relationship. A third is *philia*, or friendship, brotherly love. The fourth is *agape*, or *caritas* as the Latins called it, the love which is devoted to the welfare of the other ... Every human experience of authentic love is a blending, in varying proportions, of these four.

And there's the rub. The blends are almost infinite in variety. Freud, who did in his writings appear at times rather carelessly to confuse sex (as an appetitive drive) with love as an emotion or sentiment, was nevertheless very clear about one basic distinction (1921): 'The depth to which anyone is in love, as contrasted with his purely sexual desire, may be measured by the size of the share taken by the instincts of tenderness.'

* For the sake of simplicity, discussion is confined to heterosexual relationships.

The complexities of heterosexual attachment may be seen in other perspectives also. The psycho-analysts have insisted that, for the man, his woman is partly mate, partly mother, partly daughter, and that, similarly, for the woman, her man is partly mate, partly father, partly son (Klein & Riviere, 1937). The relationship takes its character from this fusion, now one aspect dominating, now another. Students of primate behaviour have also shown how complex the 'affectional systems' are. In their studies of monkeys the Harlows (1965) list five such systems.[4]

It was Freud's own work which above all others has enabled us to understand what is essentially a modern development and further complication. In the development of industrialized modern society, 'romantic' love, including its characteristic phase of 'falling in love' and with its emphasis on the absolute uniqueness of the partner, has become the socially accepted norm, despite the fact that it clearly represents an immature stage in the development of 'self' and in the relationship to 'other'. Whether it is a 'necessary' intermediate stage is open to question, but it is clearly a derivative of the intense Œdipal feelings developed within the nuclear family so typical of Western societies. In romantic love, the other is not known for what he or she really is, but is perceived in terms of a projected and exaggerated image of a loved parent with whom the person is, unconsciously, still partly identified. Thus in addition to being unrealistic, the other being obscured by a projected image, feeling is to a large extent narcissistic. The person is, unconsciously, enamoured of a part of himself or herself which he or she 'finds' in the other. The beloved is divine or, during a quarrel, diabolical. Two people in love, in this sense, live in a shared illusion. To say this is not to be uncharitable or to condemn, but rather to point to a fact. As the illusions fade the partners may move on to mature love of one another, they may develop a non-erotic friendship or they may simply 'fall out of love' and have no more interest in each other.

Whether the delights of this process compensate for its pains is an open question, but there is no doubt that in Western societies it seems to be a necessary stage in the growth of love from relatively uncomplicated sexual desire to the stable love and understanding of another person. The twin facts—that romantic love is central to our Western sexual experience, and that it is an unstable state—together give the key to many of our present perplexities. Since it is unstable, there must be movement, and movement can only be forward or backward, or simple repetition (sideways). Backward movements and repetitions are always easier than forward movements to more complex (mature) states. The movement towards mature love is, therefore, fraught with difficulty, for it involves giving up illusions about the self as well as about the other. There has to be genuine progress in self-knowledge and self-realization. From romantic love to 'simple' friendship (if any friendship is simple) presents in some ways as difficult a task, for the erotic component has itself largely to be denied any direct expression.

Falling out of love, however, in the sense of losing interest in the other, only requires giving up illusions about the other! But it can nevertheless be intensely painful. While self-knowledge may have been gained, this is not necessarily so, and the next step may be falling in love (and out of love) all over again—a form or repetition compulsion, or it may be a 'therapeutic' regression of a temporary nature to simpler and less intense forms of sexual relationships. Or again it may be a full regression into a cynical lust, or alternatively an almost total withdrawal from all close relationships. While it is important to identify and characterize these regressive movements, it is essential to remember that behind regression lies fear, hurt, human vulnerability.

Thus the sexual revolution, by its very emphasis on sex as a major area for the validation of personality, and by an 'enlightenment' that stresses facts rather than feelings (and so tends to divorce these), accentuates already existing conflicts and problems. Its influence is therefore inherently ambiguous. It points forward to the goal of Eros in mature creative relationships, and also backward through casual and less intense liaisons towards simple lust (with disgust as its other face), sentimentality (with cruelty as its other face), and eventually to openly manipulative and destructive relationships, i.e. towards the death of Eros. Aggression, tamed and harnessed by Eros in creative love, may break loose and endanger not only man's sexuality, but the whole of his civilized life and in this it is easily reinforced by other social factors working in the same direction.

Through the work of Klein (1960), Fairbairn (1952), Winnicott (1958, 1965) and Guntrip (1961, 1968) we have learned to amend Freud's view of man from one based on the satisfaction of instincts through tension reduction (a homeostatic model) to one in which the aim of behaviour is the formation and maintenance of relationships; if possible, 'good' relationships (an open system model). The new view does not wholly supersede the old, but reveals it as a partial truth. When societies develop tensions which threaten the well-being of individual members through undermining the relationships on which their well-being is based, the biological drives which subserve relationships are apt through fear and anxiety to turn destructive. Moreover as relationships weaken and/or the 'good' element in them diminishes, the biological drives appear in isolation and function on a 'tension reduction' model. Typically, the famous phrase, *post coitum omne animal triste est* (orgasm is followed by depression), is true only of lust. Partners who love and can satisfy one another do not have this experience.

It is quite characteristic of our times that we talk more about the sexual revolution than of love, and it is to be expected that the regressive aspects of the situation will be most clearly revealed in terms of problems of relationships. Those in turn are likely to be revealed in language, and underlying attitudes are likely to be expressed in common forms of speech. In discussing the way in which the sexual revolution insists in reducing all sexual experience to its (presumed) biological foundations, Rollo May shows how ordinary language sensitively reflects the varieties of our experience and our evaluation of it. 'The new puritanism* brings with it a depersonalization of our whole language. Instead of making love, we "have sex"; in contrast to intercourse, we "screw"; instead of going to bed, we "lay" someone, or (heaven help the English language as well as ourselves) we are laid!' And again: 'Every woman wants at some time to be "laid"—transported, carried away, "made" to have passion when at first she had none ... But if being laid is all that ever happens in her sexual life, then her experience of personal alienation and rejection of sex are just around the corner.' And then the *coup de grâce*, so to speak. 'We say "go fuck yourself" or "fuck you" as a term of contempt to show that the other is of no value whatever beyond being used and tossed aside. The biological lust is here in its *reductio ad absurdum*. Indeed, the word fuck is the most common expletive in our contemporary language to express violent hostility. I do not think this is by accident.' But it is not just language that becomes depersonalized; it is ourselves.

It is, of course, out of the question even to mention, let alone discuss, all the varieties of 'love' and their relation with sex in one short essay. There is no space to dwell on problems of dependency in love and on the nature of the mutual-interdependence characteristic of mature love, and many related topics. Our affections can, for example, embrace more than one person at a time in subtly different ways which cannot be neatly sorted out by a few standard-

* Psycho-analysis itself has, not unjustly, been criticized as being infected by puritanical attitudes. A relative of mine, the late Charles McFie Campbell, one time Professor of Psychiatry at Harvard, once declared: 'Psycho-analysis is Calvinism in Bermuda shorts'.[6] Rollo May (op. cit.) calls this an important half-truth; see also Rieff (1960).

ized adjectives. In our society where the norm is supposed to be 'one man, one woman' (a norm now challenged by a variety of sub-cultures), anxiety is quickly aroused by any departure from this and tends to produce neat classifications by attaching words like 'platonic' or 'intellectual' in front of 'relationship'. For the same reason a person is regarded as either completely 'faithful' to one partner or just 'promiscuous'. There are no situations between! The film *Jules et Jim* is a beautiful and sensitive rendering of the kinds of complexities that do exist.[5] There is, of course, anthropological evidence that adult affectional patterns are closely related to childhood experiences in different cultures. Beyond this there are ways in which personal integration can be achieved through devotion to a cause, often religious, rather than to a person, and celibacy, in some of its forms, illustrates such a successful mode of integration. He would be a bold man who would venture, in general, to assess the rewards of, and the price paid for, such ways of life, as against normal patterns of sexual relationships.

The search for satisfying relationships

Heterosexual love is, for many people, potentially the deepest of all personal relationships. It may be conceived, at its best, as an intimate fusion of the sexual drive with Eros, Philia and Agape, the creative, the comradely and the cherishing principles respectively. As such, it is a crucial source of personal integration. Sexuality in this context can be the vehicle for the most profound of human encounters and the source of unrivalled mutual ecstasy and joy. In sexual union each partner may receive an affirmation of his or her being, which may be felt to be unobtainable through any other means—'Through the Thou, a man becomes I' (Buber, 1958). Indeed it is clear that profound sexual experience and some forms of religiously described mystical experience have, psycho-dynamically speaking, much in common. A great deal of sexual experience is not of course like this at all. There is much variety and many levels. Briefly, heterosexual 'love' appears to exist today quite widely, in comparatively undeveloped and also in degenerate forms, in which Eros, Philia and Agape are only loosely associated with one another or have never grown close together, or have become wholly divorced. Eros, in the form of sexual passion, accompanied by some degree of liking, of friendship and tenderness, is capable of a life of its own, but not a very stable or long life. Divorced from comradeship and any strong and lasting degree of concern, Eros becomes unstable and tends towards lust. This is one risk attendant on casual forms of sexual relationship. Sex for its own sake, at the level only of sensual excitement and pleasure, the release of genital tension, soon ceases to be a wholly satisfying experience, although for some people it may continue as a pattern of behaviour throughout a lifetime.

In such cases (the Don Juans and so-called nymphomaniacs are extreme examples) it always conceals deeper problems. Youth, and, it is alleged, young men in particular* feel that sex is or should be wholly satisfying in itself and certainly often treat it as if it were, but all the evidence from adult, and in particular clinical, sources points to the fact that such an attitude carries its own nemesis within it. Sex treated as a separate function is apt not only to lead to satiety or to degenerate into lust, but runs the risk of losing its power as a vehicle of genuine love and intimacy. How subtle and paradoxical is this world of feeling! If sex is deliberately used as a device for making or cementing a relationship, it risks defeating its own ends. The degree of risk may differ from individual to individual but it is always there. Sexuality, however, is a much more complicated matter than even this would suggest. Because it is the vehicle *par excellence* for mature heterosexual love, it tends to be discussed, particularly by moralizers, as if this were the only function it served. In fact, sex as an activity is extremely complex and is daily used for sado-masochistic purposes, to express simple hatred, contempt, vanity, envy, competitiveness, to raise the level of self-esteem, as an almost universal source of humour (without which the world would be poorer) and above all today as a defence against anxiety and loneliness, a source of human warmth in a depersonalized world. Another notable pattern nowadays, and one by no means confined to 'youth', seems to be to use sex as a means towards forming a relationship, or of finding out whether a relationship is possible, or perhaps just as frequently as a straightforward substitute for any other kind of relationship. Such patterns express not only a longing for intimacy but also a fundamental anxiety about genuine intimacy. To be physically naked and bodily locked together is not felt as alarming, but to expose one's deepest self in emotional intimacy with another is, and the former is often apparently not felt necessarily to involve the latter. It is no longer a matter of 'now we are in love, let's go to bed', but 'let's go to bed and find out if we love each other'!

It can of course be argued that it sometimes happens that people

* 'The girl is looking for a romantic relationship, while the boy is seeking a sexual relationship' (Schofield, 1965). This is often paraphrased as: 'Boys are seeking sex and are prepared to feign love, while girls are seeking love and are prepared to feign sex.' This sounds to me like an over-simplification.

who begin a sexual relationship somewhat casually, or simply out of lust or loneliness, end up by 'falling in love', and genuinely caring for each other. But there is no evidence that this is a major pattern. It is also true moreover that this sometimes happens to one of the partners in such a casual relationship (more often the woman), the other remaining quite indifferent or even callous about it. What then? Is this just one of the risks of this particular game, which must be accepted? Perhaps. The truth in this suggestion however —that there is an inherent element of risk in all human relationships and that these are often conducted at the level of a game (Berne, 1968)—cannot conceal its essential casuistry. Again it may be urged that throughout mankind's long history, 'love', in its modern sense, was not the basis of marriage at all, and that many partners in 'arranged' marriages came to love one another deeply. But invoking just one facet of complicated and, in the industrially developed world, long extinct social systems as a justification for modern sexual casualness seems rather disingenuous. Surely it misses the fundamental issues? Are we really involved, as many apologists for the so-called permissive society suggest, in a genuine emancipation from restrictive moral codes and the discovery, at last, of the uncomplicated delights of sexuality and the simple 'naturalness' of love-making? In this respect are we returning to the Garden of Eden before the fall? There is some reason to believe that one of the gains of the sexual revolution takes this form, especially among younger people, but as a major explanation it does nothing like justice to the complexity of current phenomena. More important would seem to be the whole emphasis of modern life on externality and impersonality, on physical things, with the concomitant retreat from inwardness and from emotional intimacy.

Youth highlights what is, of course, a more general situation. With the young there is a great need to experiment and find out about relationships, and often also a shrinking from a too early emotional commitment. Urged forward by sexual desire, they yet hold back from the deeper implications of sexuality. Nowadays there is an easier compromise than formerly. Contraception is readily available and one's body can be regarded as no longer taboo (or 'sacred') in the old way. It is 'external' and so may be regarded as a relatively peripheral part of the self, which can be cut off from feelings of the deeper sort. Its urges are clamant, but can be stilled by a 'giving' which is only a 'giving in' and does not include the inner self. So, in the search for a good relationship, why not begin there? Certainly going to bed on the first date (or if not the first, then perhaps the second!) is not now so very uncommon. As one young woman put it, 'It helps to break the ice'! While we may take as a joke the thought that we may be on the way to a society where the sexual embrace has displaced the handshake as a greeting, ought we not to take seriously both the widespread fear of, and the great need for, genuine relationships which such a behaviour pattern reveals?* What perhaps should worry us here is the evident schizoid nature of the split between sensual pleasure, genital release and profound emotional response, with the concomitant inhibition of the latter. As a student put it: 'On a "one night stand" what is there to say to one another in the morning? Either you have another go, if there's time, or you beat it.'

Beyond this, what are the main features nowadays of an old and not uncommon pattern of continuing and persistent sexual adventure? In today's world, in which so much is ephemeral, in which much human contact is fleeting and superficial, and in which marriage may seem quite unattractive and unnecessary, or in which a suitable mate does not seem to turn up, then sexual 'friendships' or passing liaisons, which may well be passionate, affectionate and gentle, may satisfy immediate needs. Such patterns are quite congruent with much also in a society in which the call for commitment is not heard above the 'noise' of socially conditioned interactions or, if heard, is too weak to compel attention. This may be described as a schizoid position, but then it occurs in a culture which in many ways initiates and encourages schizoid splittings through the family and other institutions, so that schizoid features are bound to figure largely in many of its modes of adjustment.

Yet, beneath the emotional drifting which results, it is usually possible to find deeper, unsatisfied desires. Falling in love is usually the implicit aim, despite defences erected against it, and being reared in a nuclear family usually disposes people to this experience. When it happens, the lovers believe that at last their dreams have come true and the counterfeit currency, which in this condition passes for love and knowledge, is for a time wholly acceptable. Once the projected images begin to tarnish, to become unstable, and the reality of the other begins to show through, as it eventually must, then 'falling out of love' begins, and once more a new partner is sought. Student informants who have described this to me as a quite common pattern tend to comment: 'Once trouble starts with your girl (boy) friend, why bother? Why not just move on to someone else?'

As a stage in development, there is everything to be said for doing just that, in the expectation that in most cases deeper satis-

*Mutual fondling of the sexual organs as an initial greeting seems at one time to have been a custom among some tribes in New Guinea (Read, 1965, p. 19).

factions will eventually be sought, the price to be paid will be accepted, and stable relationships will form. Therefore newer patterns among the young, of couples living together for a time without formal commitments, have much to commend them. Marriage, in so far as the bringing up of children is concerned, is much too serious a matter to be left to the emotionally immature, no matter how sexually experienced they may be. For it is emotional maturity which is the issue and, unlike many aspects of so-called 'maturity', this is capable of clear definition. Full personal commitment implies, for both partners, facing and accepting the negative and relatively unlovely aspects of each other's personalities. Until this is done, no two people can be said truly to 'know' or to 'love' one another.

But neither marriage, nor any other form of prolonged intimate relationship, can guarantee such development. Dissatisfaction in marriage and outside it spring from the same emotional sources with their origins in childhood experience, and these usually include Œdipal patterns which have not been satisfactorily worked through (Dicks, 1967). Hence the notorious triangular situation, in which there are 'splits' within the self, and consequently in its love objects (other people). The man takes a mistress, the wife a lover. When this happens neither the spouse nor the lover are perceived as 'whole real people' but (in the simpler cases) only as the desirable or undesirable parts of themselves. While often these arrangements mean great unhappiness for one of the parties, and always for children where they are involved, they must occasionally 'suit' all the adults concerned—at least for a time. The cuckolded or cheated partner may be an unconscious accomplice, perhaps deriving satisfaction from being a victim and hence justified in having revengeful feelings. In such extramarital relationships, sensual pleasure is often enhanced for both partners. It is well known that people of both sexes may be more potent or passionate with mistresses or lovers, or prostitutes, than with their conjugal mates. The reasons are always complex, being in part due to the special 'spice' which secrecy may bring, to unconscious cruelty towards the cheated spouse and to the concentration of affection on the lover, while hostility is reserved for the spouse. Moreover the third party often has no burden of responsibility to bear. Usually and in the end there is a heavy price to pay, sometimes by all concerned. But this is not always so. As has been sagely remarked, 'a good many marriages, and a good many personalities, require an adulterous prop to keep them on their feet. This need may be "immature" but it is certainly widespread' (Comfort, 1964).

All these patterns, whether pre-marital, marital, or post-marital, represent a secret wish that adult life should be a long series of honeymoons, a kind of Peter-Panhood of late adolescence, prolonged, perhaps in phantasy, throughout life. Not infrequently this is disguised and rationalized as a search for an ideal mate, for the 'one who will understand', and this is a facet of a refusal to face one's own 'real' self and the selves of 'real' others. There is no emotional acceptance of the fact that love must encompass both the good and the bad in any relationship. 'For better or for worse' is a statement of the psychological truth about love, and also about deep genuine friendship of whatever sort, and not just a phrase in a formal marriage contract. Refusal to face and accept the negative side of self and others is a failure in development, a refusal to grow up. But to translate this fact into a moral judgment is, as lies a frightened infant, a damaged child. For the one who 'under-always, a stumbling-block to understanding. Behind such refusal stands' is, of course, ultimately the (good) mother. Jung points out that in German the very *verstehen* fundamentally refers to 'standing round about something' and that 'there is nothing in the world which so completely enfolds us as the mother'. The search for an ultimately satisfying adult relationship is therefore mediated by persisting images of phantasied, and therefore exaggeratedly beloved, parents.[6] Jung finds a brilliant illustration of this in Paul Verlaine's poem, *Mon Rêve familier,* here given in translation by Hinkle (Jung, 1921).

My Familiar Dream

Often I have that strange and poignant dream
 Of some unknown who meets my flame with flame—
 Who, with each time, is never quite the same,
Yet never wholly different does she seem.
She understands me! Every fitful gleam
 Troubling my heart she reads aright somehow:
 Even the sweat upon my pallid brow
She soothes with tears, a cool and freshening stream.

If she is dark or fair? I do not know.
Her name? Only that it is sweet and low,
 Like those of loved ones who have long since died.
Her look is like a statue's, kind and clear;
 And her calm voice, distant and dignified,
 Like those hushed voices that I loved to hear.

Patterns of unstable and casual relationships may of course be more complicated than this. There may be simple loneliness, and loneliness compounded by unconsummated sexual desires for which no acceptable substitute satisfactions have been found. External fate (as distinct from the internal aspect which we carry around with us) is not always obliging as regards the people we meet, or the circumstances under which we meet them. But basically, what has to be grasped is that casualness, reinforced by social pressures, is usually largely defensive. It serves to cloak a deep longing for genuine relationship. As one woman student put it in a personal paper, 'always there is the hope that someone will take me for more than the superficial body'. But this is true of both men and women (although men are often more defensively flippant about it) as the following conversation with a young man shows:

'There is this girl, very popular with men, who is always full of promises which she doesn't fulfil.'

'You mean, she is a sexual tease?'

'Not really, it's not as simple as that. She goes to bed with people all right, but there is no meeting of souls—somehow she hides her inner self, and there is just another body.'

These examples are illustrative of some of the facts habitually ignored both by moralizers and by the apostles of so-called 'free love'. Neither has ever grasped the basic facts about freedom and love, that both imply for their realization a considerable measure of integration and of responsibility, and that these desirable fruits of development are not simply there for the taking. They have to be sought for and worked at, and one needs to have some luck too, both in childhood and later. Nor must we ever forget that it is through, and by means of, our weaknesses, problems, infirmities, immaturities and disabilities that it is possible for us to grow.

The death of Eros?

The very existence of widely differing views on the relation of sex to love serves to emphasize that this is now an important issue in modern society. A recent opinion poll of youth in Massachusetts showed that while a majority of college youths do not favour sex without love, 47 per cent of men and 29 per cent of women students do. Ought we not however to be rather cautious about the interpretation of 'sex' and 'love' in this context? The distinction is rather too simple. In his recent thought-provoking book, *Love and Will*, Rollo May writes:

> it is possible to have sexual intercourse without any particular anxiety. But by doing this in casual encounters, we shut out, by definition, our eros—that is, we relinquish passion in favour of mere sensation; we shut out participation in the imaginative, personal significance of the act. If we can have

> sex without love, we assume that we escape the daimonic anxiety known throughout the ages as an inseparable part of human love. And if further, we even use sexual activity itself as an escape from the commitments eros demands of us, we may hope to have thus gained an airtight defense against anxiety. And the motive for sex, no longer being sensual pleasure or passion, becomes displaced by the artificial one of providing identity and gaining security; and sex has been reduced to an anxiety-allaying strategy. Thus we set the stage for the development of impotence and affectlessness later on.

In principle, May is surely right, but in practice, as I have tried to show, it is not always as simple as this, and dire consequences do not necessarily follow. In fact, here, May is himself adopting a somewhat puritanical stance.

But taking this perspective, what is not brought out here (although large sections of May's book are attempts to come to terms with it) is the connection between sexual behaviour and violence. It was once thought that sexual repression and inhibition were, if not the cause, at least a frequent concomitant of violence. This is no doubt true (tyrannical regimes tend to be puritanical ones also), but what has not been grasped is that sexual licence in the form of casual and loveless sex also has violence as one of its concomitants.

The close connection between sex and aggression has long been stressed by psycho-analysts, and while the slogan 'make love, not war' is a fine one so long at it really means what it says, it is quite another matter if 'love' is translated merely as 'sex'. It is surely no accident that the society in which loveless sex has become quite so common is one which is also passing through one of the most violent periods in its history? The section of youth which demands and practises 'sexual freedom' while usually denouncing 'violence' has not understood that these may be two faces of the same coin. Nor have many of their elders who profess similar views. R. D. Laing (1967) points out:

> Love and violence, properly speaking, are polar opposites. Love lets the other be, but with affection and concern. Violence attempts to constrain the other's freedom, to force him to act in the way we desire, but with ultimate lack of concern, with indifference to the other's own existence or destiny. We are effectively destroying ourselves by violence masquerading as love.

Precisely; loveless sex is one example of the violation of the integrity of the person, indeed of both persons; that is, it is a form of violence and it is none the less this, even when mutual. There have always been some individuals, and there are and always will be times in life, and youth is one of them, when all of us may be relatively insensitive about this, because of the imperious quality of our sexual desires. But there is something peculiarly contemporary about the ethos of the following extract from a recent student novel (Todd, 1970): '"Nick, I love you!" "I don't love you, Jennifer." Then I said, "I'm sorry", and I held her and then took her hand and led her over to my bed, where we undressed, and lay down, and made love.'

The extent of loveless sex in our society is of course a matter of speculation, and while researches like those of Kinsey (1953) have been severely and rightly criticized, they suggest that the incidence is considerable and indeed by the very method of enquiry used they seem to take it for granted and indeed to lend it intellectual support. Such researches have attempted to assess sexuality in terms of the kind and number of 'outlets' or occasions for the relief of sexual desire which an individual has experienced. What concerns us here is that it adopts an evidently sub-human frame of reference. Sex appears as a means of obtaining 'relief' from tension and the partner is treated only as a means to this end. Tenderness in any real depth is excluded and therefore so is love. As one of my own students put it, 'The lustful man who says he wants a woman is deceiving himself. A real woman is precisely what he does not want. What he is looking for is a piece of biological apparatus which he can use to appease his appetites. Similarly with the randy woman.'

One clearly visible influence of the sexual revolution is the tendency 'for such things as pornography, moral rules, the exploitation of sex for money and so on, to separate sex from its personal context' (Wright, 1970). The question of what is, or should be, regarded as pornography, and what should not, and what the social effects of what is so defined really are, are of course complex and changing ones. It is interesting however to note that in writing on 'The Danish experiment in pornography', H. J. Barnes (1970), while maintaining that the experiment may have had a beneficial effect in stimulating more open and tolerant discussion of sexual matters, concludes by saying: 'As to the pornography itself, the more I see of it, the more repulsive I find it, or most of it anyway. This, I have concluded, is because pornography reduces sex to an exclusively physical manifestation and excludes the feeling and commitment which are the basis of ordinary relationships.' But what is legally definable as pornography is not the central issue. What matters most is the essential meaning of the 'eroticism' to be found in plentiful supply in various branches of the entertainment industry. Sentimentality has for a long time pervaded popular literature, music and films. It is now being rivalled by the widespread appearance of paperback novels, and also of films, obviously composed to a virtually set formula, featuring themes of crude sexuality and violence. To some extent these themes are also to be found in what has quite strong claims to be considered serious art in the fields of literature and the theatre. Some of these have figured prominently in the battle over censorship.

This battle in literature seems to me to have resulted, among other things, in the publication of a number of serious, able, and sometimes brilliantly written books, full of penetrating insights, describing sexual experience in a detailed and outspoken way. I am referring here to such works as Norman Mailer's *An American Dream*, John Updike's *Couples*, Henry Miller's *Sexus* and Philip Roth's *Portnoy's Complaint*. Despite their brilliance, however, the total impact of these and similar books is, I am convinced, voyeuristic, narcissistic and sadistic. Typically, little compassion is shown for human frailty and vulnerability. *Couples*, however, is not entirely deficient in this respect, nor is it deficient in symbolic interest. It might be claimed to have clinical or anthropological significance also, but one senses in it a deliberate exploitation of voyeuristic impulses and, in its language—a calculated use of the more sexually aggressive four-letter words—an inverted prudery. Nowhere is there any attempt to illumine the conditions in a society which produce a group of people for whom love has degenerated into compulsive copulation in the form of a round game. Being flippant, one might call such works 'verbal strip-tease for intellectuals'.

Similarly the various moves to have sexual intercourse 'enacted' on the stage might incline us to ask whether perhaps sex was in danger of becoming just another 'spectator sport'! But essentially these are not comic matters for they do suggest the existence in some sections of society, at least, of a serious incapacity to find fulfilment in real-life heterosexual relationships, thereby pointing to a failure of sexuality to develop into genuine love. There is surely something grave afoot in our society when there is active support for attempts to make public entertainment out of what is potentially the most profound and private of human encounters. What may be afoot is an attack on privacy itself—'the part of the human condition that has taken the longest to grow'—as C. H. Rolph puts it. This point is made, among others equally germane, in a brilliant and penetrating article entitled 'In words begin responsibilities—aspects of literary censorship in the twentieth century' (*The Times Literary Supplement*, 10 July 1969). In reviewing Rolph's book and three others, the writer points out that 'sexual freedom of any real interest must be closely linked with social freedom and the present campaign for total sexual freedom in literature and in action, is in many ways a substitute for social freedom, as Norman Mailer has recognized.'

Typically those in the vanguard of these movements seem to be found among the middle-aged, and not notably among youth. Similarly it is reported from Denmark and Sweden that the customers for their 'sex shops'—in which illustrated publications are displayed and sold, depicting, in colour, the more usual range of variations within 'normal' sexual practices—are mainly middle-aged men (and mostly foreigners). All these trends, which are among the phenomena of the so-called permissive society and which are not in any important sense the work of youth, might be lumped together as literary and theatrical 'nudism'. They seem to me to be fundamentally anti-erotic just as nudism itself, in our kind of society, is quite explicitly a denial of sexuality.

Some of these works do of course succeed in being amusing, some are brilliant and at times even profound, but the essence of the matter seems to have been caught by the *Guardian* writer who, reviewing *Oh! Calcutta!*, entitled it 'Oh! Non-Erotica!'. There is a pathological odour of decay and defeat in all these productions, and this is not surprising if they are, as one suspects, indeed celebrating the death of Eros. When they do not invite laughter (which in any case is likely to be defensive) or give pleasure through genuine technical achievement, they invite boredom or disgust. This judgment, however, does not constitute a ground for supporting literary or theatrical censorship. These sorts of things, whatever the motivation of their authors and supporters, may perform necessary functions by serving to alert us to existing processes of decay and destructiveness in our society, processes which may be genuinely inimical to freedom. Claims that they have important cathartic and educational functions should of course be taken with rather more than a grain of salt!

Those professionally interested in literature might like to consider on what grounds one might include the books mentioned above in the anti-erotic category but would exclude Joyce's *Ulysses*, for example. How would *Lady Chatterley's Lover* stand? On the one hand the literary nudism is obvious, as is the female identification of the author (which amounts to impersonation), but its virtues as a pioneer attempt to deal descriptively, albeit implicitly, with an obsessive problem of modern man (his deep unconscious fear of woman) have to be given weight. *The Times Literary Supplement* review mentioned above makes short work of some of the more ludicrous claims in the book's defence at the time of the obscenity trial and concludes thus: 'One envisages a reply to an awkward question: Obviously when Lawrence referred to the necessity for "burning out the deepest, oldest shames, in the most secret places", he thought of this act as the necessary although disagreeable prelude to leading a Christian life.' Again, however, the comedy is not really the point. Lawrence's language 'burning out', reveals starkly his intense unconscious fear and hatred of woman (here identified with Eros) and thus ultimately of the woman in himself—the hated, and hating, bad internalized mother in Melanie Klein's sense.* But hate cannot be exorcised by further hatred, only by love. While at one level the book is clearly anti-erotic, it has value in revealing the immensity of the task with which our species is faced in enabling men and women to outgrow the primitive fears (and resultant hatreds) which stand in the way of a fuller realization of personhood.

And it would seem that in its more extreme forms the sexual revolution is pointing precisely the other way. While, in general, the activities of the so-called 'underground' are ambiguous, there is clearly much that is anti-developmental, and, curiously, anti-women. This is well brought out in a penetrating article (which is also at times brilliantly funny) by Christopher Ricks: 'It is all very well for a Yippy pamphlet to proclaim that people should have "all the time, anytime, whomever they wish".' But what about those whom nobody wishes? 'But if the underground really were to convert us all, a high proportion of such proposals would inevitably meet rebuff, and there would be people who would meet nothing but rebuff. Not to be received as a mixer in a totally promiscuous world: that has horrors which out do those of the captive housewife.' Perhaps his most telling point comes when he says, 'What *The Sex Researchers* [Brecher, 1970] really bears witness to is the Narcissism of the sexual revolution and its media. And the important thing about Narcissus is that he was a man.'

The myth of Narcissus, so well expounded psycho-analytically by Grace Stuart (1956), is really a variant on the theme of the decline and death of Eros. Rollo May approaches this conclusion also when he points out that in Greek mythology Eros sickens and becomes a puny child, virtually a 'playboy' in fact. He reminds us that except in the company of his brother Anteros, god of passion, Eros resumes childish and mischievous habits. 'This brings us to the very heart of what has gone wrong in our day: eros has lost

* Lawrence's hatred of his real mother was of course conscious and avowed.

passion, and has become insipid, childish, banal.' He also reminds us that Eros and Anteros were children of Ares, as well as of Aphrodite, and 'this is to say that love is inseparably connected with aggression.' The death of Eros becomes only too clearly a possibility for us when the creative association of love with aggression, through passion, is lost and their destructive separation is promoted and celebrated. Since Eros stands for creative power, the bridge between men and the gods, as the Greeks thought, it is not just sexuality and love, but the whole of our civilization, which is at stake.

Love's coming of age?*

If we take the psychology of human development seriously, it is plain that any adequate standards in personal relationships must be in terms of developmental criteria, and that one of the key concepts must be that of integration. This has been well expressed by Nevitt Sanford (1967) in a penetrating and wise consideration of this theme.

> Puritanism, pragmatism, the *Playboy* ethic, and other existing ideologies, seem inadequate to do the job. Some new standard is needed, one that reflects our growing understanding of man and human society. I propose that we can find this standard in the concept of integration; that here, as in the case of drinking, we should place higher value upon behaviour patterns that favour integration both in the personality and at the social level.

The adoption of developmental criteria of course means that there cannot be any single simple set of rules. At the college level, for example, and in an increasing number of cases before this level is reached, there are, and will be, young people ready for full sexual experience, and for whom this may be rewarding and integrative, and which is likely to lead in due time towards the forming of more enduring relationships. There will also be those whose development in terms of personality criteria has not reached this level, and for whom premature sexual experience can have very destructive effects. There are also always likely to be some with more or less severe personality disturbances which have sexual disturbances as one feature, and they again will complicate the issue.

This complex situation has, of course, always been with us. We are now beginning to realize it more clearly, to appreciate the prob-

* This is the title of a brilliant and provocative essay by John Wren-Lewis in *Psychoanalysis Observed*. The question mark, however, is mine.

lems it poses and to search for directions in which to look for solutions. 'Rules' laid down by adult authorities and moral exhortations about the virtues of chastity have always failed in some degree to make the young conform to an 'ideal' imposed by adults, but the 'failure' is now on a large scale. Indeed, instead of the social pressures being against pre-marital and extra-marital experience, the reverse is largely true. There has been for some time now relentless social pressure on the young, much of it transmitted through their own peer groups and aided by literature, films, plays and advertisements, to conform to the 'new morality', to be 'with it', to prove their masculinity and femininity and not to be left behind in the struggle for sexual partners. If one takes a developmental view of standards with an emphasis on the concept of integrative experiences, and also takes into account the fact that contraception is likely to become even more efficient than it already is, there are no cogent reasons for attempting to dissuade the young, in general, and as a matter of principle, from having sexual experience before marriage. Not that any such attempt would have the remotest chance of success. Nevertheless it cannot be denied that existing undiscriminating attitudes in favour of early sexual experience do result in damage to some of the more sensitive and vulnerable among the young.

The current increase in sexual freedom is, however, now also being criticized from another standpoint; that it is responsible for an alleged marked increase in the incidence of venereal disease. It would be wise to avoid the controversies surrounding the facts in this area, which concern the basis on which comparisons are made and the validity of inferences drawn from available clinical samples, and to concentrate on what is undeniably true, that a large number of people, many of them quite young, are being treated for these unpleasant diseases and, in the case of syphilis, a highly dangerous one. The fact is that our biochemical controls have not kept pace with mutations among the organisms, and current social habits, especially among the young, have compounded the danger. But the practical inferences are much less clear. Moral exhortation will simply fail, and an appeal to 'information', relying only on fear for its effectiveness, might easily defeat its own purpose, while bringing with it other highly undesirable consequences as well: i.e. an atmosphere congenial to sexual obscurantism and guilt. No reasonable person, of course, would deny the importance in this field of the widest possible dissemination of accurate information. If in doing this, instead of merely appealing to fear we were to urge the need for a positive and constructive approach to *all* the realities of sexual experience, emotional as well as physical, we would also be entitled to hope that advances in medicine, biochemical as well as social, might eventually reduce the dangers of these diseases to a minimum. In the meantime, risks should not be minimized, and practical information needs to be publicized about the means of protection available.

While in general, therefore, welcoming the beneficial effects of the sexual revolution, it is wise to recognize the risks attendant on sexual experience in quite a variety of circumstances. Educationally, in this sort of situation, the best that can be hoped for is the spread of genuine sexual enlightenment right across the generations. By this is meant not only a knowledge about sexual functions and relationships at physiological and behavioural levels, very important as this is, but also an understanding of the existential meaning of the emotional involvement of one person with another and its effects on the personal development of both. Such enlightenment can only come slowly, for it does not primarily depend on any kind of specific instruction, but on a total education which is concerned with the welfare of persons and which makes conscious concern for the welfare of others one of its basic objectives The sexual sphere could then be seen in its true setting in the personal life. This is of course the essential crux so far as the value of 'sex education' is concerned. As in other areas of education, its value depends on its quality and on the competence and sensitivity of those responsible for it. Such an education would always have to contend with the pressures of the natural appetites, the varied rates of development among the young, and contrary pressures of all kinds. Moreover it would have to contend with its own inevitable moralistic component, leading it on the one hand to a coldly clinical approach, and on the other towards a far too solemn, pious, and Sunday-school-like attitude, with a ridiculously 'precious' and unrealistic view of the whole topic. For there is in healthy sexual love, as well as sensual passion and profound feeling, an inherent element of playfulness, a rumbustiousness, an intricate fusion of tenderness and controlled aggression and a gay abandon. Sex without fun, without exuberance and simple joy, is a poor foundation for enduring love.

But the fate of Eros will not (needless to say!) be determined by the schools, for here as in other fundamental matters theirs is a secondary, if none the less important, function. The growth of love is *a*, perhaps *the*, fundamental problem in human development.* Wright, in discussing the roles of biological and social elements in sexual behaviour, says:

* Reason and love belong together, but reason is the child of love, both phylogenetically and ontologically (Murphy, 1961).

> Sexual intercourse is not something that one person does to another, or more accurately, in its most fully human form it isn't. It's rather a sequence of intermeshing actions in which two people for the time being could be said to form a single system, which is balanced and controlled by the feelings that each has for the other. The interaction itself culminates in the emotional and sensual satisfaction of both parties. The sexual component is inseparable from the other personal elements which go to make up the whole process. Of course, this implies an upbringing in which the two have been pretty consistently inseparable.

Wright is here pointing to the most fundamental consideration of all, the connection between childhood experience of relationships and patterns of adult sexuality and love. Despite differing emphases among its sects, psycho-analysis, as an approach to understanding the human condition, has consistently maintained that here lies one essential clue to the quality of human life. To put a very complex matter at its simplest—for us to be able to give and receive love at a mature adult level, someone (or, better, 'some ones') must have first loved us, at the very beginning and throughout the formative years. This insight, which has also been a feature of some religious systems, is now receiving powerful support from behavioural research like that of Bowlby and others on human infancy, and that of Harlow and others on the higher primates. All this work suggests strongly that psycho-analytic views about adult human sexuality are correct, in that the capacity for effective, meaningful and enduring relationships depends quite heavily on the experience and adequacy of relationships in early childhood (Bowlby, 1969).

But sexuality and love are never likely to cease to be problem areas. While we may legitimately hope for healthier child-rearing patterns in the future, the subtleties of emotional development are such that it is irrational to expect 'solutions' to be found there to all our problems. Indeed it is irrational to expect 'solutions' at all, except in the sense that as cultures change and develop man may evolve patterns of child-rearing and of adult sex relationships which are less damaging to the well-being of persons than most of those which have existed or exist now. This is defensible optimism in view of some recent developments, among younger persons particularly, and more especially in view of the increasing efficiency of and need for birth-control, which is an essential step towards the genuine emancipation of women. This is crucial, for where women are treated as less than persons, men who so treat them suffer a corresponding loss of their own humanity.* But as soon as we speak of our 'humanity', in this connection, of how it may be enhanced or diminished, it is evident that we have reached the crucial issue. Here we realize that ultimately the meaning of a sexual relationship transcends sexuality itself—in the sense that what is transcended is gathered up into a unity of experience of a more complete kind, without losing its identity as central to that experience. Related to this, of course is Freud's view of how sexuality comes to *inform* many fields of human activity, thereby being itself *transformed* in the process. ('Sublimation', the term often used here, is apt to be misleading.) Perhaps this is also part of the meaning of a remark which has been attributed to Jung: 'We must always remember that the penis is only a phallic symbol' ('only' is surely wrong, 'also' would be more apt). On this view, what is ultimately sought in a sexual relationship is 'communion'—a creative union of two selves, for which physical love-making is an essential vehicle. And one would want to add, a vehicle the full sensual potentialities of which are seldom available apart from a deeply shared common life.

We should not, however, take a too pessimistic view of the prospects, nor indeed of the facts of the past or the present. It is only too easy to take refuge in a morally superior attitude about what is felt to be ideal. Most of the time personal relationships fall below 'ideal' standards, yet can give much joy. Perhaps this will always be the human situation. Love in the sense here used, which alone can reconcile and transcend the good and bad in every relationship, is not so easily found. Indeed to be too exacting in one's standards is itself inimical to the growth of love. Laing (1967), in discussing the state of 'being in love' as a 'socially conditioned illusion that two actual persons are in relationship', yet admits there are 'occasions when, most lost, lovers may discover each other, moments when recognition does occur' and goes on to remark, 'at the very least, it befits Babes in the Wood to be kinder to each other, and to show some sympathy and compassion, if there is any pathos and passion left to spend.'

If one looks coolly at all the facts, this is the only view which holds out any hope. Robert Louis Stevenson perceived this at the end of last century in a remarkable essay (1888) which was entirely congruent with Freud's own findings and which was published about the time Freud began his clinical work. Speaking of 'the racy sermon against lust [which] is a feature of the age', Stevenson says,

* While man's 'humanity' may mean all his characteristics, evil as well as good, it is here used to mean that which is most 'humane' about him.

> I venture to call such moralists insincere. At any excess or perversion of a natural appetite, their lyre sounds of itself with relishing denunciations; but for all displays of the truly diabolic-envy, malice, the mean lie, the mean silence, the calumnious truth, the back-biter, the petty tyrant, the peevish poisoner of family life—their standard is quite different. These are wrong, they will admit, yet somehow not so wrong; there is no zeal in their assault on them, no secret element of gusto warms up the sermon.

He then follows this up and concludes:

> The truth is, that all these interventions and denunciations and militant mongerings of moral half truths, though they be sometimes needful, though they are often enjoyable, do yet belong to an inferior grade of duties. Ill-temper and envy and revenge find here an arsenal of pious disguises: this is the playground of inverted lusts.

Here lies the paradox of all moralizing, and especially moralizing in the sexual sphere, that it creates an atmosphere which is necessarily inimical to what it (ostensibly) seeks to promote. Freud's work is largely a detailed exposition of how this comes about.

If, in our search for the truths of love and reason in this sphere, moralizing represents the dangers of Scylla, then the radical intellectual wing of the sexual revolution perhaps represents those of Charybdis. Here the champions of oversimplification (perhaps not an apt term for their turgid works), highly honoured among some of the young, are Reich (1942), Marcuse (1955) and Brown (1959, 1966). While it will not do simply to dismiss such clever and sincere men out of hand, their major doctrines seem to me to be basically misleading. Failure to achieve sexual harmony in orgasm is a not infrequent occurrence in our culture and can lead to frustration and misery, but a satisfying sexual life is not by itself a solution to our problems, as Reich tends to suggest. Nor in any case will a knowledge of technique on its own produce sexual fulfilment. Marcuse, although drawing (selectively) on Freud, makes much of what he calls 'surplus repression'. By this he means repression over and above what he considers necessary to maintain a viable social order. He concludes that the making of a 'non-repressive civilization' will require a clear vision of libidinal liberation from the outset. He also draws (selectively) from Marx, but his does not seem quite a Marxian vision. He seems, in fact, to stand Marx on his head (consciousness determines social being, not *vice versa* as in Marx), thus getting back to Hegel! He sees the coming revolution as affecting work and all human relationships. It will, of course, replace capitalism, but it must be guided by libidinal rationality, and it will abolish man's sense of alienation, both at work and in human relationships. (For criticisms of Marcuse, see MacIntyre (1970) and Roszak (1969).)

Perhaps the most beguiling of the three is Norman Brown, who invites us to believe that if only we could create a culture which does not depend on super-ego functions, and therefore on unconscious guilt, but rather on an 'erotic sense of reality', a 'Dionysian ego', we would be free to work creatively, play creatively and love creatively. This is the 'liberation of the body'—'life against death'. Thus we could enjoy the 'sexual' pleasures of childhood (i.e. polymorphous perverse sexuality), as well as post-pubertal joys! Alas, nothing is less likely to be true, if what we have in mind is also man's mastery of nature, the creation of material abundance (the abolition of poverty and the minimizing of disease), and the highly developed cultural activities which have mainly come into being in Europe with and since the Renaissance. On this the social anthropologist Geoffrey Gorer remarks (1971b):

> Enough societies have now been studied where adolescence is undramatized, without family revolts or juvenile delinquency, so that, on an abstract level we can write the prescription for a society without adolescent problems: this prescription is the lowering of all intensity—in personal relationships, in religion, in art. Is the peace of mind of most of the population worth the price? I can answer for myself, but for nobody else.
>
> Similarly, we can enormously lower the incidence of neurosis, of character problems, if we do not cultivate autonomy, if we do not ask individuals to stand up for what they believe to be right against all social pressures. Is this worth the price?
>
> What I am convinced anthropological evidence shows is that you cannot have your cake and eat it, have an un-neurotic, gratified, un-anxious population and hope for high art, religious or erotic intensity, courageous autonomy.

We must be careful, however, not to overstate this case. In relying on the anthropological record, Gorer is making the point that from what we know of man's history, there is a connection of some sort between the control and curtailment of sexual expression and civilized achievement (see, e.g., Unwin (1934)). Yet it does not follow that we can extrapolate from existing knowledge in any simple way. The past has never been a very good guide to the future!

Some of the young will doubtless regard criticism of the views of

Reich, Brown and Marcuse as springing essentially from the sexual envy of older people. While they may in part be right, they may also be in part misled. There is, as Roszak points out, something of a poetic vision in both Brown and Marcuse, and although the vision seems over-simple it is not wholly irrational to hope for a better, freer and less exploitive social order, in which Eros, in all aspects of his creative glory, may flourish more than he does now.

By introducing Eros again, we are once more emphasizing what is missing from the whole contemporary debate about sex and society. Unwin concluded that a society could enjoy almost unlimited sexual expression *or* high civilized achievements, but not both. In all probability he was right. But love, in the sense used in this essay, cannot be equated to unlimited sexual expression, rather it is in one sense opposed to this, for it represents a canalizing and transforming of sexuality. Love and achievement are not opposed, indeed 'normally' (i.e. in health), defined as 'well-being', they go together, as Freud clearly saw, for what they express in their union is the integrity of the personality. Gorer's point about 'erotic intensity' is entirely compatible with this. Love's compatibility with achievement however is only true when *work*, without which any achievement is impossible, is itself in some measure an expression of love and this is what we mean when we describe a particular achievement as 'a work or labour of love'. Love is clearly incompatible with work in the form in which the latter is encountered by perhaps the majority of people in our technological society. In our time, work has tended to become either almost meaningless routine or else a neurotic, compulsive and, in the long run, self-destructive activity. 'Achievement', then, is often not a work of love at all, but of fear and hate, often deeply unconscious, but biding their time to erupt into violence.*

It is surely the problem of aggression, of violence, which is most pressing for modern man, and here Freud (without unfortunately benefit of Marx) is, despite all his pessimism, a wiser guide than any of his aberrant modern disciples (1933).

* The pathology of work in our kind of society needs separate treatment. In locating the seat of social ills in the pathology of 'love' and 'work' (usually misconceived as 'sex' and 'labour'), radical thinkers like Marcuse are correct (following Freud and Marx) in their global diagnosis, but mistaken in the particular inferences they draw. Similarly the puritans, past and present, are right in thinking there is a connection between the social expression of sexuality and achievement, but tragically wrong (because of their own motivation) in their approach to it. By concentrating hostility on sex, it is love which becomes unnourished, pines and dies, and fear and hate which flourish. Hence the enormous cost in human suffering of achievement based largely on 'puritan' ideals.

> From our 'mythology' of the instincts we may easily deduce a formula for an indirect method of eliminating war. If the propensity for war be due to the destructive instinct, we have always its counter agent, Eros to our hand. All that produces ties of sentiment between man and man must serve us as war's antidote. These ties are of two kinds. First such relations as those towards a beloved object, void though they be of sexual intent. The psycho-analyst need feel no compunction in mentioning 'love' in this connection; religion uses the same language; Love thy neighbour as thyself. A pious injunction easy to enounce, but hard to carry out! The other bond of sentiment is by way of identification. All that brings out the significant resemblances between men calls into play this feeling of community, identification, whereon is founded, in large measure, the whole edifice of human society.

Ultimately, however, we have each of us to work and live within a personal sphere. If love is to come of age on this planet, we have each to embark upon a personal journey, a highly individual one, at times necessarily lonely, although others on the same route accompany us. Speaking of this, Monica Furlong (1971) says:

> With pain and difficulty we establish our identity as a person, as man or woman. We are ready to love. Then, in loving, we discover how precarious, how ambiguous, is our personal and sexual identity, as we learn how to play with the boundaries of the self. Eventually we discover the joke, the paradox—the self is only the self when it forgets the boundary. Ecstasy, selfhood, are the moment when we lose the self.

She reminds us that there is 'terror and pain, as well as joy' on the road, for in loving we expose the inner self, we are ultimately vulnerable. Loving is an act of faith; there are no guarantees. She quotes Auden:[7]

> The sense of danger must not disappear,
> The way is certainly both short and steep,
> However gradual it looks from here;
> Look if you like, but you will have to leap.

Notes

1 Gorer's study referred to above gives no direct statistical evidence on this point; his general conclusions suggest that *on the whole* the sexual revolution *in England* is more a matter of the media than of behaviour.

2 'When my restless hands caress those white breasts, they grasp white civilization and dignity and make them mine', Fanon (1968), p. 63.
3 Unisex also doubtless expresses inherent human bi-sexuality and uneasiness about some aspects of sex-identity, as well as normal latent homo-sexual inclinations.
4 These systems, while distinct, 'are apt to impinge on each other, and to influence the development of each other', Bowlby (1969), p. 263.
5 Directed by François Truffaut, Films du Carosse/Sedif, France, 1961.
6 This proto-typic function of child-parent relationships has, of course, been especially emphasized in the Freudian tradition.
7 W. H. Auden, *Leap Before You Look*, Faber, 1966.

References

Barnes, H. J. (1970) 'The Danish experiment in pornography', *Encounter*, September.

Berne, E. (1968) *Games People Play*. Penguin.

Bowlby, J. (1969) *Attachment and Loss*. Vol. I. *Attachment*. Hogarth.

Brecher, E. (1970) *The Sex Researchers*. Little, Brown.

Brown, N. O. (1959) *Life Against Death*. Wesleyan University Press.

Brown, N. O. (1966) *Love's Body*. Random House.

Buber, M. (1958) *I and Thou*. Scribner.

Comfort, A. (1964) *Sex in Society*. Penguin.

Dicks, H. V. (1967) *Marital Tensions*. Routledge & Kegan Paul.

Fairbairn, W. R. D. (1952) *Psychoanalytic Studies of the Personality*. Routledge & Kegan Paul.

Fanon, F. (1968) *Black Skins and White Masks*. MacGibbon & Kee.

Freud, S. (1921) *Group Psychology and the Analysis of the Ego*. Hogarth.

Freud, S. (1933) *Civilisation, War and Death*. Hogarth.

Furlong, M. (1971) *Travelling In*. Hodder & Stoughton.

Gorer, G. (1971a) *Sex and Marriage in England Today*. Nelson (in the press).

Gorer, G. (1971b) 'The congruent society' in Sutherland, J. D. (ed.), *Towards Community Mental Health*. Tavistock.

Guntrip, H. (1961) *Personality Structure and Human Interaction*. Hogarth.

Guntrip, H. (1968) *Schizoid Phenomena, Object Relations and the Self*. Hogarth.

Harlow, H. F. and M. K. (1965) *The Affectional Systems in Behavior of Non-Human Primates*, vol. 2 (ed. Schrier, Harlow & Stolnitz). Academic Press.

Jung, C. G. (1921) *Psychology of the Unconscious* (trans. Hinkle). Kegan Paul.

Kinsey, A. C. *et al.* (1948) *Sexual Behaviour in the Human Male*. Saunders.

Kinsey, A. C. *et al.* (1953) *Sexual Behaviour in the Human Female*. Saunders.

Klein, M. (1960) *Our Adult World and its Roots in Infancy*. Tavistock.
Klein, M. & Riviere, J. (1937) *Love, Hate and Reparation*. Hogarth.
Laing, R. D. (1967) *The Politics of Experience*. Penguin.
MacIntyre, A. (1970) *Marcuse*. Fontana.
Marcuse, H. (1955) *Eros and Civilisation*. Sphere, 1969.
May, R. (1969) *Love and Will*. Norton.
Murphy, G. (1961) *Freeing Intelligence Through Teaching*. Harper.
Read, K. E. (1965) *The High Valley*. Scribners.
Reich, W. (1942) *The Functions of the Orgasm*. Panther, 1968.
Ricks, C. (1970) 'Make fun, not love', *Listener*, 26 February 1970.
Rieff, P. (1960) *Freud, the Mind of the Moralist*. Gollancz.
Rolph, C. H. (1969) *Books in the Dock*. Deutsch.
Roszak, T. (1969) *The Making of A Counter Culture*. Doubleday.
Rycroft, C. (ed.) (1966) *Psychoanalysis Observed*. Constable.
Sanford, N. (1967) *Where Colleges Fail*. Jossey-Bass.
Schofield, M. (1965) *Sexual Behaviour of Young People*. Penguin.
Stevenson, R. L. (1888) 'A Christmas sermon' in *Scribner's Magazine*. Republished by Scribner's and Chatto & Windus (various dates).
Stuart, G. (1956) *Narcissus*. Allen & Unwin.
Todd, R. (1970) 'Voices of Harvard '70', *New York Times* Magazine, 7 June 1970.
Unwin, J. D. (1934) *Sex and Culture*. Oxford University Press.
Winnicott, D. W. (1958) *Collected Papers*. Tavistock.
Winnicott, D. W. (1965) *The Maturational Processes and the Facilitating Environment*. Hogarth.
Wren-Lewis, J. (1966) 'Love's Coming of Age' (in Rycroft (ed.), 1966).
Wright, D. (1970) *Sexual Behaviour*. *Listener*, 23 July 1970.

Part III

New education and new educators

Thirteen

Promethean man
A tribute to Sigmund Freud

'There is in all greatness something forbidding and inimical to the small, and all great men have their enemies. It is only after many days that mankind resolves upon canonizing them and enters their names on the roll of those who may be invoked and must not be criticized. It is only of the dead that nothing is spoken but good.'

R. G. Collingwood, *Speculum Mentis*

Freud is not yet officially canonized, either by the community of psycho-analysts (who have been sorely tempted in this respect) or by the much wider community of those whose work and thought has been influenced by him. If he eventually escapes this fate, as he would assuredly have wished to do, this might well come to be regarded as perhaps the greatest of all tributes to what he accomplished. To my mind, Freud was, in effect, concerned above all else to bring the gods to earth, not fleetingly, as strange visitants, possessing spirits, messiahs or even archetypal symbols, but for ever, in their only possible enduring incarnation—the minds and hearts of all men everywhere. Thus man could at last come to grips with himself. Freud was concerned to reach and to fan the flame of the Olympian fire in man, and in fanning it to reveal more plainly the nature of that common human greatness which distinguishes the most humble of men from the rest of creation, and the nature of the price that has to be paid for this distinction. That greatness he revealed as essentially based on man's inner triumph over suffering. For man overcomes his primitiveness only by accepting pain, frustration and inner conflict, and renouncing unlimited pleasure, gratification and perpetual inner peace. His inner triumph is not a work of conquest but of acceptance, the full acceptance of the opposites of his greatness, of his power to love and create—namely, his littleness, his power to hate and destroy. The outstanding greatness of particular men is thus but the greatness of man himself raised to a specially high degree, and the acceptance of this point of view spells the doom of deification and canonization alike, and of all attitudes towards others and towards the self of which they are the type.

If Freud does escape canonization he will owe a very great deal to his biographer. But for Dr Jones it is doubtful whether the world would ever have known how fully Freud's life exemplified the conception of greatness to which his work naturally leads. By now it is almost superfluous to praise this magnificent book. There has been an almost uninterrupted paean since the appearance of the first volume nearly five years ago. Perhaps we may agree with Professor Henry A. Murray of Harvard that for serious students of human nature this is 'very probably the best biography ever written' and some may even venture to endorse his prophesy that it will outlive Plutarch's *Lives* and Boswell's *Johnson*. Informed opinion has thus strikingly confirmed a remarkable prediction made seven years ago by K. R. Eissler:[1]

> The total history of a man may be trivial, or it may be like a work of art. Among the immense store of biographical records scattered over the world there are only a few which concern the truly great. To make it possible for mankind to be enriched by a new and great life history, many extraordinary circumstances must conspire. The man must himself be great and the historical conjunctures opportune. Both elements were present in Freud's life ... and when he has one day found a biographer equal to his genius, no one, I surmise, will wish to have a single detail come about otherwise than it did in fact come about. This tendency towards biographical perfection which is characteristic of the lives of the great will surely not be wanting in Freud's.

Dr Jones has good cause to rest content. He is revealed as a man capable in every way of dealing justly, faithfully and brilliantly with his tremendous subject.

It is natural to ask oneself wherein Freud's greatness really lay, whether one can perceive anything of its origins and growth, and what, from a general and particularly an educational standpoint, is the significance of his contributions to the understanding of human nature. There can be little doubt of the nature of his central achievement. It was his own self-analysis resulting in, as its first fruit, the explicit discovery of the Œdipus complex, a discovery leading ultimately to the secret of the Olympian fire—to the source of creative power. Here indeed was defiance of Zeus himself. Of this Jones writes:[2]

> [when he was forty-one] Freud undertook his most heroic feat—

a psycho-analysis of his own unconscious. It is hard for us
nowadays to imagine how momentous this achievement was,
that difficulty being the fate of most pioneering exploits. Yet the
uniqueness of the feat remains. Once done it is done for ever.
For no one again can be the first to explore those depths.
In the long history of humanity the task has often been attempted.
Philosophers and writers from Solon to Montaigne, from
Juvenal to Schopenhauer, had essayed to follow the advice of
the Delphic Oracle ('know thyself'), but all had succumbed to
the effort. Inner resistance had barred advance.

Central to his achievement as it was, the remarkable degree of personal insight to which Freud attained does not by itself constitute his greatness. He did three other remarkable things. From his own lonely struggle he evolved a technique of research and therapy which enabled him to do for others what he had done for himself and enabled them in turn to bring enlightenment and a decrease in suffering to others again. Secondly, by perceiving how his discoveries related to human development in general and not just to that of the severely mentally afflicted, he was able to give a conceptual form to them which laid the foundations of a general theory of human development. Thirdly, he founded a movement and gave it an institutional framework, the International Psycho-Analytical Association, with its various affiliated national societies, within which the theory and practice of psycho-analysis could develop through the solidarity of its practitioners in the face of a hostile world. His insights, the analytical instrument he forged, the conceptual system he created and the movement he founded and sustained, each of these would have been a notable achievement for any man. Freud's success in all four fields reveals his true stature.

It is of course precisely in the directions of these great achievements that we can see the necessary limitations of his own work, and how subsequent developments have both added to and modified his own conclusions. His own analysis (carried out by himself unaided, be it remembered) would not by modern technical standards be regarded as very thorough. He was not able for example to penetrate very far into those more primitive defences which underlie the oedipus complex—given his pioneer situation and his most favourable relations with his own mother, it would have been frankly incredible had he been able to do so—and reach the very early levels of experience in which the outcome of conflicts in the infant's relation to its mother (or mother substitute) and her breast (or breast substitute) is of crucial importance for later development. It is therefore, for example, not at all surprising that he missed the full significance of the opening of the Œdipus story—the abandonment by Jocasta of her child. Analytic technique too has advanced and altered. The change might be described by saying that it is now less a matter of recovering buried memories, of merely uncovering early conflicts or traumas, than of re-activitating, re-living in feeling and phantasy, and re-patterning by means of the analytic transference, those infantile and childish relationships which are the foundations of adult character structure.

In the conceptual field also Freud's hypotheses and system of concepts (continually modified by himself in the light of fresh evidence) are undergoing extension and modification both from within the analytic movement and by discoveries and conceptual advances in related fields such as social anthropology and comparative studies of animal behaviour. As striking as the modifications are the confirmations of Freud's basic views. For example, Jones himself calls in Margaret Mead and Clyde Kluckholn, leading American anthropologists, as witnesses. He quotes the latter as saying: 'The facts uncovered in my own field-work and that of my collaborators have forced me to the conclusion that Freud and other psycho-analysts have depicted with astonishing correctness many central themes in motivational life which are universal. The styles of expression of these themes and much of the manifest content are culturally determined, but the underlying psychologic drama transcends cultural differences', and 'I am convinced that the essential universality of the oedipus complex and of sibling rivalry are now established by the anthropological record.' I might add also that no serious student of human behaviour should omit to consult a comparative study of developments in instinct theory by Fletcher[3] which shows how closely related are Freud's formulations based on certain aspects of human behaviour to those arrived at quite independently through recent observations of animal behaviour.

It is fascinating too to follow in Jones's account the growth of the psycho-analytical movement, and how in much of their behaviour its members displayed (and even to some extent still display) precisely those intolerances, jealousies and hostilities displayed by every small tightly knit in-group which faces a hostile larger society, particularly if it possesses valuable but highly disturbing knowledge. The cabalistic manoeuvres, defections, loyalties, schisms and alliances are powerfully reminiscent of religious and political life, and there are those who are foolish enough to jeer on this account. There is no occasion even for surprise, let alone a heavily defensive moral superiority. The powerful primitive passions which are the daily pre-occupations of analysts are of course precisely those which are at work (in a more or less sublimated form) in family, religious, political and scientific organization. The insight into and control of primitive feeling which analysts acquire through their own analysis is relative only, and comes most fully into play in the analytic situation itself in dealing with the counter-transference. To expect such insight and control to be other than partial in most of the situations in life is to fail altogether to understand what analysis can achieve—it is to suppose that it is a gospel of salvation. The group behaviour of analysts is just what would be predicted on their own hypotheses, but as one might also expect with the growth of a climate of more or less informed public and scientific opinion favourable to psycho-analytic thought, the tensions and acerbities of the earlier years are tending to diminish. Freud's creation of a secret militant sect or cult (which is how the analytical organization has often appeared to those outside it) was fully justified by his own hypotheses regarding the hostilities and resistances his discoveries would necessarily encounter, and has been vindicated by the progress of the movement to the present time when all over the world analysts and non-analytic students of human nature are beginning to develop far reaching forms of co-operation in research.

Is it possible to understand, from Freud's own childhood and education and from his developed adult character, how his unique achievement came about? Here Dr Jones has done a truly magnificent job and his account cannot be appreciated without reading it in its entirety. Even so there is much that is obscure, and this emphasizes how far short of completeness is our present understanding of human beings, and one feels that Freud would be the first to agree. Certain matters however stand out with great clarity. Freud was faced with an astonishingly complex family situation. He was the first child of his father's second marriage, and was born an uncle. His younger half-brother was the same age as his mother—his father being of course much older—and this fits in very well with the hypothesis that because his oedipal jealousy of his father could be easily displaced on to his half-brother, he was able to develop an exceedingly close and affectionate relationship with his real father. In this way the anxieties and therefore the defences inherent in the negative side of the oedipus complex may have been substantially reduced—accounting in part for the insight he eventually obtained into these early relationships. He was temporarily displaced in his mother's affection at eleven months by a young brother who eventually died at eight months old when Freud was nineteen months. Freud (in a letter to Fliess, 1897) 'admits the evil wishes he had against his rival and adds that their fulfilment in his death had aroused self-reproaches, a tendency to which had remained ever since.' Jones adds: 'In the light of this confession it is astonishing that Freud should write twenty years later how almost impossible it is for a child to be jealous of a newcomer if he is only *fifteen* months old when the latter arrives.'[4] Such is the recurrent power of man's primitive defences, against self-knowledge.

Further complexities were introduced by the existence of his nephew John, one year older than himself, who was the constant playmate of his youth and towards whom his feelings were deeply ambivalent. He later remarked himself how 'an intimate friend and a hated enemy have always been indispensable to my emotional life.' We now know how, in the beginning, these two are usually one and the same person, and how frequently in later development the conflicting impulses become separated and directed towards different persons. One fact is perhaps of overriding importance in understanding Freud's powerful and resilient adult character, and his indomitable courage in the face of the savage hostility which his discoveries aroused, and later in the face of protracted and intense physical suffering. This was the deep and secure relation he enjoyed with his mother, which was but transitorily disturbed by the arrival of other children. He wrote: 'A man who has been the indisputable favourite of his mother keeps for life the feeling of a conqueror, that confidence of success that often induces real success.'

Although research among school records has revealed almost all the external facts about his scholastic progress, nothing is really known of the inner aspect of this important part of his life. There is an Essay on Schoolboy Psychology which he wrote for the fiftieth anniversary of his secondary school, and from this emerges a lively picture of the adolescent emotional relationships between boys and their teachers, which is doubtless based on his own experience; but nothing emerges of specific importance for his own development. Of his later education at the university a great deal more is known, and Jones gives a vivid picture of the influence of his teachers in science and medicine, particularly in physiology which was his first love. It is worth remarking, however, that Freud, before becoming a scientist, had mastered a large number of languages, a fact which is probably of great significance when we attempt to understand the catholicity and depth of his knowledge and interest in humanity. In addition to being a distinguished stylist in his native German, he was completely at home in Latin and Greek, had a thorough acquaintance with French and English, and could read Italian, Spanish and Hebrew. His intellectual appetite and capacity were enormous. Besides ranging widely in biology (far beyond what was required by the medical curriculum) he attended seminars in philosophy, and after having been a university student for two and a half years he began the first of his numerous researches on the gonadic structure of eels. He wrote in his paper: 'No one has ever found a mature male eel—no one has yet seen the testes of the eel in spite of innumerable efforts through the centuries.' How eagerly will this revelation be seized upon by those of his detractors who base their attacks on his alleged pre-occupation with sexual themes!

Of his courtship and marriage, his difficulties in choice of a career, the extraordinary incident of his discovery of the properties of cocaine, and of his long uphill struggle in his chosen field, there is too much to be said for comment here. What of the man himself as he emerges into maturity, achievement and old-age? In his courtship he displayed the most intense and unjustifiable jealousy, and here again we are reminded of the situation and events of his childhood. Nevertheless, he was a splendid husband and father, affectionate to a degree, deeply attached and utterly faithful to his wife and all his family. He was a loyal and generous friend, extending unfailing courtesy and displaying extreme personal kindness to all who sought his aid. He was a prodigious worker, but it is a relief to lesser mortals to be told that after working as was his custom well into the small hours, he did not spring fresh and vigorous from his bed in the morning. He was extremely difficult to rouse and reluctant to get started. But he was never late!

A number of characteristics, however, stand out above all others. The first was his deep rationality. The irrational side of man's nature could only have been explored by someone whose own rationality was unusually secure. His intellectual integrity was uncompromising and unquestionable. Perhaps only Darwin, whom he deeply revered, could compare with him in this respect. Students of psycho-analysis know well the severe test to which he was put by finding that the stories of infantile seduction which all his early patients produced had practically no foundation in fact, and how, through pondering on this tremendous apparent reverse, and re-weighing all the evidence, he made one of his greatest discoveries—the universal existence and power of childish phantasy. This discovery was the basis for the growth of the concept of psychological reality. His courage has already been mentioned and Jones regards his combination of courage and scepticism as one of the keys to his success. But his rationality and scepticism only just balanced a quite extraordinary vein of credulity, and it is in this fine balance that Jones finds another important key. But the great secret Jones considers to have lain in the immense strength of his truth-seeking impulse, formed undoubtedly on his deep attachment to his mother and his complete confidence in her love. It is only when such confidence exists that curiosity, which is sexual and aggressive in origin, can safely be allowed untrammelled play.

But that confidence was bought of an inner struggle in which Freud had persistently to assert his independence and subdue his inclination to believe in others more than in himself. Many of those he trusted betrayed him—and they were without exception men. Where was the prototypic experience which predisposed Freud to form relationships with those who would eventually fail him, and which may also have enabled him eventually to overcome this disposition? Assuredly not with his own father, Jones concludes: 'There was his half-brother, Philip, so given to joking as Freud himself remarked, whom he suspected of being his mother's mate and whom he tearfully begged not to make his mother again pregnant. Could one trust such a man, who evidently knew all the secrets, to tell the truth about them? It would be a curious trick of fate if this insignificant little man—he is said to have ended up as a pedlar—had through his mere existence proved to have fortuitously struck the spark that lit the future Freud's determination to trust himself alone, to resist the impulse to believe in others more than in himself, and in that way to make imperishable the name of Freud.'[5]

The story of his long and painful but stoical fight against an encroaching cancer is the closing episode of an assuredly heroic career. His fortitude was immense. Granted asylum in England in 1938 from Nazi persecution, he died in 1939 in his eighty-third year, at work upon his 'Outline of Psycho-Analysis'.

From one point of view, Freud's significance for education is simply a reflection of his significance for a general understanding of human nature. His work has profoundly altered our whole outlook on behaviour and development, much more so than many of us realize. We are primarily indebted to him (although others from Plato onwards have glimpsed its importance) for the whole notion of an unconscious dimension in personality functioning, and hence for our understanding of the dynamics of behaviour. It was he too who first gave us a clear conception of the *modus operandi* of the moral function, its growth in childhood, and the variety of its forms, many of them of crucial importance in the study and treatment of mental illness and of pathological behaviour generally. There is scarcely a branch of modern thought concerning human affairs which does not show traces of his influence. Moreover, his promethean act of laying bare the springs of belief, the way in which symbols grow, and whence they derive their power has not of course gone unpunished. Although brought to earth, the gods are not mocked. On us has fallen the cruelly hard task of reinterpreting symbols in a way which does justice both to their infantile origins and to their potential significance as vehicles of truth, for the development of adult attitudes to life and for the deeper enjoyment of it. In all such legacies of Freud's work educators have an inescapable share.

Nevertheless, as teachers we have a right to ask for more. In what respects is Freud's work of direct importance in the everyday work of educating children? He himself had very little indeed to say about it, and his own direct work with children was minimal. Large numbers of people associate his name with certain views on the upbringing of children, views which as often expressed are either gross distortions of what he said, or quite illegitimate deductions from his theory of personal development. Educationists, particularly in this country, know of the direct influence on work with young children in nursery and infant schools which has been inspired by the pioneer labours of his daughter Anna, and of Susan Isaacs and Melanie Klein. His ideas too lay behind the work of many of the progressive schools which sprang up after World War I, and while much that was done in these schools was based on misconceptions of Freud's views, the attempt to gain a deeper understanding of childhood which inspired these efforts has had a not inconsiderable and valuable effect on schooling generally. Yet perhaps the majority of teachers and many students of education, when they are not actually hostile to psycho-analysis, fail to understand how Freud's work can have much practical consequence in the ordinary affairs of school life. Against this failure has to be set what would appear to be the potential consequences of his revolutionary discoveries about the nature and development of human personality. What is the explanation of this apparent contradiction? Must one accept the suggestion which is often made that by their emphasis on the importance for character formation of the first five years of life, psycho-analysts have drastically reduced the importance of the teacher and the school in children's development? On the contrary, I would suggest that this idea, which misrepresents the whole analytic conception of what is entailed in development, is a defence against the need which would arise if psycho-analytic views were really accepted, to alter in a most radical way many of our prevailing assumptions regarding the nature of education itself.

What is the central concern of education, its supreme aim? Surely its central concern is with personal development, and its supreme aim the growth of children into mature persons. We see this growth taking place when children are truly engaged or absorbed in what they are learning, and we wonder what is the secret of learning of this kind, and why some teachers can evoke it more readily than others. Freud's ideas suggest that the secret lies in an inner freedom, a freedom possible only in a setting of personal relationships which have a particular quality. The provision of this setting is the contribution of the good teacher. What then is the essence of the relationship between teacher and children which makes such inner freedom possible? Its essence would appear to be the teacher's capacity for unconditional acceptance of each child as he is—an acceptance which the child is able to feel, and through which he is unconsciously convinced that the teacher is on his side —on the side of that part of himself which is trying to gain control over primitive impulses and over the irrational and inhibiting demands of the most primitive levels of his own emerging conscience.

Being on the child's side has of course nothing to do with either sentimentality about children or letting them do exactly as they please. In Freud's terms the teacher's capacity to accept children as they are is essentially his capacity to accept both their love and hate—love and hate which is continually being expressed in countless disguised forms in all their learning and relationships. A necessary condition of this capacity to accept children's love and hate is that the teacher can accept his own love and hate, that is that he is able to accept the child within himself. Most of the time the crux of the matter is his capacity to acknowledge and accept the existence of hate, of hostile feelings, both the child's and his own, albeit this acceptance is usually an unconscious matter. Only when the child feels that he is fully, wholly and unconditionally accepted in this way, is he free to develop his powers. It is only when hate is accepted that love can work its creative miracles. This is incidentally the key to the real meaning of the idea of redemption. In the creative learning of a good home and a good classroom where the duality of human feelings is fully accepted, the world is redeemed every day, haltingly, intermittently, but significantly. In the long run this is the only way in which its redemption is possible.

This capacity for the acceptance of the duality of feeling presupposes that the teacher is primarily concerned with the child's welfare rather than with his own needs, that he himself is mature enough to be able to fulfil his own nature through another's growth. This is readily recognized as the distinguishing mark of a good parent; it is no less the distinguishing mark of the good teacher. Again, in Freud's terms we are here recognizing that personal maturity is achieved when our capacity for loving others is greater than our own need for love. Now none of this is new truth, but it is truth which is very difficult really to accept and which hitherto we have glimpsed but fleetingly, and usually in a mythological form (e.g. in Christianity). Nor has it necessarily anything to do with being analysed. Good teachers have always existed. What Freud's work has done is to reveal the secret of the good teacher, and he has therefore in principle provided the key with which more and more ordinary teachers may be able to discover the good teacher within themselves. Again this is not something requiring a personal analysis in any technical sense. What it does imply is an education for teachers, both initially and through refreshment, which enables them more and more to understand, accept and hence modify their own feelings towards children, towards one another and towards themselves.

Freud's work was concerned at bottom with setting free man's creative powers, powers epitomized in everything implied by the term reason. Fundamentally this means setting free man's power to love. His promethean feat lay in the discovery that there is no freedom for love except through the acceptance of its opposite, hate. But Freud's work has given us no grounds whatever for supposing that the task of making love and reason supreme in human affairs is anything but Herculean. It suggests rather an unending struggle, an unending drama of redemption, in which education has a leading part to play. One wonders how he would have met the news of the fate of his elderly sisters whom he had to leave behind in occupied Vienna when he came to this country. He did not live to hear the news that they had been incinerated by the Nazis. Probably with courage and resignation as he met every other blow. He knew better than anybody else that, in revealing the secret of the Olympian fire in man, he was inviting man to come to grips not only with the divine in himself, but also with the diabolic. Ernest Jones has given him a splendid epitaph. It seems to me appropriate to add that accorded by Shelley to Prometheus:

> To suffer woes which Hope thinks infinite;
> To forgive wrongs darker than death or night;
> To defy Power, which seems omnipotent;
> To love and bear . . .
> . . . This like thy glory Titan is to be
> Good, great, joyous, beautiful and free;
> This is alone Life, Joy, Empire and Victory.

Originally published in the *New Era*, vol. 39, no. 3, March 1958; I have published a rather more technical appreciation of Freud's significance for education in A. V. Judges (ed.), *The Function of Teaching*, Faber, 1959.

References

1 K. R. Eissler, 'An unknown biographical letter by Freud and a short comment', *International Journal of Psycho-analysis*, vol. 32, pt. 4 (1951), pp. 319–24.

2 E. Jones, *Sigmund Freud: Life and Work*, Hogarth Press, 1954–7, vol. 1, p. 351. On the question of priority, Eissler has this to say:

> From time to time it is urged that Freud's self analysis had historical precursors and that others had been aware of their oedipal ties. Stendhal is certainly a very striking example. But closer scrutiny reveals that, notwithstanding all the unsolved problems in Stendhal's life, his knowledge of his oedipus complex rested on an entirely different mechanism from that of Freud. Stendhal was repeatedly exposed to his mother's seduction, and her passionate kisses overstimulated the boy's highly sensuous temperament far into the latency period. There can be do doubt that a large, if undetermined, number of men have remembered erotic feelings towards their mothers stemming from their mothers' seductive stimulation.

3 Ronald Fletcher, *Instinct in Man*, Allen & Unwin, 1953.

4 Jones, op. cit., p. 8.

5 Ibid., vol. 2, p. 483.

Fourteen

Scholar and teacher
A tribute to William Boyd

There is a perennial tension in academic life between scholarship and teaching. At times, for individuals, their conflicting demands may become almost unbearable. Yet, all of us who have thought about the nature and purpose of education, particularly higher education, know that this tension is, in general, both ineradicable and utterly necessary. Students may, on occasion, be the bane of our lives, yet they are our main, if not our only, justification as scholars, and are also the source of our deepest satisfactions as teachers. Whatever our field of scholarship, the arts or the sciences, scholarly activity represents the satisfaction of a deep need within us. It is probably true that the scholar gives of his best when concerned primarily with scholarship, and his own personal vision, rather than primarily with the needs of students. This does not mean that he cannot or should not consider the student at all, or that he may not sometimes with advantage deceive himself as to the inner purpose of his work. If he is to communicate his vision effectively, there is a sense in which the needs of students must always inform his work. And to be an effective teacher he himself must always continue to be a student. Yet, scholar, teacher, student do not have identical needs. In a wide and general sense they have an identity of purpose which is perhaps best expressed by saying that they require one another.

Within most of us, scholar, teacher, student most of the time achieve a somewhat limited concordat, and it is rare indeed to find scholar, teacher, student *and* man of action effectively combined in one person. They were so combined in William Boyd, educational thinker, historian and pioneer who, as head of the Education Department in Glasgow University for close on forty years, had a deep influence on generations of students and teachers. Boyd's most scholarly writing, as in *The Educational Theory of Jean-Jacques Rousseau* (1911), for example, reveals the same enthusiasm, the same sense of life that filled his teaching and inspired his students and is imbued with the same intellectual integrity and moral conviction that made him such a force in Scottish educational affairs, notably as a member of the education committees of Dunbartonshire and Ayrshire, on the Glasgow and West of Scotland Provincial Committee for the Training of Teachers, and in the Educational Institute of Scotland, of which he was President in 1920.

His was a truly creative life, from its humble beginnings in Ayrshire to its peaceful but fertile close in Devon. In him, rich native endowment received the finest educational nurture. At Kilmarnock Academy and Glasgow University his studies were both broad and deep in the best Scottish tradition, and in the remarkable galaxy of his teachers were to be numbered Edward Caird, Lord Kelvin, Gilbert Murray and A. C. Bradley. He was fond, too, of recalling that among his first students, when he taught as an assistant to Henry Jones in the Philosophy Department in Glasgow, was A. D. Lindsay. Such was Glasgow University at the turn of the century, and it was from such men that Boyd's own mind took fire. Much as he drew, in his own thinking, upon the neo-Hegelianism of Caird and Jones, and greatly as Rousseau and later even Dewey influenced him, it was Plato who challenged and engaged him most deeply. No Platonist—his was too critical and independent a mind for discipleship—he yet never ceased to learn from the ancient master. His first book was *An Introduction to the Republic of Plato* (1904) and the last published during his life was *Plato for Today* (1962).

Between these events were packed fifty-eight years of what he himself described as educational adventure—adventure in thought, word and deed. A student of philosophy all his working and thinking life, he became a distinguished educational theorist in his own right—yet never just a theorist. A sound experience as class teacher and headmaster behind him, he continued right throughout his nearly forty years of university teaching to engage in a range of other activities as diverse as the production of the 'Standard Spelling List' (1924), still widely used today, and the Clydebank Mutual Service Association in the dark days of unemployment in the thirties. A brilliant lecturer, he was continually experimenting with new ways of teaching and examining, and was a pioneer user of group discussion methods long before they became fashionable.

His great *History of Western Education*, first published in 1921, which has gone through many editions and been translated into many languages, and his *Education in Ayrshire Through Seven Centuries* (1961), are genuine works of scholarship drawing upon original sources. In the former work he set himself the task of displaying the history of education as a record of evolution—a record which in its own mode offers an account of the development of our western society. His method was to present, against a background of sociologically based chronology, the contrapuntal development of theory and practice from Hellenic times to the present day. Such a task would have been impossible without employing a guiding set of general concepts. These, however, remain only partly explicit and are never allowed to assume an abstract life of their own—there is here no ghostly dance of bloodless categories—but are depicted as being specified uniquely in the actions of peoples and in the ideas of their pioneers. The result is a profound and moving story, history in the grand manner. That William Boyd believed in the capacity of mankind to maintain the supremacy of constructive action over destructive impulse, the continual, hard won, and always partial victory of love over hate, is obvious. But his was no facile optimism, and he displayed the evolution he perceived in all its unevenness, its triumphs in all their fragility; the retrogressions and blind alleys were seen as integral parts of the whole.

In a final chapter he attempted to assay the first half of the present century, both in its achievements and disasters, as well as its implications for future good and evil. He did not shrink from accepting the fact that it may only be stark fear which in the end will bring man's now limitless power of destruction under constructive control. An atomic holocaust apart, he perceived the central threat of totalitarianism to our way of life to be the possibility that through the rigours of conflict, political as well as military, or through defeat even without occupation, that unique institution, so laboriously evolved and now spread across the earth —the European school—might disappear. The creation of the school as we know it, an instrument of collective purpose able to reflect, yet contain within bounds the tensions of a democratic society, he saw as one of the cardinal achievements of the civilizing spirit of the West. To him it was both instrument and symbol of democracy. Were he alive today, he would surely be among the first to assert that the school must continue to change its character, in the direction in which he had always advocated, if it is to retain its force as a civilizing influence throughout the world.

Firmly rooted in the past he was yet the most ardent of educational pioneers. He introduced child guidance to Scotland, was active in the development of the movement for parent-teacher associations, stood firmly for graduate status for the teaching profession, was himself an original researcher in child study, in testing and in teaching methods, and was a powerful member of the Scottish Council for Research in Education.

Such a nature immediately found itself at home among the other pioneers being gathered together by Beatrice Ensor in the N.E.F. just after the end of World War I. His work for the Fellowship and interest in its affairs, continuing right up to his death, is well known and is commemorated in his *New Era* articles and in his editorship of *Towards a New Education* (1930), a report of the N.E.F. World Conference at Elsinore. The Fellowship was for him not only a meeting place of kindred spirits but also a major instrument for that continual renewal and reform of education in which he saw man's greatest hope.

Unambitious for himself, he spared no efforts to secure wider acceptance of the importance of educational study. It was characteristic of him that he arranged for the royalties from his 'Standard Spelling List' to be paid into a fund for the foundation of a Chair of Education in the University of Glasgow. When the Chair was eventually founded, the university decided that the sum of over £2,000 which had accrued from this fund should be invested to provide the income for a William Boyd Prize in Education.

Possessed of a formidable intellect, his was yet always a philosophy of action. He was a practising socialist and regarded himself as a practising Christian, although he had little time for the dogmas of either party or Church. He fought all his life for freedom, both social and personal. From the description that he was socially a radical and religiously a Presbyterian agnostic he would probably not have dissented, but such words and phrases cannot adequately characterize his passion for social justice and the deep personal warmth of his humanism. It was above all this warmth, this bigness of mind and heart that endeared him to his students. He gave them not only the vision and the encouragement needed for them to find a way of life for themselves, but his personal friendship as well. His most enduring memorial will surely be in the influence he has had in their lives, within Scotland and all over the world. This is as he himself would have wished it. His loyalties were at once intensely homely and also completely universal. He summed it up himself at the end of *America in School and College* when he wrote: 'My desire for Scottish well-being is bound up with a desire for human well-being. In that sense I pray with greater comprehensiveness, "Thy Kingdom come. Thy will be done, on earth as in Heaven."'

During the last decade of his life William Boyd was planning and writing a book to be called 'The New Education of the Twentieth Century'. He never completed it, but most fortunately, and at Boyd's own wish, the manuscript passed to an old friend and collaborator, Wyatt Rawson, himself a pioneer educator. Rawson edited Boyd's manuscript and added a good deal of material of his own (much of which had in substance been discussed with Boyd) and the book was published jointly as *The Story of the New Education* (Heinemann, 1965).* In his preface, Rawson remarks that 'Boyd planned to preface his book with a chapter explaining what the New Education is. He thought two points fundamental: First, in all education the personality of the child is an essential concern; second, education must make for human betterment, that is for a New Era.' There could be no more succinct summing up of Boyd's faith. For him the person was paramount and in one of his last letters to Rawson he wrote: 'the great need is still to make education personal and creative'. This takes us back to the heart of this tribute—only when education is personal and creative can the ideal identity of scholar, teacher, student and man of action be realized.

Rawson himself points out that we have learned two major lessons during this century—the first, 'that schools by themselves cannot hope to build a new society' and the second, 'that the key to the changes required lies in the education of the teacher in a new attitude and a new faith.' William Boyd would have agreed entirely. He saw with singular clarity that it is only through the life and work of men and women who are both free in themselves, and who live in a free society, that love and reason can become enduringly manifest in the world.

William Boyd, M.A., B.Sc., D.Phil., LL.D., was appointed the first Lecturer in Education in the University of Glasgow in 1907. He became Reader in Education and was head of department until his retirement in 1946. Born in 1874, Boyd had a world-wide reputation as a scholar in the history of Education and was one of the foremost of the 'new educators' of the twentieth century. I became his student in 1933, later his colleague in the university, and remained a close personal friend until his death in 1962. This is a revised and slightly enlarged version of an appreciation published in *The New Era*, vol. 43, no. 8, October 1962.

* Some of Boyd's views about the New Education were in fact published by him as 'The Basic Faith of the New Education Fellowship', chapter 6 of *Year Book of Education 1957*, part II, Evans.

Fifteen

Objectives and perspectives in education
A tribute to Winifred Mercier[1]

When I received the invitation to come here this evening, extended to me from you through the Principal of the College, I was pleased. I am now grateful. I was pleased, because this is the first time I have ever had an opportunity of visiting Whitelands. The reason for my gratitude is that the invitation has provided me with an opportunity to come to know something of the life and work of a very remarkable woman, about whom I willingly confess I knew very little. To have come to know something about Winifred Mercier is cause enough for gratitude.

All pioneers are people of vision. They have a view of life which leads out beyond the immediate issues and perplexities of the present and of the purely local scene and this enables them to perceive those elements in the here and now which are not obvious but which are fraught with possibilities for the future. To be effective pioneers, they need both clarity, realism and great courage. That is to say that their vision has to be in terms of quite definite objectives, and of the routes by which these may be reached, and that the vision has to be energized by endless devotion. Quite often, however, such people are committed to single objectives in the pursuit of which they ignore everything else, including the objectives of others, and in triumphantly reaching their own objectives they may leave behind much wreckage on the way. Sometimes too in such cases the goal aimed at turns out in the end to be of very questionable value, because the price which has had to be paid for it is found to be much too high. One might say perhaps that the pursuit of a just and valid method of selecting children for a grammar-school education has turned out to be an objective of just this kind. Is it not possible that our pursuit of a similar test for entry to higher education will in the long run turn out to be a mistake of the same nature?

Pioneers with too much singleness of mind and heart may have clear objectives but their vision lacks the perspectives that would enable them to see the chosen goal as only one among a large range of inter-related goals and one which needs interpretation in the light of all the rest. They habitually neglect the wisdom of the ancient Chinese proverb which cautions those who would erect earthen walls lest they find that they only succeed in digging a pit.

Winifred Mercier was a great pioneer and an effective one, but she was also the kind of pioneer, rather rare in education, who brought her personal objectives within a wide and embracing perspective. In honouring her tonight I thought that it might be appropriate if we were to attempt to review some of our own educational objectives, many of which she shared, in the light of some of the perspectives into which they fit. I propose therefore to discuss some of the major issues in the education and training of teachers and in the functioning of our educational system with which teacher education is so intimately linked.

The education and training of teachers

Teacher education is a field in which Winifred Mercier laboured magnificently and in which in this College she found the crown of her career. In her day the great objectives were the prolongation of the education of the teacher, involving the abolition of the pupil-teacher year, the universalizing of the two years of professional preparation and the establishment of an unbreakable link with the university world. She was a member of the Departmental Committee of 1925 which ultimately led to the creation of the Joint Examining Boards centred on the universities, and, as we all know, these were the forerunners of our present Institutes of Education. Now all these objectives were achieved and the educational price was on the whole, I think, minimal. The reason for the smallness of this price was, I believe, that the perspective in which these several objectives found their place, itself formed an element in a grand strategy embracing the purposes of education as a whole. What of our own times? What are the objectives on which we have recently set our hearts? We now rejoice in the establishment of a three-year course of education and training for teachers, as the logical continuation of the work to which Winifred Mercier gave so much. We are also seeing, at this very moment, the establishment of a fourth-year degree course for some college of education students, involving even closer links with the universities.

The three-year course is now an established fact: it has been accepted. In seeking to establish it our immediate objective was substantially the same as in Winifred Mercier's time: an adequately educated and trained profession. But did this objective for the three-year course give us a wide enough perspective by itself?

What of the price? We do not yet know the full price, but I confess to a certain uneasiness. It is often said that even with the accompanying expansion of the colleges (and only those who have lived and worked in them in the last five or six years know what this means) the three-year course contributes fundamentally to our dire teacher shortage. This shortage is indeed dire.[2] But beyond this it seems to me that the attempt to extend the education of teachers has not been accompanied by a willingness to examine fully such questions as what the teacher's role should be and what other kinds of people we need in our schools today. No proper examination of the school as a functioning community has as yet been made, although the new Nuffield-sponsored project on resources for learning may make a significant contribution. This links up of course with the sheer enormity of the demand for teachers which our present educational objectives seem to require. We may well ask, I think, whether it is conceivable that any society can allow one single profession to swallow up such a large proportion of its own product. The implication is that we are still reluctant to examine what the function of the teacher should be *vis-à-vis* other sorts of people, auxiliaries of various kinds. Or do we perhaps dream that in the grand automated society of tomorrow everyone will be free to teach everyone else? To teach them what, I wonder? I think these are dangerous and misleading phantasies. And so I continue to be haunted by the feeling that the price for our single-mindedness about the three-year course may well turn out to be too high. Personally, however, I would still be unrepentant about the extension to three years, provided that we now tackle the other related problems which have been sadly neglected.[3]

What about the latest development—the fourth year for some of the students, giving the opportunity to study for a Bachelor of Education degree? I feel that Winifred Mercier would have rejoiced at this development. I myself have been and still am in the thick of the struggle which surrounds the creation of this degree and it may be that my own vision has been so foreshortened that I under-estimate the dangers attendant on the achievement of this objective. I am convinced of the rightness of the objective itself. A significant proportion of our college students are capable of deeper study and of achieving a sharper intellectual edge to their educational understanding through degree level work. None the less, I think that the dangers are serious. Foremost among them is what we could call the backwash effect which the struggle for high academic standards for relatively few students may have upon the rest of college work. Shall we see a false academicism gradually undermine the professional competence and vision which at its best the three-year course is now achieving? Will the pursuit of high standards in the 'academic' sense by students and their tutors drain away vital energy from the essential focus upon learning and curriculum studies? We will need to be extremely vigilant and determined if these things are not to happen. Winifred Mercier herself foresaw the danger in 1923 when the question of university education for all teachers was being canvassed. She was unreservedly against it and I am sure she was right—for her time and for our time too—and by that I mean the immediate present and the near future. Yet the creation of this fourth year and the possibility of degree studies for some students is an essential step forward.

What of the future in teacher education? One of our recently passionately pursued objectives was the full implementation of the main recommendations on teacher training made in the Robbins Report: the entry of colleges of education as self-governing bodies into the federal structure of university schools of education. Many of us, including myself, have been grievously disappointed here and we may well be going to be disappointed further if all the local education authorities do not fully implement the recommendations of the National Study Group on the Government of Colleges of Education. I doubt very much if all will willingly do so. This particular objective—of responsible and dignified self-government for colleges—is one which I would personally pursue to the end, however bitter the struggle and whatever the price.

What can briefly be said with regard to the larger issue, the place of teacher training in our system of higher education and of the problems of what has come to be called the 'binary system'? I sometimes wonder where this metaphor comes from. Is it derived, perhaps, from astronomy? Is it a case of a dark star revolving round a bright one, and if so which is which? We shall have to live with this system for a while. In it the world of teacher education lies in an uneasy middle position partly within the so-called autonomous sphere of the universities, and partly within the sphere controlled by local government and to some extent by central government. In terms of the great sweeping perspective which is necessary here I think this binary system is fundamentally destructive. It seems to be the product not of government in the political sense but of the policies of the permanent powers that be in Curzon Street—those whom I sometimes like to think of as 'the new Mayfair set'. Many of these people are brilliant public servants, and all are I am sure devoted and well intentioned. Some of them are my good friends, and yet I think their present policies seem to have no regard for the kind of institutional structure which a free society requires. The issues here of course are exceedingly complex and any of us could be wrong.

Nevertheless on one issue I have myself no doubts. The education and training of teachers must ultimately be brought within that sector of higher education erroneously and mischievously called private, for it is only within this sector that the freedom necessary in the education of a great profession can be guaranteed. The freedom necessary in educating for a profession is not only intellectual or academic, but is also a freedom of conscience, in the best sense of that term, and this is incompatible with any form of direct political control. Where the members of a profession will for the most part subsequently be employed in a public service which is under political control, then the arguments for preparing them in institutions outside direct political control apply with even greater force. Certainly, of course, a profession owes equal loyalty to its own conceptions of integrity and to the public weal. In the long run it must be accountable to society as a whole, and hence freedom in the preparation of its members implies a condition of *relative* autonomy, the essential nature of which depends on respect for the similar autonomy of others, and of the whole.

Of course we must have national policies in the education and training of teachers. These must be resolutely pursued, but unless education itself is to be degraded in the process, the partners in a national policy—and in our kind of society central government is only one of these—must be free to enter into a continuous dialogue together in the pursuit of a true consensus. Moreover, such a dialogue must be effectively institutionalized. While a representative central government must have ultimate responsibility, the commission offered to 'autonomous' institutions must be genuine, generous and long term. Many of us also believe that such arrangements are not only necessary conditions of freedom but, in the long run, the best guarantee of national policies which are both right and effective. That is, we believe that freedom and right and effective national policies are essentially identical objectives. This is, I believe the perspective necessary in the field of higher education, and our current failure is the failure to develop a grand strategy which encompasses the basic conditions of freedom. This seems to me a very menacing failure indeed. It arises less from sinister intentions than from a weakness of vision.

Finally, in this sector of our endeavours can we look forward to a fully graduate teaching profession? This is a stated aim of policy of some at any rate of the teachers' organizations. It is of course a loaded question, one loaded with unanalysed ideas. Unless we are prepared to rethink the functions of those we want to continue to call teachers, and unless the universities themselves are prepared to re-examine the whole nature, purpose and standards of first degrees, then I think a fully graduate profession is a hopeless quest and one which if successful under present conditions would entail a ruinous price. There are stirrings in the universities. In time, I believe many will come to see that the so-called high standards of degrees and also the so-called high standards of A level GCE involve questionable values, questionable because the actual standards are so largely phoney. They are for many students pseudo standards which do not represent genuine personal achievements. We see the proof of this every day in our university work. Given new conceptions of teaching and of teachers and given a new form of university education which I believe must entail some kind of two-tier system (that means first degrees for a much greater proportion of the population with advanced studies for the abler ones), then a fully graduate profession is feasible without debasing the true coinage of personal and professional achievement. Of course, if this objective is achieved in these terms it may well turn out to be less important than many now think it to be, because of the other profound changes now going on in our society as a whole.

Among the arguments levelled against the introduction of the three-year course was that the goal of expanded teacher education would be better sought not through the expansion of initial training but through in-service education later on in the teacher's career. As an argument against the three-year course, I always thought this was a poor one, but the idea which it enshrines seems to me to be of enormous importance. Given the rate of change in modern society it is absolutely necessary on grounds both of professional competence and of personal well-being that all teachers should go on being educated—re-educated, if you like—throughout their lives. I will not, however, traverse this ground further since it has recently been so brilliantly done by Derek Morrell in his Joseph Payne Memorial Lecture. However much some people may wish to find fault with the present operations of the Schools Council, we must surely acclaim its foundation as a great event and we must surely play out part wholeheartedly in helping to work out the many and varied objectives which it brings together in one grand perspective. In any adequate conception of teacher education this in-service dimension is absolutely indispensable.

The scope of the school system: the comprehensive ideal

Let us now turn to certain issues concerning our school system. Because of the impending publication of the Plowden Report on the primary school I am going to focus attention elsewhere, and I would like to offer some observations on the ideal of a comprehensive system of education. To the pursuit of the objective of a truly comprehensive system of education in its proper and widest sense I would give my full and whole-hearted assent. Nothing less it seems to me is commensurate with the dignity of human beings. Many (but I think not all) institutionalized privileges in education can be got rid of and should be got rid of. We have of course to watch the price. There are already grave signs that short-sighted and too single-minded devotion to what are only parts of this grand design may well bring disaster in their train. Thus, we are now apparently committed to bringing into being, with quite insufficient time and absurdly inadequate financial means, a comprehensive system within the secondary stage of education. I do not intend to elaborate on this aspect. Instead I want to bring this objective into perspective from a different point of view. We may recall here with advantage Mark Twain's remark to the effect that you must be careful not to let your children's schooling interfere with their education. The function of the school is to provide only one part of a young person's education, the other parts being contributed by the home and the community, social and industrial. The objectives outlined in the Newsom Report concerning the relations of school and community are quite indispensable elements for an adequate perspective here. Yet I think that Newsom did not pay enough attention to Mark Twain. Mere chronological age is so often a quite misleading criterion of development that I believe that full-time schooling should be a variable and not a fixed element in the grand perspective of the comprehensive ideal. Otherwise the whole of education is in danger of being tyrannized by the school. I believe we are beginning to see the need for greater flexibility on the question of when 'school' should begin. Why not a similar flexibility as to when it should end?

May we now turn and look at the other end of the system, at the position of the under fives? Here indeed it seems to me is one of the darkest sectors of our whole endeavour. We are now agreed I think that a child's primary need is for adequate relationships first with a few and later on with an increasing number of older people, and alongside this, an increasingly wide social experience of children of his own age. Yet these needs do not begin at five years or later. The primary need of stable relationships begins at birth and the wider needs only a little later. Can any of us pretend that these needs are being adequately met for all children in our society? The Nursery School movement was a brave and pioneer effort to deal with this problem. Winifred Mercier was closely associated with it, being a member from its inception in 1924 to the end of her life, and she laboured valiantly for the cause. It may be that we will need to extend and redefine the scope of the movement if we are to fulfil our obligations to the very young. At present the play group movement voluntarily sponsored is gaining momentum but the effort is tiny compared with the need. The changing status and roles of women, and especially married women, in our society has, I am quite sure, come to stay. In this area of our concern for the young, health and education are quite obviously inextricably mixed, although of course they are always more closely related than the conduct of our school system would seem to suggest. Any government which takes the welfare of all its people as its supreme purpose must in the end be driven to act in this area if only for the sake of diminishing the incidence of crime, violence and overt mental illness. Let us hope that the Plowden enquiry into the primary stage of schooling may throw light into this dark area of our society.*

The organization of learning

I would like now to turn away from problems of educational provision, which are so largely problems for administrators and politicians, to look at what is happening within our educational institutions and to consider a few of the objectives and perspectives currently claiming our devotion there. This is the general field of what one may call the organization of learning.

First of all let us look at the objectives of teaching. I say objectives of teaching rather than aims of education. Aims are on the whole out of fashion now in educational thought, and for the most part for good reasons. I would largely agree here with Richard Peters's view of the matter. There is a wide and ominous gap between the objectives we publicly proclaim to be ours—development of the whole individual, etc.—and the actual *objectives implied by what we do*. What we do is still predominantly concerned with factual knowledge and with the passing of examinations and this emphasis involves a grave distortion of our declared objectives. Such a judgment is true of course to a diminishing extent in our primary schools, but it is still I think a judgment which remains true of the system as a whole. I am not here going to inveigh against examinations. The practical task is so to transform our conception of subjects and the teaching of subjects that examinations come to take their proper place in the whole process as a means for evalu-

* The Plowden Report, published in January 1967, does indeed do this, but society's response through governmental action has, so far, been pitiably inadequate.

ating and re-evaluating our objectives. This implies the reform of examinations, a process which now seems to be gaining some momentum. It obtained an initial impetus from the establishment of the Certificate of Secondary Education. Many people, however, still believe that the introduction of CSE was a retrograde step. If one reads all the evidence, however, it is very difficult to maintain this view. My main grounds for thinking that the CSE offers some hope for the future is of course the provision in it for schools to conduct their own examinations with the assistance of external moderators. In effect it has been suggested that there is no valid reason why we should not extend to schools a system of examination which holds good in all universities and in a great many colleges of education—the system of internal examinations externally moderated. In this field of examination reform lies another reason for welcoming the establishment of the Schools Council, for its terms of reference include both curriculum and examinations—two aspects of a single process which should never be pulled asunder.

Curriculum reform implies examination reforms, which in turn implies an analysis of objectives in teaching. It is in these terms that we are now beginning to understand how to set about closing the gap between our declared intentions and our actions. We can do so by learning how to spell out in detail what we are up to, and we can do this by a type of rigorous analysis of our subject syllabuses aimed at revealing the actual connections which exist between ends and means. For ends are inherent in all that we do. If ends, aims or objectives, call them what you will, are to be really effective in guiding our actions, they cannot remain as lofty and unanalysed aspirations to be referred to on speech days and in old-fashioned lectures on the philosophy of education. In this field we owe a great deal to the studies of Professor Bloom of Chicago and his colleagues. Their book, *The Taxonomy of Educational Objectives*, in its two parts, Cognitive Domain and Affective Domain, is now becoming extensively used in courses for advanced qualifications in education. Bloom and his co-workers have explored in detail the intricate ramifications of the goals we set in education. For example, the ability to interpret information, not just to remember it, can be shown to be highly complex and require the cultivation of a host of skills, none of which can be learned by devotion to particular subjects in isolation. In general our wider objectives in education all belong to a level of complexity which involve a many-sided approach. This indeed is not a new thesis. Assuredly not. Winifred Mercier herself had something to say about it. 'Educationists lament the strangle-hold which the separate subjects have gained on education. As the subjects grow from more to more, less of knowledge in us dwells. Happy only is the infant who has no subjects.'*

But the situation is different today. Bloom's analysis is a detailed account of the connections not between the separate subjects, but between the distinctive skills towards which many subjects contribute and which, acting together, constitute intellectual power. The Bloom analysis is a beginning only. It is an excellent beginning for theoretical study but even in theory it does not go far enough; for one thing, intellectual and emotional qualities should not be divorced. If they are, both will suffer. A still wider perspective is needed therefore to give us truly inclusive objectives for teaching, in which at last may be disclosed the whole human being. In our practice we have also made a beginning, largely due to the initiative of the Nuffield Foundation and now (and in the future increasingly) through work being made possible by the Schools Council. This development encompasses, for example, science, both junior and senior; mathematics for all ages; and modern languages from eight or nine upwards. In all these areas we are beginning the long task of adequately describing what it is we want to achieve and of identifying the means whereby we hope we may achieve it. The leaving age programme, too, as it is mistakenly and misleadingly called, is about to receive a powerful impetus from the same source. Beside these advances are of course obvious dangers, particularly in calling to our aid new and powerful tools which might be put into the service of too narrowly conceived ends. We will I hope remind ourselves of the often mistaken uses to which in the recent past we have put our powerful tools of psychological testing. To counteract the overweening claims of purely technical analyses we have to develop a perspective which embraces the curriculum as a whole and this has to be a perspective which sees the curriculum not only in terms of a timetable of activities and subjects, but in terms also of the qualities of heart and mind which we are endeavouring to foster.

Here we go back to Bloom and to the developments which ought to flow from his work. We are brought up short at this point, however, by an ominous dichotomy in our thinking. In all I have said so far about the organization of learning I have been speaking from the teachers'—from the adults'—point of view. This is an inescapable point of view in education. We are necessarily in a relatively much stronger position than our pupils to understand the complex development of thought and feeling which lies ahead of them and which is the means of initiating them into the world of adult

* Lynda Grier, *The Life of Winifred Mercier*, Oxford University Press, 1937, p. 189.

achievements and experience. Yet it is a platitude in our profession that all our analysis and preparation is brought to nought if we fail to take account of the process of human development and its vicissitudes. Without an intimate knowledge of the awakening being and his or her still largely unpredictable course of development, we not only fail to achieve our objectives in teaching, we often foist on the young objectives which are not properly *theirs* at all, and which irreparably distort their personal development. I will not here attempt to justify this statement, but I do believe that such failure and such distortion exist on a large and frightening scale in our educational institutions, and from this I certainly do not exclude the universities. Of course a great deal of stress is placed on studies in child development in colleges of education and this is a job which is by and large well done. Yet our educational practices often show very little result for it all. This suggests that the study of subjects and of the curriculum comes under one perspective, while the study of learning and of the growth of pupils' powers comes under a quite different perspective and that the two perspectives have little to do with each other. Do our teaching arrangements take much account of the second perspective? Here I would like to quote Winifred Mercier. On the question of organization: *

> Young pupils under 13 or 14 need a class teacher who knows them well and teaches them most of the subjects they learn. If they are taught by as many as five or six different teachers their general training will suffer. On the other hand, if they are in the exclusive charge of only one teacher for six months or a whole year, both they and she will suffer. The cricketer will never become a batsman if he faces one type of bowling only; children will lack mental alertness if in effect the bowling is not occasionally changed.

Yet in the primary school we are still aghast if more than one teacher is thought appropriate for a class, and in the earliest years of the secondary school we are seemingly quite happy with seven or eight or even more teachers. Do we really take account of personal growth in our teaching? Again may I quote from a document which owes much to Winifred Mercier's inspiration: †

> We must first clear our minds by studying the Beatitudes, and the standard of values revealed to us in the Parables. We can then ask ourselves pertinent questions as to our methods of

* Ibid., p. 188.

† *The Cambridge Syllabus of Religious Teaching for Schools*, Cambridge University Press, 1924, pp. 38–9.

> organization and discipline, and as to the value set in the school on the various interests that move children and the actions that result. Does the school routine encourage emulation and competition? or is it organized so as to make co-operation easy? Are there opportunities for the stronger to help the weaker?

I see this great divide, this separation of a perspective of adult teaching and a perspective of youthful learning and experiment as the profoundest danger attendant on our current endeavours. Am I merely trotting out the old arguments about adult-centred versus child-centred education? Not at all. I am pointing to the fact that the great divide still exists and that in maintaining it both protagonists reveal that they have missed the essential point about the whole educational enterprise. With furious and learned arguments still proceeding on both sides, most of which misunderstand the basic issues, can we devise an inclusive perspective for education to which all our objectives must be submitted? I think we can. The necessary perspective has always been before our eyes, although it is true I think that the social sciences have recently helped greatly to clarify it for us. What we have to do is recognize it and embrace it as our own. The key question to be answered is this: What is our educational enterprise really all about? Most of our answers are, I think, mistaken. It is not, in any but a subordinate sense, about training minds and equipping the citizens of the future. And neither is it about carefully tending the budding flower of the human personality in some sort of vacuum. In any particular society, and in the great human society as a whole, the educational enterprise is essentially a huge and complicated transaction between the generations, each learning from and modifying the vision of the other. Education is a two-way process: a transaction out of which the future grows. Adult and young person, pupil and teacher, are together involved in every step and all the time both must be prepared to change and learn from the other.

Education then, as a *transaction between the generations*, is the enterprise through which men seek to transform and redefine their patterns of life and value. Now although obvious this is in fact no simple concept, and the responsibility for fully grasping and applying the perspective it implies lies inescapably on the adult side. By and large we do not accept or even recognize this perspective yet. The division of 'we' and 'they' which exists on both sides in many schools and colleges (not, I am glad to say, in all) is only one symptom of our failure. But it is a crucial one.

Let me point to just one example of the problems affecting relationships between the generations. Today the young are openly struggling to redefine the ethics of personal relationships, in particular the sexual ethics. Yet what understanding and help do we give? How well equipped are we to give such help? Would it be accepted if it were offered? It will not be accepted and the split between the generations will not be healed unless we try to understand some of the fundamentals at stake. These fundamentals have very little to do with the formal teaching of the churches or with the moral law. But they have an enormous amount to do with the teaching of the founder of Christianity in the sense that they concern emotional and intellectual honesty, mutuality and love. Our society is still savagely moralistic and deeply hypocritical in sexual matters. It is my belief that the young today are seeking, in however a groping and confused way, to redefine the spheres of love and responsibility. They are reaching towards that union of Eros and Agape which alone holds the key to the maintenance of human dignity and to love's coming of age on this planet. Their search, however, is less effective than it might be because so few adults show enough understanding to be acceptable as senior partners in the enterprise.

This is only an example. The major question is whether we can attain a perspective that will allow us to see anew problems such as this. Can we accept as our all-inclusive perspective for education the vision of it as a living transaction between the generations which nourishes the whole of human society? This is, I think, the great perspective we have to master and its mastery will not be easy; for many it will be painful. The price in emotional terms is likely to be high but unless we are prepared to pay it I see no genuine grounds for hope in the future. At the heart of the educational enterprise lies our endeavour as adults to enable the young to fashion their own objectives and perspectives—not to get them to take on ours. The supreme test is whether what we do furthers this end or thwarts it.

Winifred Mercier was a woman of great courage and fortitude. She faced and overcame many setbacks and endured great physical pain. Our task of fashioning an inclusive and liberalizing perspective for education in our time is no less hard than the tasks she faced in hers. The only honour that she would ever accept from us would, I am sure, be that we should face our tasks with the same clear vision, with the same unflinching resolve, and with the same great hopes.

The Winifred Mercier Memorial Lecture delivered at Whitelands College, Putney, London, 26 October 1966.

Notes

1 Principal of Whitelands College, London, 1918–34.

2 Not now of course (1972), at least in the official view of what shortage means! A perceptive analysis of some of the salient issues of the recruitment, training and organization of a large teaching force has been made by my colleague, William Taylor (*Half a Million Teachers*, Bristol University, 1968).

3 Among these are problems of teaching practice (school experience) investigated by my colleague Edith Cope (*Education for Teaching*, Autumn 1969), and the equally pressing problems of probationary teachers, also studied by my colleagues Alan Brimer, Roger Dale and John Taylor (*A Survey of Teachers in their First Year of Service*, University of Bristol School of Education, 1969) and Ray Bolam (*Trends in Education*, January 1971).

Sixteen

Towards a creative education
A tribute to Sir Herbert Read

I think that for many educators Sir Herbert Read, through his writings, has been an immensely liberating influence. My own early education was almost entirely innocent of any activity that could be called artistic. Occasionally there was something called 'singing' but here my absence was much preferred to my presence. I did 'drawing' but I was hopeless at it. My representation of bottles, oranges, and human figures had little resemblance to the actual objects before me. Even today I don't believe that because of this they would have qualified me to be regarded in certain circles as a great artist in the making! Yet somewhere in the files of the Scottish Education Department, if anyone ever bothered to look, there would be found a record of the fact that I once obtained a pass in drawing at training college. This was a miracle. I did this course as an extra, after I had qualified as a teacher, because I found that I had not the slightest idea of what to do with children during the timetable period so marked. My college teacher was something of a genius. He must have been. Perhaps the only plausible reason for my passing was the fact that no one who had diligently attended ever failed. Nevertheless, something had happened to me. My complete conviction of my utter incapacity in this field had received a jolt. The idea took root that somewhere within me was the tiny germ of something that had never had a chance to flower.

Those of us whose experience was in any way similar to mine must feel when we look at schools today, particularly at infant and primary school, that we were cheated of a large part of our human inheritance. How different, how much better things are now, and how clear it is that among those responsible for this change, no one has been a more powerful influence than Sir Herbert Read. Yet we have still far to go.

My theme is 'towards a creative education'. What do we mean by creative education? What would it be like if we had one? Is such a thing possible? We often use the word creative and sometimes we say we use it about education for lack of a better word. We are apologetic. But can there be a better word? Our apologies sound like a defensive dodge. Don't we fight shy of the term 'creative' because we are deeply afraid and suspicious of what it means? Nowadays, of course, you may say that 'creativity' is all the rage, especially among psychologists. Yet note the great effort put into attempts to measure it and to predict its development, compared with the efforts directed to attempting to discover the conditons which nourish it. Measurement in education often seems to be to some extent a way of wrapping up abilities and labelling them, of making sure that they can be pinned down, and rendered harmless perhaps, harmless because predictable, and therefore to some extent controllable. Now I am sure that this is not necessarily the basic aim of measurement and assessment in education, but it does lend itself very easily to this misuse. What I am objecting to here, of course, is the idea that creative powers in any worthwhile degree are the possession of only some children, who therefore must be spotted and specially encouraged. This will not do. We must take as our point of departure, the belief that all children are naturally creative, and that if we do not nourish the creativity of all, we explicitly condemn some to a less than human life; implicitly we may go far to condemn all to a failure to perceive the creative spark in their fellow men.

What is creative education?

What do we mean by a creative education? The shortest and most satisfactory answer is to point to examples and say, 'There it is!' Nowadays we can point to many examples. We might go back quite a long way. In art for example we might begin with Cizek in Vienna. Then we have Sir Herbert's famous book which is teeming with illustrations.[1] We have also the wonderful examples from accounts of children's work by our chairman, Miss Seonaid Robertson, in her book *Rose Garden and Labyrinth.*[2] Nowadays we are surely all convinced of this kind of achievement.

In literature and particularly in poetry we have the work inspired by Miss Marjorie Hourd beginning with *The Education of the Poetic Spirit*[3] and carried on with Gertrude Cooper in *Coming into their Own.*[4] In music we could find many examples, but I have particularly in mind some primary schools in the West Riding inspired by the vision of Sir Alexander Clegg. These, of course, are all examples from the arts in the broadest sense, and it is right that they should come first, for it is in the arts that this work began.

Creative work is however now going on in many of our infant and junior schools, covering the whole range of the curriculum. Experiment and discovery by children lies at the heart of modern thought about education. The scientific activities of looking, observing, finding out, asking questions, comparing, naming and classifying, go on without that fearsome abstraction 'science' to deter them. The same is true in the social studies, in the exploration of our human world. Mathematical understanding too is beginning to grow and blossom in some of our junior schools where it is not stunted by an enormous, irrelevant, and wholly premature burden of calculation. It may well be that one of the most fruitful matrices in which the mathematical mind can have time and nourishment to grow is one in which arts and crafts play a prominent part. I feel that Sir Herbert would probably support that idea.

Again there is physical education, with its emphasis on free and natural movement, on rhythm, and on expressive dance, a development closely allied to dramatic art in which we have again discovered the natural powers of children. In foreign languages there is a strong movement for the only natural way in which to begin to learn a language, by speaking it, and this movement is spreading into the primary schools. What of secondary education? Creative work is spreading upwards, slowly perhaps, but it is, and some of our secondary modern schools have much to show. There is great hope here too in the development of special courses for secondary teachers arising from the Newsom Report. There is one of them in this college which lays stress on creative work for teachers themselves, particularly in the arts. Such work with teachers is surely one of the foci of educational development. Lastly, the idea that creative learning is the best kind of learning is spreading to grammar schools and grammar forms of comprehensive schools. As witness of this we have the new developments initiated by the Nuffield Foundation and by the Schools Councils in many parts of the country in mathematics, science, and modern languages with other subjects to follow. In all these ways in our national system we are at last reaping the reward of years of effort by pioneers, many of whom worked in independent progressive schools.

An interesting question arises at this point. Has programmed learning, one of the newest 'with it' things, something creative to contribute? Programmed learning, like every technique, is a double-edged device. It can, I am sure, be used for creative ends, but it could lend itself with disastrous ease to exploitation in the service of mere mechanical efficiency, defined as mastery of what adults think children should know and be able to do. So long as it is seen as only one tool amongst others, and its sphere of usefulness understood, we need not fear it but welcome it.

I think if we are honest we will admit that we can recognize creative education at once when we see it, but can we define it? To try to define it too closely might be a dis-service, but I think we can say this about it. Creative education is concerned with the joyful discovery by children of their human powers of construction and expression, of imagination and reason, freely exercised and uncoerced by neurotic adult pressures for premature results which can be defined beforehand. It is concerned with personal development, with the discovery by every child of what he has it within him to become. It is thus concerned with being and becoming, with the right to enjoy every stage of our development for, and in, itself, as well as a preparation for further stages. This is of course an idea whose currency today owes much to Rousseau's initial advocacy of it.

This leads to the next question. What is the basis of our belief in this kind of education? As we have seen and despite the sceptics, this kind of education works when conditions are right for it. But has it any firmer basis in ideas? Can we give it any rationale? I think so. The central notion is that children under certain conditions of relationship with adults and with each other, and with example and encouragement, will create for themselves the very substance of civilization and in the process recreate and revitalize the civilization they inherit. The basic belief is that it is *natural* for children to shape, to mould, to draw, to dance and sing. These activities do not have to be imposed upon them. It is natural for them to explore the external world in both its human and non-human manifestations. It is natural for them to explore human thought and achievement. It is natural for them to experiment with and make discoveries in human relationships, which lead them to moral and social values. We believe that all this is natural, but that it only happens given certain conditions.

In making such statements the word 'natural' appears again and again. Some educators, their wits having been sharpened by a little analytic philosophy, tell us that this is an almost empty word, or that alternatively it means too much, for it means all that human beings are capable of. They will point out that this includes the capacity for hatred, mutual exploitation, destruction, distortion of the truth, the creation of ugliness, pain and suffering. All this is, of course, true. Who would be likely to deny it today? This is one of the ways in which the word 'natural' can be used, but it is not what is meant by it in this context.

In the context of creative education, 'natural' means in line with developments which do not, in the long run, lead to destructiveness, and maladaptation, to frustration and neurosis, to the stultifying of powers and the withering of promise. What is natural to man in this sense are the achievements which promote well-being in persons, in communities and in the human species as a whole. It is of course a value-laden concept, but one in which what is matter of fact and what is matter of value are subtly inter-linked. We will, I am quite sure, discover that there are long term developmental and evolutionary criteria of what is natural to man in terms of increased awareness and constructiveness, and of the capacity for love and co-operation on which his very continued existence depends. In creative education our position is simply this. Man can improve his lot, he can go on from strength to strength in constructive achievement and happiness, or he can degenerate, stultify and ultimately destroy himself. Which of these paths would you say is natural? The first one is natural, only if we want to make it ours. Our nature is not wholly given; in an important sense we create it as we go along. 'In my beginning is my end', said Eliot at the start of *East Coker*, but he finished by saying, 'In my end is my beginning.' In other words our natures are in an important sense defined by what we conceive our ends to be, and by what we are prepared to make an effort to achieve.

What characterizes the kind of learning on which creative education must be based? Briefly, I would say that it is learning mediated by relationships between young and old, which are founded on trust, respect and love, and a belief that all children can partake in the adventure of creation. It is characterized by personal expression, personal experience, and personal discovery. It is informed by purpose and activity which is meaningful to the learner. To begin with it always takes the shape of participation in projects and not in the learning of subjects. Have we forgotten what subjects are? They are human achievements, human creations, and to approach them effectively children have to discover how they are created, through some experience of acts of creation, and not merely by coming to learn the results of other people's creative work. In a word this kind of learning is productive rather than reproductive, and ideally it leads to vocations on the basis of intrinsic interests. This is another point which Sir Herbert has often made.

I wish finally to characterize creative learning in this way. It is the kind of learning in which the next step must, in an important sense, always be essentially indeterminate from the teacher's point of view, indeterminate because it is the child who must make it. What the teacher does is to accept what the child does, while trying to enlarge the background out of which he does it, and to enhance the skills which he uses to do it.

What stands in the way of a wider establishment of creative education? Basically our difficulties seem to be these. Many children come to us malformed, their natures distorted by early experience in home and (we are prone to think) in other people's schools. Many of us have suffered the same fate in our childhood, in home and school, and cannot liberate ourselves easily to educate creatively. We are faced all the time by public demands for premature results, for what I call pseudo achievements. Above all there is the demand that education should primarily provide the way to enhance social status and a materially safe way of life. Now these are very formidable difficulties. They go to the heart of contemporary society. None of us is in any position to sneer at or feel superior about them, merely because we may have been relatively lucky ourselves. We have to learn to face these difficulties, to try to understand them and to discover how they may be overcome. There can of course be no panaceas, no easy solutions. All I can do here is to suggest some of the directions in which we should turn and some of the tasks we shall have to undertake. Here are some of the leading questions we have to ask ourselves. What are the guiding notions we require in order to develop our understanding of creative work, its preconditions, the means to be employed in facilitating it, and the ends towards which it is directed? What is essentially required of teachers who would educate creatively, and lastly what kind of image of man do we require to sustain us in our task?

What are the preconditions of creativity?

First of all, what can we say about the necessary preconditions for creativity? We could list all sorts of things, of course, and psychologists and sociologists will go on listing them, but I want to put forward just one single idea. The major precondition is the preservation of man's natural openness towards the world. What do we mean when we say that some people are more open than others, to experience, and to other people, just as others are more shut in and withdrawn? What is hinted at in this popular thinking? We see openness at its best in children, and in artists, and in those who are artists in the world of science or scholarship. These display for us an acceptance of the world in all its glorious variety and the capacity to seize upon individual things and perceive them with freshness, a sustained naturalness, fullness and simplicity. I am referring here, among other things, to what is often called the innocent eye. This is the title which Sir Herbert used for one of his books and is of course something which he has pre-eminently preserved in himself.

Ernest Schachtel, an American psycho-analyst who has been radically revising some classical Freudian conceptions, has this to say of the adult in his very important book *Metamorphosis*.[5]

> Only the adult who is able to be completely absorbed again and again, often for many hours and days, in an object that arouses his interest, will be the one who enlarges his and sometimes men's scope of perception and experience. A painter may spend many days, weeks or months or even years in looking at the same mountain, as Cézanne did, or at blades of grass, or bamboo leaves, or branches of a tree, as many of the Chinese or Japanese masters did, without tiring of it, and without ceasing to discover something new in it. The same is true of the poet's or the writer's devoted love for his object, of the naturalist's perception of the plant or animal with which he has to live for long periods of time in order to acquire that intimate knowledge from which eventually new meaning and understanding will be born. This applies to all men who want to learn to know something or somebody truly and deeply.

How can this quality, this precondition of creative work be preserved throughout childhood and into adulthood? What are the influences which cause its disappearance in so many of us? Basically, of course, we humans require to protect ourselves against the blinding light of reality. In our perceptual acts we deploy selective devices, and we develop quite natural and proper defences to limit our vision and other senses. We might here recall Eliot in *Burnt Norton*:

> And the pool was filled with water out of sunlight,
> And the lotos rose, quietly, quietly,
> The surface glittered out of heart of light,
> And they were behind us, reflected in the pool.
> Then a cloud passed, and the pool was empty,
> Go, said the bird, for the leaves were full of children,
> Hidden excitedly, containing laughter.
> Go, go, go said the bird; human kind
> Cannot bear very much reality.

Or we may say simply and equally symbolically, 'No man can look upon the face of God and live.'

But our concern here is a very much more limited one. It is

symptomatic of the human condition that many of our powers have to develop out of others, and may do so at their expense. Conception grows out of perception, and the shadow cast by thought on man's world is familiar to the psychologists in the truth that successful concept formation, both facilitates and inhibits perception. As rational thought grows, we tend to lose our innocent eye. But need we? The artists are there to give the lie to this. Schachtel, whom I have already quoted, would agree. Speaking of the child's early acquaintance with the objects of his world, he speaks of how their significance is enhanced as the child apprehends their meaning in his culture. But he says: 'On the other hand they (these meanings) also increasingly supplant the child's original approach to the objects and especially in our time entail the danger of closing his openness to the world and reducing all experience to the perception of such preformed cliches as make up the world of reality as seen by his family, peer group and the society in which he grows up.' Primary perception, he says, tends to stagnate and to atrophy. He goes on:

> In our time this stagnation takes the form of an alienation of man from the objects and from his own sensory capacities. The danger of this alienation is that man's dulled senses may no longer encounter the objects themselves, but only what he expects and already knows about, the labels formed by his society. The closed world of this perspective ceases to hold any wonder, everything has its label, and if one does not know it, the experts will tell him.

Some psycho-analysts then tend to see the dulling of our perceptions as due to the over-development of our natural defences; an over-development which seeks to limit and relieve the pain of enduring interpersonal tensions and inner strivings. The remedy they suggest is that somehow we must learn to decrease the severity of the often unnecessary conflicts which face children, and, even more important, help them to tolerate and live with the inner stresses that are quite inescapable in the development of modern man. This then, we may suggest, is the means required to maintain our natural creativity; a tolerance of conflict and the use of conflict to create a new synthesis, a new wholeness in which the 'conscious and the depth minds co-operate', as Marion Milner has put it. This is not at all to suggest that art creations are just symptoms of conflict, or that the meaning of a work of art is to be found in the unconscious conflicts of the artist. (That idea is completely outmoded, particularly among psycho-analysts.) What is suggested is that the creative person is able to make constructive use of his inner stresses—these need not result in conscious conflict —as means to create something new and valuable for himself and the world. What is created has usually a symbolic quality, but again the meaning of the symbol is not simply that it mirrors unconscious conflicts. It does this, inevitably, but only incidentally. The larger meaning of the symbol is that it proclaims new truth about our perception of the world. As an embodied truth it is a work of art, because it has attained what Suzanne Langer has called 'significant form'.[6]

Following up a remark of Sir Herbert Read's, about art as the finding of significant symbols, Marion Milner in her essay 'Psychoanalysis and Art'[7] says this: 'It is a fact that more and more analysts are now becoming concerned with the way in which symbols are created. Analysts find that in their most deeply disturbed patients, the process of symbol formation has been interfered with or perhaps never properly established.' The moral for education is I think painfully clear. We have practically everything still to learn about understanding the stresses and conflicts of childhood in the sense of trying to help children to tolerate them and use them, not defensively to limit and shut out reality, but constructively to reveal reality through creation and discovery. If we have to learn how to do this with children, have we not first in fact to learn how to do it to some extent with ourselves, and this is likely to be a promethean task? A great deal of the time, however, we are apt to deny that there is any such task. Our defences against inner reality in particular are often so good that for long spells we exist by accepting complacently the deadening routine of our formal educational procedures.

What are the aims of creative activity? I would suggest three. Our creative strivings are directed in the first place I think to the production of significant form in music, and the plastic arts, in literature and dance, in science and mathematics and in historical understanding. In the second place they are directed to the achievement of an objective sympathy with the world of things, with living creatures, and with our fellow men. It is in our creative moments that we see the world most clearly in all its astonishing variety, in its glory, and in its tragedy. Louis MacNeice put this beautifully in his poem 'Snow'.

> World is crazier and more of it than we think,
> Incorrigibly plural. I peel and portion
> A tangerine and spit the pips and feel
> The drunkenness of things being various.

Finally, our creative efforts are directed to the attainment of a wholeness which is the consummation of our relatedness to the world and to other human beings. To talk more about this would be to start on a very long story indeed. These ideas, the preservation of openness, the tolerance of stress, and the striving for significant form, for objective sympathy, and for wholeness, do express, I think, something of the essence of creative work.

What is required of the creative educator?

In my kind of job we are never tired of exhorting teachers, and student teachers, to do this, and the next thing, to be this and to be that. Naturally they get tired of us and our exhortations, and rightly so. We seem to be inexhaustible exhorters. Let me instead then put the question another way. If we are to educate creatively, is it not the case that we need more than anything else to have time and opportunity to refresh our own vision, to recover the pristine feeling of encountering new life in our contacts with children, our fellow men, and the achievements of men? Have we not to recapture and keep the feeling we may have on a sun-drenched May morning when we feel that we have stepped suddenly into the beginning of the world? We must allow time for such refreshment and actively seek it, but beyond this there are things upon which we must reflect, and work, and experiment a great deal more if we are going to increase our powers to educate creatively.

The first of these is our capacity to accept children and young people as they are. Sir Herbert and others have constantly pointed out that this must often mean accepting the poorest of poor work, because at the moment it is all that a child can do. Discrimination is needed of course, but to reject the work is often to reject the person. The idea of acceptance of people, not only children, as they are and not as we would wish them to be, is however a very profound one, and it is difficult to put into practice. It lies at the heart of Christian teaching about God's relation to man, which at least, whatever else it may mean, is a symbolic way of talking about the relation between man and man. It is clear that humanity has not progressed very far as yet in this direction. The difficulty is not far to seek. The rejection we mete out so much of the time to children and young people is a concealed way of rejecting something in ourselves that we do not wish to acknowledge, something based on fear or hate or envy. For example, the behaviour of some young people may openly express all that we have denied about ourselves. Consequently, we may not only condemn the behaviour (which we may be right to do) but reject the person also. The child indeed lives on in each of us as an unacknowledged part of ourselves, and this means that our capacity to create and destroy, to love and to hate, and to feel joy and pain at the child level, is still there.

Absolute acceptance of all children, by all teachers, is a Utopian idea, and it is enough to learn to increase our capacity for such acceptance. Failure to progress in this is failure to learn more fully how to accept ourselves as we are, with all our imperfections. It is a failure in self-knowledge in the deepest sense. Let us recall Freud's words about this: 'Only someone who can feel his way into the minds of children can be capable of educating them, and we grown up people cannot understand children because we can no longer understand our own childhood.' Coming from him, this was of course a challenge. Without some measure of understanding of the child within us we cannot begin to accept children and young people as they are, and without a measure of such acceptance, there is no real life, no partnership, no creativity.

The second thing seems to me to be a much greater willingness to let the spirit blow where it listeth. In her fascinating analysis of Blake's illustrations to the Book of Job, Marion Milner says this:

> There are moments when the spirit bloweth where it listeth (like Blake's God in the whirlwind). They cannot be induced either by teacher or child, but they can be allowed for, and if psycho-analytical experience is right, they are most likely to occur in a particular kind of setting, one in which there is not too great fear of a tyrannical authority, so that the spontaneous life is either denied, or expressed in defiant rebellion: not yet too much licence, which would mean that the child is kept too busy with unshared responsibility for his own aggression to dare to give his imagination its head; in fact, in a setting in which it is safe sometimes to be absent-minded.

The third thing we have to ponder is the nature of the relation in education between teachers and children. The teacher stands for authority. He simply cannot help this, and there is much self-deception about it among some even very brilliant educators. But the teacher also stands for love. Neither of these alone will do, as Marjorie Hourd points out. What is necessary is a special kind of partnership which aims at mutuality. Again Miss Hourd points out this cannot be a full mutuality because of the inherent inequality of teacher and child, but I would prefer to say that the necessary partnership is one which bears the stamp of a mutuality which transcends inequalities. For there is a basic mutuality in the common purpose of education. It is perhaps Buber who puts the matter best when he emphasizes the crucial role of trust. 'Trust in the world because this human being exists. That is the most inward achievement of the relation in education.'[8] Thus many tasks lie before us, tasks of developing and preserving our openness towards the world, of learning to tolerate and use conflict, of accepting ourselves and children as we and they are, of letting the spirit blow where it listeth, and of seeking to create the basic trust which must permeate all that we do. These are immense and hard undertakings, yet inescapably they mark the way forward.

What image of man does creative education require?

I am going to be quite categorical here. We have to reject as inadequate the kind of image with which we are presented every day, in particular by some of the vociferous champions of the behavioural sciences, who glory in presenting man as *nothing but* a 'machine' or a homeostatic organism, and in fostering the notion that civilized achievements are *nothing but* the sublimation of animal and infantile drives. Such limited models of man may be necessary for specific and limited purposes within scientific work itself, but they are quite inappropriate as the basis of an image of all that man is and may become. Moreover, the conceptual idiom in which Freud himself clothed many of his most pregnant and important insights has through unsophisticated interpreters unhappily contributed much to this kind of image and this kind of error. We must reject too the image of ourselves as merely producers and consumers, anxious only to maintain the material values of, for example, a middle-class way of life as it is known in our society in the West. Such images inevitably add their influence to all the already existing tendencies to dehumanize education.

Instead we must proclaim our faith in the primacy of the personal in human life. Nothing short of a personal image of man will do to sustain ourselves as persons, to enable us to live and move and have our being in and through relationships with other persons. To erect and proclaim a dehumanized image of man is already to promote our own actual dehumanization. As I suggested earlier, our nature is not wholly given; in part we create ourselves. Only an image of man as a person can sustain our efforts to become enjoyers of life, discoverers of meaning in the world, and creative educators.

In conclusion, it seems to me that we need above all to sustain within ourselves a sense of wonder and mystery, the sense of indeterminancy, of life without end. Eliot puts this issue superbly in *The Family Reunion*:

> Thus with most careful devotion
> Thus with precise attention

To detail, interfering preparation
Of that which is already prepared
Men tighten the knot of confusion
Into perfect misunderstanding,
Reflecting a pocket-torch of observation
Upon each other's opacity
Neglecting all the admonitions
From the world around the corner
The wind's talk in the dry holly-tree
The inclination of the moon
The attraction of the dark passage
The paw under the door.

Let us then embrace wonder, and let us embrace hope, the kind of hope for which Sir Herbert has always stood. Hope creates and children, normal children, are always full of hope. I have just come across a beautiful and inspiring book called *In the Early World* by a creative teacher, Elwyn Richardson.[9] It is a record of yet one more of these conquests in the field of creative education, this time in a little village school in the North Island, New Zealand. In his introduction, the author says: 'I now realize that what I have learned from my children and recorded here supports some well established educational beliefs. For what I myself learned during these years I have mainly my children to thank.' This is a lesson that Sir Herbert has been trying to teach us all his life.

The text of a lecture given at Goldsmiths' College London as part of a tribute to Sir Herbert Read. Originally published in *The New Era*, vol. 49, no. 3, March 1968.

References

1 Sir Herbert Read, *Education Through Art*, Faber & Faber, 1943, 1964.
2 Seonaid Robertson, *Rose Garden and Labyrinth*, Routledge & Kegan Paul, 1963.
3 Marjorie Hourd, *The Education of the Poetic Spirit*, Heinemann, 1949.
4 Marjorie Hourd and Gertrude Cooper, *Coming into their Own*, Heinemann, 1959.
5 Ernest Schachtel, *Metamorphosis*, Routledge & Kegan Paul, 1963.
6 Susan K. Langer, *Philosophy in a New Key, A Study in the Symbolism of Reason, Rite and Art*, Mentor Books, 1955.
7 Marion Milner. 'Psycho-analysis and Art' in J. D. Sutherland (ed.), *Psycho-Analysis and Contemporary Thought*, Hogarth, 1958.
8 Martin Buber, *Between Man and Man*, Beacon Press, 1955.
9 Elwyn Richardson, *In the Early World*, NZ Council for Educational Research, Wellington, 1964.

Seventeen

Renewal and new horizons

When I stepped out of the aeroplane that brought me to Australia, just over six weeks ago, I immediately encountered three things characteristically Australian. I was warmly welcomed as a friend by people I had never met before, and then I was confronted by a newspaper reporter. 'What is your opinion of Australian teachers?' he asked. Thinking hurriedly of some of the few I had met in England, I unguardedly replied: 'They remind me of Scottish teachers.' 'That is a compliment, I suppose,' he said. 'Not entirely, it might have been more of a compliment twenty or thirty years ago,' I managed to add, before I was rescued by my new friends and taken in the glorious Perth sunshine to breakfast. This was the third thing. To a fruit and coffee man like myself that breakfast seemed remarkably like lunch.

You Australians have large appetites—not only for your traditional and nourishing food, now having fresh tastes and flavours injected into it by New Australians—but large appetites for life, for work and for friendship. This gusto of yours and your personal kindness and stimulating conversation have formed the background against which I have been trying to find out exactly what I did mean by those first rash remarks about Australian teachers. I think perhaps I was really trying to make a guess at how far the ideas of the new education, about which I had come to talk, have influenced the work of Australian schools. How accurate was my guess, and what is the new education anyway? I now think that Australian teachers are much like teachers anywhere else. What that means you must judge for yourselves from what I have to say about the new education.

The first point about the new education is that it is very old—I do not know how old. Socrates for example was a new educator, one of the greatest; and we may trace the new education through a long list of famous names and through a vastly longer list, of nameless devoted and inspired teachers, who in each generation have tried to restate, through their practice, man's fundamental insights into his own nature and development. That is one aspect of the new education—a re-statement of old truths, and their re-embodiment in new practices appropriate to a particular age. But the new education also looks forward. It looks to new horizons, to the ever new horizons opening before mankind, and it seeks with some quite new insights to prepare the children of men for the complex changing world of today, for the unknown world of tomorrow. And these new horizons are to be seen nowhere more clearly, than in Australia.

Where can we find this new education? We find it wherever we find parents and teachers who see in their children and their pupils, growing, striving, creative beings. Such parents and teachers may be found everywhere in the world and certainly in Australia. While their numbers may seem small at first, one finds on closer inspection that there are many who achieve some measure of new education in their work, often without being aware of it and in spite of adverse circumstances. To some people concerned with children the statements of the new education appear wildly idealistic and unpractical. They will point out that children have to be taught to read, write and count whether they like it or not, that schools must concentrate on bringing them up to the required standards of attainment and getting as many as possible of them through public examinations. They will add that to do these things children must be disciplined and made to work. That, they will say, is the real business of education, and personal growth, whatever that may be, must be left to look after itself. Yet, judged by the kind of results it itself values, as many studies have shown, this traditional way of looking at education has not proved very efficient, nor does personal growth seem to look after itself very well either.

We have no reason to be particularly proud of the state of the world today. Fear, cruelty, prejudice and intolerance abound in it. Delinquency and crime are wide-spread. In every civilized community there is a burden of mental ill-health—the extent of which we are only just beginning to realize. In England, half our hospital beds are occupied by patients whose illnesses involve some degree of emotional disturbance and about one third at least of the population suffers at one time or another from some form of maladjustment. Do you believe that in Australia conditions are so very different? How many of us are satisfied with the quality of our own lives in work and personal relationships? How many of us have fully developed our potentialities? Are we so naive as to believe that this burden of human distress and personal shortcomings is wholly unrelated to our educational systems? Is it not likely that an improved education—improved in its inward quality—has something to contribute to the welfare of mankind?

How can we improve the quality of education? The most characteristic feature of the new education is the stress it puts on individual development and on the inward and emotional nature of that development. We see this exemplified best in the work of the modern kindergarten. In the later stages however, many schools, and this is true everywhere in the world, seem to lose sight of the fact that every child is different in capacity, interests and rate of development. As a result, the individual tends to disappear into the mass.

Mass teaching dooms many children to repeated failure and hence to a disbelief in their own powers and personal worth. It may also give to others a sense of a quite false superiority. Anxiety over failure, lack of faith in oneself, a false sense of superiority—from these spring many personal difficulties in life and many of the world's ills.

The development of confidence in one's own genuine powers—however limited these may be—is the first essential of personal growth, and such confidence is rooted in an attitude to the world which finds it a good place and the people in it worthy of trust and love. In the beginning, belief in ourselves depends on someone else having believed in us, having cared for us, having loved us. This—the first responsibility of parents and teachers—is the theme of a moving book by an Australian new educator, Donald McLean—with the arresting title *Nature's Second Sun*, a quotation from a sixteenth-century playwright which is worth giving in full. 'Love is nature's second sun, causing a spring of virtues where he shines.'*

Assured of love and concern on the part of parents and teachers—concern which shows itself in suiting tasks to individual capacity, in offering the security of sensible rules, in awakening interests and sometimes in a wise neglect—children spontaneously develop interests and abilities which correspond to the great activities and achievements of mankind. Given the right start, children want to grow up; they want to learn to use their own bodies skilfully, to create in clay, paint, dance and music; they want to learn to read, write and count, to explore the world around them, to master ideas and to help one another. The clues to how to educate our children are given to us by the children themselves, in the unfolding of their powers under appropriate stimulation and encouragement. We know too, that children see the world with the eye of the poet much more easily than most adults. In his poem, 'The Orange Tree', one of your own poets, John Shaw Nielsen, says:

> The young girl stood beside me. I
> Saw not what her young eyes could see

* George Chapman (1559–1634), *All Fools*, Act I, Sc. 1.

A light she said, not of the sky,
Lives somewhere in the orange tree.

This inward light, which illumines the world for children and for poets, is shared also by new educators. They see with the inward eye, the latent powers of children—of all children—awaiting the conditions under which they can blossom.

There is plenty of evidence to show that given the right conditions children do not have to be driven to learn the things we want them to learn. The driving is necessary only when things have already gone wrong, when the adults are in too much of a hurry and the children are not ready.

Not ready! Many children are unready for a great many of the things we adults, in our anxiety about so-called standards, force upon them in primary and secondary schools. At present secondary education in particular seems to be involving pupils in a sort of rat-race for formal examination achievements, achievements which are often insecurely based, and are but little related either to the requirements of life or even of higher education itself. Sir Alexander Todd, Regius Professor of Chemistry in Cambridge, has recently complained that his students come to him knowing far too many chemical facts and with far too little ability to think. He was pointing to a very grave danger. The present stress on raising standards in science may easily result in just the opposite being achieved unless we realize that the growing scientist needs time and carefully selected and restricted material through which to develop his own powers of thought. You cannot make good scientists, or good poets, or good businessmen or simply good human beings in a hurry. They have to have time to grow.

So new educators strive to enable their pupils to experience achievement in discovery and creation, in appreciation, in understanding and in thinking for themselves, rather than in the memorizing of facts. And not only in thinking for themselves, but in feeling for themselves. The ills of life spring even more from warped feelings and loss of the power to feel, than they do from inability to think. The new education is as much an education of the heart as of the head. To become fully human we have to learn to deepen our sympathies and widen our loyalties, we have to learn how to cooperate with one another even more than to compete. We have to discover our own personal destinies, and strive to express in our behaviour worthwhile values, which are nevertheless genuinely our own.

To enable our children to develop in this way, we will need both in Australia and in Britain to re-fashion much of our education. We need to reconsider how best to educate and train our teachers and we need to work out how teachers can be given more freedom and responsibility in the education of their pupils, how they can be given more confidence to use the freedom they already possess and how they can be helped to overcome unfavourable circumstances. For in the free and unfettered relations between pupils and teachers lies the key to true personal growth for both. Both need to grow. Teachers have continually to deepen their understanding of children. Surely this is something of which we are all at least potentially capable.

Education, truly conceived, is something altogether beyond mere instruction. It is an adventure in human mutuality. For far too much of the time, life in our schools seems like a laborious trek across a desert land, instead of being a joyous adventure into a world teeming with life and possibility. How far has the new education gone in Australia; how far has it gone anywhere?

In 'Portrait of a Country' the poet Max Dunn wrote:

> Yet in this unpeopled island
> In this insular people, the seeds
> of promise, undelivered, wait
> for the tolerant season.
> O'turn the mirages into lakes,
> Turn back, turn back, the rivers
> Into the centre, into the dry heart.

He was speaking of your Australia, land of immense promise, but I would take his words to express rather the needs of all men everywhere. Turn back the rivers, the rivers of joy, of creativeness, of love; turn back the rivers into the dry heart of the world. That is the message and the task of the new education.

The text of a broadcast given as National Guest of Honour, Australian Broadcasting Commission, Sydney, March 1960. First published in *New Horizons in Education*, the journal of the New Education Fellowship in Australia, no. 23, Autumn 1960.

Indices

Name index

Subject index